EIGHT YEARS IN CEYLON

A LEOPARD KILLED BY A COW

EIGHT YEARS IN CEYLON

SIR SAMUEL W. BAKER, M.A. F.R.S. F.R.G.S.

PACHA AND MAJOR-GENERAL OF THE OTTOMAN EMPIRE:
GOLD MEDALLIST OF THE ROYAL GEOGRAPHICAL SOCIETY,
AND GRANDE MEDAILLE D'OR DE LA SOCIETE DE
GEOGRAPHIE DE PARIS:
AUTHOR OF 'RIFLE AND HOUND IN CEYLON' 'ALBERT
N'YANZA, GREAT BASIN OF THE NILE' 'NILE TRIBUTARIES
OF ABYSSINIA' 'ISMAILIA'

NEW EDITION

WITH ILLUSTRATIONS

GYAN

Published by

GYAN

Gyan Publishing House
5, Ansari Road
Daryaganj, New Delhi-110002
Phone: 011-47034999, 9811692060
E-mail: books@gyanbooks.com

Distribution Network
gyanbooks.com
India, USA, Canada, UK, Australia, France

ISBN : 978-81-212-4518-0 (HB)
First Published, 1891

2nd Impression 2020

Printed at: Gyan Press, Delhi.

Eight Years in Ceylon
Author: Sir Samuel W. Baker

PREFACE

TO

THE NEW EDITION.

NEARLY twenty years ago, when settled in the island of Ceylon, I wrote this book.

The lapse of this interval of time has produced many important changes; Ceylon has progressed, and is become one of our most prosperous colonies.

My work published in 1855, closed with these words—'For me Ceylon has always had a charm, and I shall ever retain a vivid interest in the colony.

'I trust that a new and more prosperous era has now commenced, and that Ceylon, having shaken off the incubus of mismanagement, may, under the rule of a vigorous and enterprising governor, arrive at that prosperity to which she is entitled by her capabilities.

'The governor recently appointed (Sir Henry

Ward), has a task before him which his well-known energy will doubtless enable him to perform.'

Upon the arrival of Sir Henry Ward in the colony, he quickly entered upon reforms; among which he adopted my suggestions for the restoration of ancient irrigation works.

From the advent of Sir H. Ward, the colony has been blessed with good government, and under the able administration of energetic governors, railways have opened up the interior; excellent roads have cut through the dense jungles, connecting distant points of the island with the capital; ancient tanks have in several districts been repaired, and the system of artificial irrigation has been successfully renewed.

The result of irrigation has been an immense increase in the production of rice. I have been informed that in a district that was in my time a dense jungle redolent of malaria, and only inhabited by wild animals, there is now a vast plain comprising 25,000 acres of rice cultivation.

This satisfactory advancement is a proof of the correctness of my theories expressed twenty years ago, and the future will develop the extraordinary resources of the country.

The recent famine in India is a severe lesson that

should be a warning to every administration. Ceylon has suffered from the high prices caused by the scarcity of imported grain; this grave event should determine the necessity of a home production.

Should the magnificent irrigation works of the ancients be gradually restored, the population may be relatively increased, not only by the coolies of Malabar, but by an importation of the industrious Chinese. The introduction of that energetic race would infuse a new spirit of rivalry, and the more indolent Cingalese would either be outstripped by their competitors, or would be excited to extra exertion.

There can be no doubt that Ceylon should be independent of a rice supply from without, and the day will, I believe, arrive when the colony will export instead of importing that great staple of the East.

The change that has taken place throughout the coffee districts is extraordinary. Vast forests in which I formerly hunted the elk (sambur deer), and boar, have entirely disappeared. Mountains that were clothed with jungles, damp and dreary solitudes, pathless, and then unknown, are now thriving plantations of coffee that have rewarded the industry of their proprietors. The stride of civilization during the past twenty years has been enormous—'the wilderness has blossomed as the rose.'

It is already difficult to procure forest land that is adapted for coffee cultivation,.and the time will arrive when every available acre will be made productive.

My old home in the mountains of Newera Ellia has shared in the general prosperity, and has benefited by the increased wealth of the country. It is now an important station, and is approached by excellent roads, which extend direct to the sea-coast at Batticaloa.

The formerly swampy plain of Newera Ellia is about to be converted into a large lake, by the formation of a dam that will prevent the escape of the river. This is intended as an ornament to the now fashionable sanitorium, but a reservoir of water at that elevation (6,200 feet above the sea-level) may be of important service for the future irrigation of the lower country.

The Cinchona plant is successfully cultivated in the neighbourhood of Newera Ellia. Tea has been grown of the finest quality, and it is supposed that it will eventually supplant the wild forests of the higher mountains, in the same manner that coffee has usurped their place on lower altitudes.

Such is the faint outline of the present condition of Ceylon, which I give upon hearsay; I have not seen the colony since twenty years. The success of that important island is the happy result of good management; and the able and energetic administrator, Mr. Gregory, who at this moment represents the government, is one under whom Ceylon cannot fail to advance in material prosperity.

I give my old work to the public in its original integrity, as written many years ago when I worked as an early pioneer, and assisted in the advancement of the colony by opening a future for the now prosperous mountain settlement of Newera Ellia.

SAM. W. BAKER.

October, 1874.

PREFACE.

EIGHT YEARS' wanderings in Ceylon have created a love for this beautiful island which can only be equalled by my affection for Old England, from which the independence of a wild life, combined with an infatuation for rambling into every unvisited nook and corner, sentenced me to a term of voluntary exile.

During this period my delight has been in tracing the great natural resources of the country, in observing the immense relics of its former prosperity, and contrasting the past grandeur and energy of an extinct race with the apathetic and selfish policy of our present system.

It is the false economy of our present government to leave untested the actual capabilities of its possessions. Thus, while Ceylon remains with ruined tanks, deserted cities, and vast tracts of uncultivated rice lands, India, governed by the Company, is advancing in cultivation. New tanks are formed, new canals for irrigation penetrate through hitherto barren jungles, and arouse the soil to fertility. In fact the vigilant eye of the Company is directed to the true resources of the country, and every acre of available land should yield its proportion to the revenue.

Without the statistical details which would render a description laborious to the general reader, I shall endeavour to give an impartial picture of Ceylon as it is, touching lightly upon the past, in order to prove the possibility of improvement for the future. Having given an account of the sports of the country in the 'Rifle and Hound,' I shall not dwell at too great length upon this topic, how tempting soever it may be.

In these days, when the enterprise of Englishmen is exhibited on so large a scale by the stream of emigration to foreign shores, a few hints may not be uninteresting to the intending settler. We are all more or less sanguine, and, if unguided by the experience of age, we are apt to paint the future too brightly. This is an error which entails disappointment and regret upon the hasty emigrant, who may discover, when far from his deserted home, that the paradise which he had pictured to himself is but earthly after all, and is accompanied by drawbacks and hardships which he had not anticipated.

It is not every temperament that is fitted for the anxieties of a wild life in a strange land. This many persons who have left England confident in their own strength have discovered, unfortunately, when too late.

Englishmen, however, are naturally endowed with a spirit of adventure. There is in the hearts of all a germ of freedom which longs to break through the barriers that confine us to our own shores; and as the newborn wildfowl takes to water from its deserted egg-shell, so we wander over the world when launched on our own resources.

This innate spirit of action is the mainspring of the power of England. Go where you will, from north to south and from east to west, you meet an Englishman. Sail round the globe, and upon every point of strength the Union Jack gladdens your eye, and you think with wonder of the vast possessions which have been conquered, and the immense tracts of country that have been peopled by the overflow of our little island.

Among the list of possessions, Ceylon is but a

speck; nevertheless, the act of settling in one colony is a fair sample of the general hardships of emigration. I shall therefore introduce a slight sketch of a settlement in Ceylon, which may give some insight into the little disappointments, inseparable from a new enterprise. The reader will, I trust, wander with me in my rambles through this lovely country, and endeavour to pass an idle hour among the scenes portrayed.

CONTENTS.

CHAPTER I.

CHAPTER II.

CHAPTER III.

CHAPTER IV.

CHAPTER VIII.

CHAPTER IX.

CHAPTER X.

CHAPTER XI.

CHAPTER XII.

CHAPTER XIII.

ILLUSTRATIONS.

EIGHT YEARS IN CEYLON.

CHAPTER I.

Colombo—Dulness of the Town—Cinnamon Gardens—A Cingalese Appo—Ceylon Sport—Jungle Fever—Newera Ellia—Energy of Sir E. Barnes—Influence of the Governor—Projected Improvements.

IT WAS in the year 1845 that the spirit of wandering allured me towards Ceylon;—little did I imagine at that time that I should eventually become a settler.

The descriptions of its sports, and the tales of hair-breadth escapes from elephants, which I had read in various publications, were sources of attraction against which I strove in vain; and I at length determined upon the very wild idea of spending twelve months in Ceylon jungles.

It is said that the delights of pleasures in anticipation exceed the pleasures themselves: in this case doubtless some months of great enjoyment passed in making plans of every description, until I at length arrived in Colombo, Ceylon's seaport capital.

I never experienced greater disappointment in an expectation than on my first view of Colombo. I had spent some time at Mauritius and Bourbon previous to my arrival, and I soon perceived that the far-famed Ceylon was nearly a century behind either of those small islands.

Instead of the bustling activity of the Port Louis harbour in Mauritius, there were a few vessels rolling about in the roadstead, and some forty or fifty fishing canoes hauled up on the sandy beach. There was a peculiar dulness throughout the town,—a sort of something which seemed to say, 'coffee does not pay.' There was a want of spirit in everything. The ill-conditioned guns upon the fort looked as though not intended to defend it; the sentinels looked par-boiled; the very natives sauntered rather than walked; the bullocks crawled along in the mid-day sun, listlessly dragging the native carts. Everything and everybody seemed enervated, except those frightfully active people in all countries and climates, 'the custom-house officers:' these necessary plagues to society gave their usual amount of annoyance.

What struck me the most forcibly in Colombo was the want of shops. In Port Louis the wide and well-paved streets were lined with excellent 'Magazins' of every description; here, on the contrary, it was difficult to find anything in the shape of a shop until

I was introduced to a *soi-disant* store, where everything [that] was to be purchased, from a needle to a crowbar, and from satin to sail-cloth ; the useful predominating over the ornamental in all cases. It was all on a poor scale ; and after several inquiries respecting the best hotel, I located myself at that termed the Royal or Seager's Hotel. This was airy, white, and clean throughout ; but there was a barn-like appearance, as there is throughout most private dwellings in Colombo, which banished all idea of comfort.

A good tiffin concluded, which produced a happier state of mind, I ordered a carriage for a drive to the Cinnamon Gardens. The general style of Ceylon carriages appeared in the shape of a caricature of a hearse ;—this goes by the name of a palanquin carriage. Those usually hired are drawn by a single horse, whose natural vicious propensities are restrained by a low system of diet.

In this vehicle, whose gaunt steed was led at a melancholy trot by an equally small-fed horsekeeper, I traversed the environs of Colombo. Through the winding fort gateway, across the flat Galle Face (the race-course), freshened by the sea-breeze as the waves break upon its western side ; through the Colpetty,—topes of cocoa-nut trees shading the road, and the houses of the better class of European residents to the right and left; then turning to the left,—a few minutes of expectation,—and behold the Cinnamon Gardens!

What fairy-like pleasure-grounds have we fondly anticipated!—what perfumes of spices, and all that our childish imaginations had pictured as the ornamental portions of a cinnamon garden!

A vast area of scrubby low jungle, composed of cinnamon bushes, is seen to the right and left, before and behind. Above, is a cloudless sky and a broiling sun; below, is snow-white sand of quartz, curious only in the possibility of its supporting vegetation. Such is the soil in which the cinnamon delights;—such are the Cinnamon Gardens, in which I delight not. They are an imposition, and they only serve as an addition to the disappointments of a visitor to Colombo. In fact, the whole place is a series of disappointments. You see a native woman clad in snow-white petticoats, a beautiful tortoiseshell comb fastened in her raven hair; you pass her—you look back—wonderful!—she has a beard! Deluded stranger, this is only another disappointment; it is a Cingalese Appo—a man—no, not a man,—a something male in petticoats; a petty thief, a treacherous, cowardly villain, who would perpetrate the greatest rascality had he only the pluck to dare it. In fact, in this petticoated wretch you see a type of the nation of Cingalese.

On the morning following my arrival in Ceylon, I was delighted to see several persons seated at the 'table-d'hôte' when I entered the room, as I was most anxious to gain some positive information respecting the game of the island, the best localities, &c. &c. I was soon engaged in conversation, and one of my first questions naturally turned upon sport.

'*Sport!*' exclaimed two gentlemen simultaneously, —'*sport!* there is no sport to be had in Ceylon!'— 'at least, the race week is the only sport that I know of,' said the taller gentleman.

'No sport!' said I, half energetically and half despairingly. 'Absurd!—every book on Ceylon mentions the amount of game as immense; and as to elephants!'——

Here I was interrupted by the same gentleman: 'All gross exaggerations;' said he, 'gross exaggerations; in fact, inventions to give interest to a book. I have an estate in the interior, and I have never seen a wild elephant. There may be a few in the jungles of Ceylon, but *very* few, and you never see them.'

I began to discover the stamp of my companion from his expression 'you never see them.' Of course I concluded that he had never looked for them; and I began to recover from the first shock which his exclamation 'there is no sport in Ceylon!' had given me.

I subsequently discovered that my new and non-sporting acquaintances were coffee planters of a class then known as the Galle Face planters, who passed their time in cantering about the Colombo race-course and idling in the town, while their estates lay a hundred miles distant, uncared for, and naturally ruining their proprietors.

That same afternoon, to my delight and surprise, I met an old Gloucestershire friend in an officer of the 15th Regiment, then stationed in Ceylon. From him I soon learnt that the character of Ceylon for game had never been exaggerated, and from that moment my preparations for the jungle commenced.

I rented a good airy house in Colombo as head-quarters, and the verandahs were soon strewed with jungle-baskets, boxes, tent, gun cases, and all the paraphernalia for a shooting trip.

* * * * * *

What unforeseen and apparently trivial incidents may upset all our plans for the future, and turn our whole course of life!

At the expiration of twelve months my shooting trips and adventures were succeeded by so severe an attack of jungle fever, that from a naturally robust frame I dwindled to a mere nothing, and very little of my former self remained. The first symptom of convalescence was accompanied by a peremptory order from my medical attendant to start for the highlands, to the mountainous region of Newera Ellia, the sanatorium of the island.

A poor, miserable wretch I was upon my arrival at this elevated station, suffering not only from the fever itself, but from the feeling of an exquisite debility that creates an utter hopelessness of the renewal of strength.

I was only a fortnight at Newera Ellia. The Rest-house or inn was the perfection of everything that was dirty and uncomfortable. The toughest possible specimen of a beefsteak, black bread, and potatoes were the choicest and only viands obtainable for an invalid. There was literally nothing else; it was a land of starvation. But the climate! what can I say to describe the wonderful effects of such a pure and unpolluted air? Simply, that at the expiration of a fortnight, in spite of the tough beef and the black bread and potatoes, I was as well and as strong as I ever had been; and in proof of this, I started instanter for another shooting excursion in the interior.

It was impossible to have visited Newera Ellia, and to have benefited in such a wonderful manner by the climate, without contemplating with astonishment its poverty-stricken and neglected state.

At that time it was the most miserable place conceivable. There was a total absence of all ideas of comfort or arrangement. The houses were for the most part built of such unsubstantial materials as stick and mud plastered over with mortar; pretty enough in exterior, but rotten in ten or twelve years. The only really good residence was a fine stone building erected by Sir Edward Barnes when governor of Ceylon. To him alone indeed are we indebted for the existence of a sanatorium. It was he who opened the road, not only to Newera Ellia, but for thirty-six miles further on the same line to Badulla. At his own expense he built a substantial mansion, at a cost, as it is said, of 8,000*l.*, and, with provident care for the health of the European troops, he erected barracks and officers' quarters for the invalids.

Under his government Newera Ellia was rapidly becoming a place of importance, but, unfortunately, at the expiration of his term the place became neglected. His successor took no interest in the plans of his predecessor; and from that period, each successive governor, being influenced by an increasing spirit of parsimony, Newera Ellia has remained 'in statu quo,' not even having been visited by the present governor.

In a small colony like Ceylon, it is astonishing how the movements and opinions of the governor influence the public mind. In this instance, however, the *movements* of the governor (Sir G. Anderson) cannot carry much weight, as he does not move at all, with the exception of an occasional drive from Colombo to Kandy. His knowledge of the colony and of its wants or resources must therefore, from his personal experience, be limited to the Kandy road. This apathy, when exhibited by her Majesty's representative, is highly contagious among the public of all classes and colours, and cannot have other than a bad moral tendency.

Upon my first visit to Newera Ellia in 1847 Lord Torrington was the governor of Ceylon, a man of active mind, with an ardent desire to test its real capabilities, and to work great improvements in the colony. Unfortunately, his term as governor was shorter than was expected. The elements of discord were at that time at work among all classes in Ceylon, and Lord Torrington was recalled.

From the causes of neglect described, Newera Ellia was in the deserted and wretched state in which I saw it; but so infatuated was I in the belief that its importance must be appreciated when the knowledge of its climate should be more widely extended, that I looked forward to its becoming at some future time a rival to the Neilgherries station in India. My ideas were based upon the natural features of the place combined with its requirements.

It apparently produced nothing except potatoes. The soil was supposed to be as good as it appeared to be. The quality of the water and the supply were unquestionable; the climate could not be surpassed for salubrity. There was a carriage road from Colombo 115 miles, and from Kandy forty-seven miles, the last thirteen being the Ramboddé Pass, arriving at an elevation of 6,600 feet, from which point a descent of two miles terminated the road to Newera Ellia.

The station then consisted of about twenty private residences, the barracks and officers' quarters, the Rest-house and the Bazaar, the latter containing about 200 native inhabitants.

Bounded upon all sides but the east by high mountains, the plain of Newera Ellia lay like a level valley of about two miles in length by half a mile in width, bordered by undulating grassy knolls at the foot of the mountains. Upon these spots of elevated ground most of the dwellings were situated, commanding a view of the plain, with the river winding through its centre. The mountains were clothed from the base to the summit with dense forests, containing excellent timber for building purposes. Good building-stone was procurable everywhere; limestone at a distance of five miles.

The whole of the adjacent country was a repetition of the Newera Ellia plain with slight variations, comprising a vast extent of alternate swampy plains and dense forests.

Why should this place lie idle? Why should this great tract of country in such a lovely climate be untenanted and uncultivated? How often I have stood upon the hills and asked myself this question when gazing over the wide extent of undulating forest and plain! How often I have thought of the thousands of starving wretches at home who here might earn a comfortable livelihood! and I have scanned the vast tract of country, and in my imagination I have cleared the dark forests, and substituted waving crops of corn, and peopled a hundred ideal cottages with a thriving peasantry.

Why should not the highlands of Ceylon, with an Italian climate, be rescued from their state of barrenness? Why should not the plains be drained, the forests felled, and cultivation take the place of the rank pasturage, and supplies be produced to make Ceylon independent of other countries? Why should not schools be established, a comfortable hotel be erected, a church be built? In fact, why should Newera Ellia, with its wonderful climate, so easily attainable, be neglected in a country like Ceylon, proverbial for its unhealthiness?

These were my ideas when I first visited Newera Ellia, before I had much experience in either people or things connected with the island.

My twelve months' tour in Ceylon being completed, I returned to England delighted with what I had seen of Ceylon in general; but, above all, with my short visit to Newera Ellia, *malgré* its barrenness and want of comfort, caused rather by the neglect of man, than by the lack of resources in the locality.

CHAPTER II.

Past Scenes — Attractions of Ceylon — Emigration — Difficulties in Settling—Accidents and Casualties—An Eccentric Groom—Insubordination—Commencement of Cultivation—Sagacity of the Elephant — Disappointments— 'Death' in the Settlement — Shocking Pasturage—Success of Emigrants—'A Good Knock-about Kind of a Wife.'

I HAD not been long in England before I discovered that my trip to Ceylon had only served to upset all ideas of settling down quietly at home. Scenes of former sports and places were continually intruding themselves upon my thoughts, and I longed to be once more roaming at large with the rifle through the noiseless wildernesses in Ceylon. So delightful were the recollections of past incidents, that I could scarcely believe that it lay within my power to renew them. Ruminating over all that had happened within the past year, I conjured up localities to my memory which seemed too attractive to have existed in reality. I wandered along London streets, comparing the noise and bustle with the deep solitudes of Ceylon, and I felt like the sickly plants in a London parterre. I wanted the change to my former life. I constantly found myself gazing into gunmakers' shops, and these I sometimes entered abstractedly to examine some rifle exposed in the window. Often have I passed an hour in boring the unfortunate gunmakers to death by my suggestions for various improvements in rifles and guns, which, as I was not a purchaser, must have been extremely edifying.

Time passed; and the moment at length arrived when I decided once more to see Ceylon. I determined to become a settler at Newera Ellia, where I could reside in a perfect climate, and nevertheless enjoy the sports of the low country at my own will.

Thus, the recovery from a fever in Ceylon was the hidden cause of my settlement at Newera Ellia. The infatuation for sport, added to a gipsy-like love of wandering and complete independence, thus dragged me away from home and from a much-loved circle.

In my determination to reside at Newera Ellia, I hoped to be able to carry out some of those visionary plans for its improvement which I have before suggested; and I trusted to be enabled to effect such a change in the rough face of Nature in that locality as to render a residence at Newera Ellia something approaching to a country life in England, with the advantage of the whole of Ceylon for my manor, and no expense of gamekeepers.

To carry out these ideas, it was necessary to set to work; and I determined to make a regular settlement at Newera Ellia, sanguinely looking forward to establishing a little English village around my own residence.

Accordingly I purchased an extensive tract of land from the Government at twenty shillings per acre. I engaged an excellent bailiff, who with his wife and daughter, with nine other emigrants, including a blacksmith, were to sail for my intended settlement in Ceylon.

I purchased farming implements of the most improved descriptions, seeds of all kinds, saw-mills, &c. &c., and the following stock:—A half-bred bull (Durham and Hereford), a well-bred Durham cow, three rams (a Southdown, Leicester, and Cotswold), and a thorough-bred entire horse by Charles XII.; also a small pack of foxhounds, and a favourite greyhound ('Bran').

My brother had determined to accompany me; and with emigrants, stock, machinery, hounds, and our respective families, the good ship 'Earl of Hardwicke,' belonging to Messrs. Green and Co., sailed from London in September, 1848. I had previously left England by the overland mail of August to make arrangements at Newera Ellia for the reception of the whole party.

I had as much difficulty in making up my mind

to the proper spot for the settlement, as Noah's dove experienced in its flight from the Ark. However, I wandered over the neighbouring plains and jungles of Newera Ellia, and at length I stuck my walking-stick into the ground where the gentle undulations of the country would allow the use of the plough. Here, then, was to be the settlement.

I had chosen the spot at the eastern extremity of the Newera Ellia plain, on the verge of the sudden descent towards Badulla. This position was two miles and a half from Newera Ellia, and was far more agreeable and better adapted for a settlement, the land being comparatively level, and not shut in by mountains.

It was in the dreary month of October, when the south-west monsoon howls in all its fury across the mountains; the mist boiled up from the valleys and swept along the surface of the plains, obscuring the view of everything, except the pattering rain which descended without ceasing day or night. Every sound was hushed, save that of the elements and the distant murmuring roar of countless waterfalls; not a bird chirped, the dank white lichens hung from the branches of the trees, and the wretchedness of the place was beyond description.

I found it almost impossible to persuade the natives to work in such weather; and it being absolutely necessary that cottages should be built with the greatest expedition, I was obliged to offer an exorbitant rate of wages.

In about a fortnight, however, the wind and rain showed flags of truce, in the shape of white clouds set in a blue sky. The gale ceased; and the skylarks warbled high in air, giving life and encouragement to the whole scene. It was like a beautiful cool midsummer in England.

I had about eighty men at work; and the constant click-clack of axes, the falling of trees, the noise of saws and hammers, and the perpetual chattering of coolies, gave a new character to the wild spot upon which I had fixed.

The work proceeded rapidly; neat white cottages soon appeared in the forest; and I expected to have everything in readiness for the emigrants on their arrival. I rented a tolerably good house in Newera Ellia, and so far everything had progressed well.

The 'Earl of Hardwicke' arrived after a prosperous voyage, with passengers and stock all in sound health; the only casualty on board had been one of the hounds. In a few days all started from Colombo for Newera Ellia. The only trouble was, how to get the cow up? She was a beautiful beast, a thorough-bred 'short horn,' and she weighed about 13 cwt. She was so fat that a march of 115 miles in a tropical climate was impossible. Accordingly a van was arranged for her, which the maker assured me would carry an elephant. But no sooner had the cow entered it than the whole thing came down with a crash, and the cow made her exit through the bottom. She was therefore obliged to start on foot in company with the bull, sheep, horse, and hounds, orders being given that ten miles a day, divided between morning and evening, was to be the maximum march during the journey.

The emigrants started per coach, while our party drove up in a new clarence which I had brought from England. I mention this, as its untimely end will be shortly seen.

Four government elephant carts started with machinery, farming implements, &c. &c., while a troop of bullock bandies carried the lighter goods. I had a tame elephant waiting at the foot of the Newera Ellia Pass to assist in carrying up the baggage and maid-servants.

There had been a vast amount of trouble in making all the necessary arrangements; but the start was completed, and at length we were all fairly off.

In an enterprise of this kind many disappointments were necessarily to be expected, and I had prepared myself with the patience of Job for anything that might happen. It was well that I had done so, for it was soon put to the test.

Having reached Ramboddé, at the foot of the

Newera Ellia Pass, in safety, I found that the carriage was so heavy that the horses were totally unable to ascend the Pass. I therefore left it at the Rest-house while we rode up the fifteen miles to Newera Ellia, intending to send for the empty vehicle in a few days.

The whole party of emigrants and ourselves reached Newera Ellia in safety. On the following day I sent down the groom with a pair of horses to bring up the carriage; at the same time I sent the elephant to bring some luggage from Ramboddé.

Now this groom, 'Henry Perkes,' was one of the emigrants, and he was not exactly the steadiest of the party;—I therefore cautioned him to be very careful in driving up the Pass, especially in crossing the narrow bridges and turning the corners. He started on his mission.

The next day a dirty-looking letter was put in my hand by a native, which, being addressed to me, ran something in this style:—

Honor[d] Zur

I'm sorry to hinform you that the carrige and osses has met with a haccidint and is tumbled down a precippice and its a mussy as I didn't go too. The precippice isn't very deep being not above heighty feet or therabouts—the hosses is got up but is very bad—the carrige lies on its back and we can't stir it nohow. M[r].—— is very kind, and has lent above a hunderd niggers, but they aint no more use than cats at liftin. Plese Zur come and see whats to be done.

Your Humbel Serv[t],

H. PERKES.

This was pleasant certainly; a new carriage and a pair of fine Australian horses smashed before they reached Newera Ellia!

This was, however, the commencement of a chapter of accidents. I went down the Pass, and there sure enough I had a fine bird's-eye view of the carriage down a precipice on the road side. One horse was so injured that it was necessary to destroy him; the other died a few days after. Perkes had been intoxicated; and, while driving at full gallop round a corner, over went the carriage and horses.

On my return to Newera Ellia I found a letter informing me that the short-horn cow had halted at Amberpussé, thirty-seven miles from Colombo, dangerously ill. The next morning another letter informed me that she was dead. This was a sad loss after the trouble of bringing so fine an animal from England; and I regretted her far more than both carriage and horses together, as my ideas for breeding some thorough-bred stock were for the present extinguished.

There is nothing like one misfortune for breeding another; and what with the loss of carriage, horses, and cow, the string of accidents had fairly commenced. The carriage still lay inverted; and although a tolerable specimen of a smash, I determined to pay a certain honour to its remains, by not allowing it to lie and rot upon the ground. Accordingly I sent the blacksmith with a gang of men, and Perkes was ordered to accompany the party. I also sent the elephant to assist in hauling the body of the carriage up the precipice.

Perkes, having been much more accustomed to riding than walking during his career as groom, was determined to ride the elephant down the Pass; and he accordingly mounted, insisting at the same time that the Mohout should put the animal into a trot. In vain the man remonstrated, and explained that such a pace would injure the elephant on a journey: threats prevailed, and the beast was soon swinging along at full trot, forced on by the sharp driving-hook, with the delighted Perkes striding across its neck, riding an imaginary race.

On the following day the elephant-driver appeared at the front door, but *without* the elephant. I immediately foreboded some disaster, which was soon explained. Mr. Perkes had kept up the pace for fifteen miles to Ramboddé, when, finding that the elephant was not required, he took a little refreshment in the shape of brandy and water, and then, to use his own expression, 'tooled the old elephant along till he came to a stand-still.'

He literally forced the poor beast up the steep Pass for seven miles, till it fell down and shortly after died.

Mr. Perkes was becoming an expensive man: a most sagacious and tractable elephant was now added to his list of victims; and he had the satisfaction of knowing that he was one of the few men in the world who had ridden an elephant to death.

That afternoon Mr. Perkes was being wheeled about the bazaar in a wheelbarrow, insensibly drunk, by a brother emigrant who was also considerably elevated. Perkes had at some former time lost an eye by the kick of a horse, and to conceal the disfigurement he wore a black patch, which gave him very much the expression of a bull terrier with a similar mark. Notwithstanding this disadvantage in appearance, he was perpetually making successful love to the maid-servants, and he was altogether the most incorrigible scamp that I ever met with, although I must do him the justice to say he was thoroughly honest and industrious.

I shortly experienced great trouble with the emigrants; they could not agree with the bailiff, and openly defied his authority. I was obliged to send two of them to gaol as an example to the others. This produced the desired effect, and we shortly got regularly to work.

There were now about a hundred and fifty natives employed in the tedious process of exterminating jungle and forest, not felling, but regularly digging out every tree and root, then piling and burning the mass, and levelling the cleared land in a state to receive the plough. This was very expensive work, amounting to about 30*l.* per acre. The root of a large tree would frequently occupy three men a couple of days in its extraction, which at the rate of wages, at one shilling per diem, was very costly. The land thus cleared was a light sandy loam, about eighteen inches in depth, with a gravel subsoil, and was considered to be far superior to the patina (or natural grass land), which was in appearance black loam on the higher ground, and of a peaty nature in the swamps.

The bailiff (Mr. Fowler) was of opinion that the patina soil was the best; therefore, while the large native force was engaged in sweeping the forest from the surface, operations were commenced according to agricultural rules upon the patinas.

A tract of land known as the 'Moon Plains,' comprising about two hundred acres, was immediately commenced upon. As some persons considered the settlement at Newera Ellia the idea of a lunatic, the 'Moon Plain' was an appropriate spot for the experiment. A tolerable level field of twenty acres was fenced in, and the work began by firing the patina and burning off all the grass. Then came three teams as follows:—

Lord Ducie's patent cultivator, drawn by an elephant; a skim, drawn by another elephant; and a long wood plough, drawn by eight bullocks.

The field being divided into three sections, was thus quickly pared of the turf, the patent cultivator working admirably, and easily drawn by the elephant.

The weather being very dry and favourable for the work, the turf was soon ready for burning; and being piled in long rows, much trouble was saved in subsequently spreading the ashes. This being completed, we had six teams at work, two horse, two bullock, and two elephant; and the ploughing was soon finished. The whole piece was then sown with oats.

It was an interesting sight to see the rough plain yielding to the power of agricultural implements, especially as some of those implements were drawn by animals not generally seen in plough harness at home.

The 'cultivator,' which was sufficiently large to anchor any twenty of the small native bullocks, looked a mere nothing behind the splendid elephant that worked it, and it cut through the wiry roots of the rank turf as a knife peels an apple. It was amusing to see this same elephant doing the work of three separate teams when the seed was in the ground. She first drew a pair of heavy harrows; attached to these and following behind were a pair of light harrows; and behind these came a roller. Thus the land had its first and second harrowing and rolling at the same time.

This elephant was particularly sagacious; and her farming work being completed, she was employed in making a dam across a stream. She was a very large animal, and it was beautiful to witness her wonderful sagacity in carrying and arranging the heavy timber required. The rough stems of trees from the lately-felled forest were lying within fifty yards of the spot, and the trunks required for the dam were about fifteen feet long and fourteen to eighteen inches in diameter. These she carried *in her mouth*, shifting her hold along the log before she raised it until she had obtained the exact balance; then, steadying it with her trunk, she carried every log to the spot, and laid them across the stream in parallel rows. These she herself arranged, under the direction of her driver, with the reason apparently of a human being.

The most extraordinary part of her performance was the arranging of two immense logs of red keenar (one of the heaviest woods). These were about eighteen feet long and two feet in diameter, and they were intended to lie on either bank of the stream parallel to the brook and close to the edge. These she placed with the greatest care in their exact positions, unassisted by any one.[1] She rolled them gently over with her head, then with one foot, and

[1] Directed of course by her driver.

keeping her trunk on the opposite side of the log, she checked its way whenever its own momentum would have carried it into the stream. Although I thought the work admirably done, she did not seem quite satisfied, and she presently got into the stream, and gave one end of the log an extra push with her head, which completed her task, the two trees lying exactly parallel to each other, close to the edge of either bank.

Tame elephants are constantly employed in building stone bridges when the stones required for the abutments are too heavy to be managed by crowbars.

Many were the difficulties to contend against when the first attempts were made in agriculture at Newera Ellia. No sooner were the oats a few inches above ground than they were subjected to the nocturnal visits of elk and hogs in such numbers that they were almost wholly destroyed.

A crop of potatoes of about three acres on the newly-cleared forest land was *totally* devoured by grubs. The bull and stock were nearly starved on the miserable pasturage of the country, and no sooner had the clover sprung up in the new clearings than the Southdown ram got hoven upon it and died. The two remaining rams, not having been accustomed to much high living since their arrival at Newera Ellia, got pugnacious upon the clover, and in a pitched battle the Leicester ram killed the Cotswold—and remained solus. An epidemic appeared among the cattle, and twenty-six fine bullocks died within a few days ; five Australian horses died during the first year, and everything seemed to be going into the next world as fast as possible.

Having made up my mind to all manner of disappointments, these casualties did not make much impression on me, and the loss of a few crops at the outset was to be expected ; but at length a deplorable and unexpected event occurred.

The bailiff's family consisted of a wife and daughter ;—the former was the perfection of a respectable farmer's wife, whose gentle manners and amiable disposition had gained her many friends ; the daughter was a very pretty girl of nineteen.

For some time Mrs. Fowler had been suffering from an illness of long standing, and I was suddenly called to join in the mournful procession to her grave. This was indeed a loss which I deeply deplored.

At length death left the little settlement, and a ray of sunshine shone through the gloom which would have made many despond. Fortune smiled upon everything. Many acres of forest were cleared, and the crops succeeded each other in rapid succession. I had, however, made the discovery that without manure *nothing* would thrive. This had been a great disappointment, as much difficulty lay in procuring the necessary item.

Had the natural pasturage been good, it would soon have been an easy matter to procure any amount of manure by a corresponding number of cattle; but as it happened, the pasturage was so bad that no beast could thrive upon it. Thus everything, even grass-land, had to be manured, and, fortunately, a cargo of guano having arrived in the island, we were enabled to lay down some good clover and seeds.

The original idea of cultivation driving the forests from the neighbourhood of Newera Ellia was therefore dispelled. Every acre of land must be manured, and upon a large scale at Newera Ellia that is impossible. With manure everything will thrive to perfection excepting wheat. There is neither lime nor magnesia in the soil. An abundance of silica throws a good crop of straw, but the grain is wanting; Indian corn will not form grain from the same cause. On the other hand, peas, beans, turnips, carrots, cabbages, &c., produce crops as heavy as those of England. Potatoes, being the staple article of production, are principally cultivated, as the price of 20*l.* per ton yields a large profit. These, however, do not produce larger crops than from four to six tons per acre when heavily manured; but as the crop is fit to dig in three months from the day of planting, money is quickly made.

There are many small farmers, or rather gardeners, at Newera Ellia who have succeeded uncommonly well. One of the emigrants who left my service returned to England in three years with three hundred pounds; and all the industrious people succeed. I am now without one man whom I brought out. The bailiff farms a little land of his own, and his pretty daughter is married; the others are scattered here and there, but I believe all are doing well, especially the blacksmith, upon whose anvil Fortune has smiled most kindly.

By the bye, that same blacksmith has the right stamp of a 'better half' for an emigrant's wife. According to his own description, she is a 'good knock-about kind of a wife.' I recollect seeing her, during a press of work, rendering assistance to her Vulcan in a manner worthy of a Cyclops' spouse. She was wielding an eighteen-pound sledge-hammer, sending the sparks flying at every blow upon the hot iron, and making the anvil ring again, while her husband turned the metal at every stroke, as if attending on Nasmyth's patent steam hammer.

It has been a great satisfaction to me that all the people whom I brought out are doing well; even Henry Perkes, of elephant-jockeying notoriety, is, I believe, prospering as a groom in Madras.

CHAPTER III.

Task Completed—The Mountain-top—Change in the Face of Nature—Original Importance of Newera Ellia—'The Path of a Thousand Princes'—Vestiges of Former Population—Mountains—The Highlands of Ouva—Ancient Methods of Irrigation—Remains of Aqueducts—The Vale of Rubies—Ancient Ophir—Discovery of Gold—Mineral Resources—Native Blacksmiths.

IN a climate like that of Newera Ellia, even twelve months make a great change in the appearance of a new settlement; plants and shrubs spring up with wonderful rapidity, and a garden of one year's growth, without attendance, would be a wilderness.

A few years, necessarily, made a vast change in everything. All kinds of experiments had been made, and those which succeeded were persevered in. I discovered that excellent beer might be made at this elevation (6,200 feet), and I accordingly established a small brewery.

The solitary Leicester ram had propagated a numerous family, and a flock of fat ewes, with their lambs, throve to perfection. Many handsome young heifers looked very like the emigrant bull in the face, and claimed their parentage. The fields were green; the axe no longer sounded in the forest; a good house stood in the centre of cultivation; a road of two miles in length cut through the estate, and the whole place looked like an adopted 'home.' All the trials and disappointments of the beginning were passed away, and the real was a picture which I had ideally contemplated years before. The task was finished.

In the interim, public improvements had not been neglected; an extremely pretty church had been erected, and a public reading-room established; but, with the exception of one good house which had been built, private enterprise had lain dormant. As usual, from January to May, Newera Ellia was over-crowded with visitors, and nearly empty during the other months of the year.

All Ceylon people dread the wet season at Newera Ellia, which continues from June to December.

I myself prefer it to what is termed the dry season, at which time the country is burnt up by drought. There is never more rain at Newera Ellia than vegetation requires, and not one-fourth the quantity falls at this elevation compared to that of the low country. It may be more continuous, but it is of a lighter character, and more akin to 'Scotch mist.' The clear days during the wet season are far more lovely than the constant glare of the summer months, and the rays of the sun are not so powerful.

There cannot be a more beautiful sight than the view of sunrise from the summit of Pedrotallagalla, the highest mountain in Ceylon, which, rising to the height of 8,300 feet, looks down upon Newera Ellia, some two thousand feet below upon one side, and upon the interminable depths of countless ravines and valleys at its base.

There is a feeling approaching the sublime when a solitary man thus stands upon the highest point of earth, before the dawn of day, and waits the first rising of the sun. Nothing above him but the dusky arch of heaven. Nothing on his level but empty space,—all beneath, deep beneath his feet. From childhood he has looked to heaven as the dwelling of the Almighty, and he now stands upon that lofty summit in the silence of utter solitude; his hand, as he raises it above his head, the highest mark upon the sea-girt land; his form above all mortals upon this land, the nearest to his God. Words, till now unthought of, tingle in his ears,—'He went up into a mountain apart to pray.' He feels the spirit which prompted the choice of such a lonely spot, and he stands instinctively uncovered, as the first ray of light spreads like a thread of fire across the sky.

And now the distant hill-tops, far below, struggle through the snowy sheet of mist, like islands in a fairy sea; and far, how far his eye can scan, where the faint line upon the horizon marks the ocean! Mountain and valley, hill and plain, with boundless forest, stretch beneath his feet, far as his sight can gaze, and the scene, so solemnly beautiful, gradually wakens to his senses: the birds begin to chirp; the dew-drops fall heavily from the trees, as the light breeze stirs from an apparent sleep; a golden tint spreads over the sea of mist below; the rays dart lightning-like upon the eastern sky; the mighty orb rises in all the fulness of his majesty, recalling the words of Omnipotence,—'Let there be light!'

The sun is risen! the misty sea below mounts like a snowy wreath around the hill-tops, and then, like a passing thought, it vanishes. A glassy clearness of the atmosphere reveals the magnificent view of Nature, fresh from her sleep; every dewy leaf gilded by the morning sun, every rock glistening with moisture in his bright rays, mountain and valley, wood and plain, alike rejoicing in his beams.

And now, the sun being risen, we gaze from our lofty post upon Newera Ellia, lying at our feet. We trace the river winding its silvery course through the plain, and for many miles the alternate plains and forests joining in succession.

How changed are some features of the landscape within the few past years, and how wonderful the alteration made by man on the face of Nature!

Comparatively but a few years ago, Newera Ellia was undiscovered—a secluded plain among the mountain-tops, tenanted by the elk and boar. The wind swept over it, and the mists hung around the mountains, and the bright summer with its spotless sky succeeded, but still it was unknown and unseen except by the native bee-hunter, in his rambles for wild honey. How changed! The road encircles the plain, and carts are busy in removing the produce of the land. Here, where wild forest stood, are gardens teeming with English flowers; rosy-faced children and ruddy countrymen are about the cottage doors; equestrians of both sexes are galloping round the plain, and the cry of the hounds is ringing on the mountain-side.

How changed! There is an old tree standing upon a hill, whose gnarled trunk has been twisted by the winter's wind for many an age, and so screwed is its old stem, that the axe has spared it, out of pity, when its companions were all swept away, and the forest felled. And many a tale that old tree could tell of winter's blasts and broken boughs, and storms which howled above its head, when all was wilderness around. The eagle has roosted in its top, the monkeys have gambolled in its branches, and the elephants have rubbed their tough flanks against its stem in times gone by; but it now throws a shadow upon a Christian's grave; and the churchyard lies beneath its shade. The church bell sounds where the elephant trumpeted of yore. The sunbeam has penetrated where the forest threw its dreary shade, and a ray of light has shone through the moral darkness of the spot.

The completion of the church is the grand improvement in Newera Ellia.

Although Newera Ellia was in the wild state described when first discovered by Europeans, it is not to be supposed that its existence was unknown to the Cingalese. The name itself proves its former importance to the kings of Kandy, as Newera Ellia signifies 'Royal Plains.' Kandy is termed by the Cingalese 'Newera,' as it was the capital of Ceylon, and the residence of the king.

Although the country is wild, and in many portions unvisited by Europeans, still every high mountain, and every little plain, in this wilderness of forest, is not only known to the natives of the adjacent low country, but has its separate designation. There is no feature without its name, although the immense tract of mountains are totally uninhabited, and the nearest villages are some ten or twelve miles distant, between two and three thousand feet below.

There are native paths from village to village, across the mountains, which, although in appearance no more than deer-runs, have existed for many centuries, and are used by the natives even to this day.

The great range of forest-covered Newera Ellia mountains divides the two districts of Ouva and Kotmalee, and these paths have been formed to connect the two by an arduous ascent upon either side, and a comparatively level cut across the shoulders of the mountains, through alternate plain and forest for some twenty-five miles. These paths would never be known to Europeans were it not for the distant runs of the hounds, in following which, after some hours of fatiguing jungle work, I have come upon a track. The notches on the tree-stems have proved its artificial character, and by following its course I have learnt the country.

There is not a path, stream, hill, or plain within many miles of Newera Ellia, that I do not know intimately, although when the character of the country is scanned by a stranger from some mountain-top, the very act of traversing it appears impossible. This knowledge has been gained by years of unceasing hunting, and by perseveringly following up the hounds wherever they have gone. From sunrise till nightfall I have often ploughed along through alternate jungles and plains, listening eagerly for the cry of the hounds, and at length discovering portions of the country which I had never known to exist.

There is a great pleasure in thus working out the features of a wild country, especially in an island like Ceylon, which, in every portion, exhibits traces of former prosperity and immense population. Even these uninhabited and chilly regions, up to an elevation of 7,000 feet, are not blank pages in the book of Nature, but the hand of man is so distinctly traced, that the keen observer can read with tolerable certainty the existence of a nation long since passed away.

As I before mentioned, I pitched my settlement on the verge of the highland, at the eastern extremity of the Newera Ellia plain, where the road commences a sudden descent towards Badulla, thirty-three miles distant. This spot, forming a shallow gap, was the ancient native entrance to Newera Ellia from that side, and the Cingalese designation for the locality is interpreted 'the Path of a Thousand Princes.' This name assists in the proof that Newera Ellia was formerly of some great importance. A far more enticing name gives an interest to the first swampy portion of the plain some three hundred paces beyond, viz., 'the Valley of Rubies.'

Now, having plainly discovered that Newera Ellia was of some great importance to the natives, let us consider in what that value consisted. There are no buildings remaining, no ruins, as in other parts of Ceylon, but a liquid mine of wealth poured from these lofty regions. The importance of Newera

Ellia lay, first, in its supply of *water*, and, secondly, in its gems.

In all tropical countries, the first principle of cultivation is irrigation, without which the land would remain barren. In a rice-growing country like Ceylon, the periodical rains are insufficient, and the whole system of native agriculture depends upon the supply of water. Accordingly, the mountains being the reservoirs from which the rivers spring, become of vital importance to the country.

The principal mountains in Ceylon are Pedrotallagalla, 8,280 feet; Kirigallapotta, 7,900; Totapella, 8,000; and Adam's Peak, 7,700, &c.; but although their height is so considerable, they do not give the idea of grandeur which such an altitude would convey. They do not rise abruptly from a level base, but they are merely the loftiest of a thousand peaks towering from the highlands of Ceylon.

The greater portion of the highland district may therefore be compared to one vast mountain; hill piled upon hill, and peak rising over peak; ravines of immense depth, forming innumerable conduits for the mountain torrents. Then, at the elevation of Newera Ellia, the heavings of the land appear to have rested, and gentle undulations, diversified by plains and forests, extend for some thirty miles. From these comparatively level tracts and swampy plains, the rivers of Ceylon derive their source, and the three loftiest peaks take their base; Pedrotallagalla rising from the Newera Ellia Plain, Totapella, and Kirigallapotta from the Horton Plains.

The whole of the highland district is thus composed of a succession of ledges of great extent at various elevations, commencing with the highest, the Horton Plains, 7,000 feet above the sea.

Seven hundred feet below the Horton Plains, the Totapella Plains and undulating forests continue at this elevation as far as Newera Ellia for about twenty miles, thus forming the second ledge.

Six miles to the west of Newera Ellia, at a lower elevation of about nine hundred feet, the district of Dimboola commences, and extends at this elevation over a vast tract of forest-covered country, stretching still further to the west, and containing a small proportion of plain.[1]

At about the same elevation, nine miles on the north of Newera Ellia, we descend to the Elephant Plains;—a beautiful tract of fine grass country, but of small extent. This tract and that of Dimboola form the third ledge.

Nine miles to the east of Newera Ellia, at a lower elevation of 1,500 feet, stretches the Ouva country, forming the fourth ledge.

[1] The forests have now been cleared, and this district is in coffee cultivation.

The features of this country are totally distinct from any other portion of Ceylon. A magnificent view extends as far as the horizon, of undulating open grass land, diversified by the rich crops of paddy which are grown in each of the innumerable small valleys formed by the undulations of the ground. Not a tree is to be seen except the low brushwood which is scantily distributed upon its surface. We emerge suddenly from the forest-covered mountains of Newera Ellia, and, from a lofty point on the high road to Badulla, we look down upon the splendid panorama stretched like a waving sea beneath our feet. The road upon which we stand is scarped out of the mountain's side. The forest has ceased, dying off gradually into isolated patches, and long ribbon-like strips on the sides of the mountain, upon which, rich grass is growing in vivid contrast to the rank and coarse herbage of Newera Ellia, distant only five miles.

Descending until we reach Wilson's Plain, nine miles from Newera Ellia, we arrive in the district of Ouva, as much like the Sussex Downs as any place to which it can be compared.

This district comprises about six hundred square miles, and forms the fourth and last ledge of the highlands of Ceylon. Passes from the mountains which form the wall-like boundaries of this tableland descend to the low country in various directions.

The whole of the Ouva district upon the one side, and of the Kotmalee district on the other side, of the Newera Ellia range of mountains, are, with the exception of the immediate neighbourhood of Kandy and Colombo, the most populous districts of Ceylon.

This is entirely owing to the never-failing supply of water obtained from the mountains, and upon this supply the wealth and prosperity of the country depend.

The ancient history of Ceylon is involved in much obscurity; but, nevertheless, we have sufficient data in the existing traces of its former population to form our opinions of the position and power which Ceylon occupied in the Eastern Hemisphere, when England was in a state of barbarism. The wonderful remains of ancient cities, tanks, and water-courses throughout the island all prove that the now desolate regions were tenanted by a multitude—not of savages, but of a race long since passed away, full of industry and intelligence.

Among the existing traces of former population few are more interesting than those in the vicinity of Newera Ellia.

Judging from the present supply of water required for the cultivation of a district containing a certain population, we can arrive at a tolerably correct idea of the former population by comparing this supply with that formerly required.

Although the district of Ouva is at present well populated, and every hollow is taken advantage of for the cultivation of paddy, still the demand for water in proportion to the supply is comparatively small.

The system of irrigation has necessarily involved immense labour. For many miles the water is conducted from the mountains through dense forests, across ravines, round the steep sides of opposing hills, now leaping into a lower valley into a reservoir, from which it is again led through this arduous country until it at length reaches the land which it is destined to render fertile.

There has been a degree of engineering skill displayed in forming aqueducts through such formidable obstacles; the hills are lined out in every direction with these proofs of industry, and their winding course can be traced round the grassy sides of the steep mountains, while the paddy fields are seen miles away in the valleys of Ouva stretched far beneath.

At least eight out of ten of these water-courses are dry, and the masonry required in the sudden angles of ravines has in most cases fallen to decay. Even those aqueducts still in existence are of the second class; small streams have been conducted from their original course, and these serve for the supply of the present population.

From the remains of deserted water-courses of the first class, it is evident that more than fifty times the volume of water was then required that is in use at present, and in the same ratio must have been the amount of population.

In those days rivers were diverted from their natural channels; opposing hills were cut through, and the waters thus were led into another valley to join a stream flowing in its natural bed, whose course, eventually obstructed by a dam, poured its accumulated waters into canals which branched to various localities. Not a river in those times flowed in vain. The hill-sides were terraced out in beautiful order; these are now waving with wild vegetation and rank lemon grass.

The remaining traces of stone walls point out the ancient boundaries far above the secluded valleys now in cultivation.

The nation has vanished; and with it the industry and perseverance of the era.

We now arrive at the cause of the former importance of Newera Ellia, or the 'Royal Plains.'

It has been shown that the very existence of the population depended upon the supply of water, and that supply was obtained from the neighbourhood of Newera Ellia. Therefore a king in possession of Newera Ellia had the most complete command over his subjects; he could either give or withhold the supply of water at his pleasure by allowing its free exit, or by altering its course.

Thus during rebellion he could starve his people into submission, or lay waste the land in time of foreign invasion. I have seen in an impregnable position the traces of an ancient fort, evidently erected to defend the pass to the main water-course from the low country.

This gives us a faint clue to the probable cause of the disappearance of the nation.

In time of war or intestine commotion the water may have been cut off from the low country, and the exterminating effects of famine may have laid the whole land desolate.

It is therefore no longer a matter of astonishment that the present vale of Newera Ellia should have received its appellation of the 'Royal Plain.' In those days there was no very secure tenure to the throne, and by force alone could a king retain it. The more blood-thirsty and barbarous the tyrant, the more was he dreaded by the awe-stricken and trembling population. The power of such a weapon of annihilation as the command of the waters may be easily conceived, as it invested a king with almost divine authority in the eyes of his subjects.

There is little doubt that the existence of precious gems at Newera Ellia may have been accidentally discovered in digging the numerous water-courses in the vicinity: there is, however, no doubt that at some former period the east end of the plain, called the 'Vale of Rubies,' constituted the Royal 'Diggings.'

That the king of Kandy did not reside at Newera Ellia there is little wonder, as a monarch delighting in a temperature of 85° Fahr. would have regarded the climate of a mean temperature of 60° Fahr. as we should that of Nova Zembla.

We may take it for granted, therefore, that when the king came to Newera Ellia his visit had some object, and we presume that he came to look at the condition of his water-courses, and to superintend the digging for precious stones; in the same manner that Ceylon governors of past years visited Arippo during the pearl fishing.

The 'diggings' of the kings of Kandy must have been conducted on a most extensive scale. Not only has the Vale of Rubies been regularly turned up for many acres, but all the numerous plains in the vicinity are full of pits, some of very large size and of a depth varying from three to seventeen feet. The Newera Ellia Plain, the Moon-stone Plain, the Kondapallé Plain, the Elk Plains, the Totapella Plains, the Horton Plains, the Bopatalava Plains, the Augara Plains (translated the 'Diggings'), and many others, extending over a surface of thirty miles, are all more or less studded by deep pits formed by the ancient searchers for gems, which in those days were a royal monopoly.

It is not to be supposed that the search for gems would have been thus persevered in unless it was found to be remunerative; but it is a curious fact that no Englishmen are ever to be seen at work at this employment. The natives would still continue the search, were they permitted, upon the 'Vale of Rubies;' but I warned them off on purchasing the land; and I have several good specimens of gems which I have discovered by digging two feet beneath the surface.

The surface soil being of a light peaty quality, the stones, from their greater gravity, lie beneath, mixed with a rounded quartz gravel, which in ages past must have been subjected to the action of running water. This quartz gravel, with its mixture of gems, rests upon a stiff white pipe-clay.

In this stratum of gravel an infinite number of small, and for the most part worthless, specimens of gems are found, consisting of sapphire, ruby, emerald, jacinth, tourmaline, chrysoberyl, zircon, cat's-eye, 'moon-stone,' and 'star-stone.' Occasionally a stone of value rewards the patient digger; but, unless he thoroughly understands it, he is apt to pass over the gems of most value as pieces of ironstone.

The mineralogy of Ceylon has hitherto been little understood. It has often been suggested as the

'Ophir' of the time of Solomon, and doubtless, from its production of gems, it might deserve the name.

It has hitherto been the opinion of most writers on Ceylon that the precious metals do not exist in the island; and Dr. Davy in his work makes an unqualified assertion to that effect. But from the discoveries recently made, I am of opinion that it exists in *very large* quantities in the mountainous districts of the island.

It is amusing to see the positive assertions of a clever man upset by a few uneducated sailors.

A few men of the latter class, who had been at the gold-diggings both in California and Australia, happened to engage in a ship bound for Colombo. Upon arrival, they obtained leave from the captain for a stroll on shore, and they took the road towards Kandy, and when about half-way, it struck them, from the appearance of the rocks in the uneven bed of a river, called the Maha Oya, 'that gold must exist in its sands.' They had no geological reason for this opinion; but the river happened to be very like those in California, in which they had been accustomed to find gold. They accordingly set to work with a tin pan to wash the sand, and to the astonishment of everyone in Ceylon, and to the utter confusion of Dr. Davy's opinions, they actually *discovered gold!*

The quantity was small; but the men were very

sanguine of success, and were making their preparations for working on a more extensive scale, when they were all prostrated by jungle fever; a guardian-spirit of the gold at Ambepussé, which will ever effectually protect it from Europeans.

They all returned to Colombo, and, when convalescent, they proceeded to Newera Ellia, naturally concluding that the gold which existed in dust in the rivers below must be washed down from the richer stores of the mountains.

Their first discovery of gold at Newera Ellia was on the 14th of June, 1854, on the second day of their search in that locality. This was found in the 'Vale of Rubies.'

I had advised them to make their first search in that spot for this reason: that, as the precious stones had there settled in the largest numbers, from their superior gravity, it was natural to conclude that, if gold should exist, it would, from its gravity, be somewhere below the precious stones, or in their vicinity.

From the facility with which it has been discovered, it is impossible to form an opinion as to the quantity or the extent to which it will eventually be developed. It is equally impossible to predict the future discoveries which may be made of other minerals. It is well known that quicksilver was found at Cotta, six miles from Colombo, in the year 1797. It was in small quantities, and was neglected by the Government, and no extended search was prosecuted. The present search for gold may bring to light mineral resources of Ceylon which have hitherto lain hidden.

The minerals proved to exist up to the present time are gold, quicksilver, plumbago, and iron. The two latter are of the finest quality, and in immense abundance. The rocks of Ceylon are primitive, consisting of granite, gneiss, and quartz. Of these the two latter predominate. Dolomite also exists in large quantities up to an elevation of 5,000 feet, but not beyond this height.

Plumbago is disseminated throughout the whole of both soil and rocks in Ceylon, and may be seen covering the surface in the drains by the road-side, after a recent shower.

It is principally found at Ratnapoora and at Belligam, in large detached kidney-shaped masses, from four to twenty feet below the surface. The cost of digging and the transport are the only expenses attending it, as the supply is inexhaustible. Its component parts are nineteen of carbon and one of iron.

It exists in such quantities in the gneiss rocks, that upon their decomposition it is seen in bright specks like silver throughout.

This gneiss rock, when in a peculiar stage of decay, has the appearance and consistency of yellow brick, speckled with plumbago. It exists in this state in immense masses, and forms a valuable building-stone, as it can be cut with ease to any shape required, and though soft when dug, it hardens by exposure to the air. It has also the valuable property of withstanding the greatest heat; and for furnace building it is equal to Stourbridge fire-bricks.

The finest quality of iron is found upon the mountains in various forms, from the small ironstone gravel to large masses of many tons in weight, protruding from the earth's surface.

So valuable is that considered at Newera Ellia and the vicinity, that the native blacksmiths have been accustomed from time immemorial to make periodical visits for the purpose of smelting the ore. The average specimens of this produce about eighty per cent. of pure metal, even by the coarse native process of smelting. The operations are as follow:—

Having procured the desired amount of ore, it is rendered as small as possible by pounding with a hammer.

A platform is then built of clay, about six feet in length by three feet in height and width.

A small well is formed in the centre of the platform, about eighteen inches in depth and diameter; egg-shaped.

A few inches from the bottom of this well is an air-passage, connected with a pipe and bellows.

The well is then filled with alternate layers of

charcoal and pulverised iron ore; the fire is lighted, and the process of smelting commences.

The bellows are formed of two inflated skins, like a double 'bagpipe.' Each foot of the 'bellows-blower' is strapped to one skin, the pipes of the bellows being fixed in the air-hole of the blast. He then works the skins alternately by moving his feet up and down, being assisted in this treadmill kind of labour by the elasticity of two bamboos, of eight or ten feet in length, the butts of which, being firmly fixed in the ground, enable him to retain his balance by grasping one with either hand. From the yielding top of each bamboo, a string descends attached to either big toe; thus the downward pressure of each foot upon the bellows strains upon the bamboo top as a fish bears upon a fishing-rod, and the spring of the cane assists him in lifting up his leg. Without this assistance, it would be impossible to continue the exertion for the time required.

While the 'bellows-blower' is thus getting up a blaze, another man attends upon the well, which he continues to feed alternately with fresh ore and a corresponding amount of charcoal, every now and then throwing in a handful of fine sand as a flux.

The return for a whole day's puffing and blowing will be about twenty pounds weight of badly smelted iron. This is subsequently remelted, and is eventually worked up into hatchets, hoes, betel-crackers, &c. &c., being of a superior quality to the best Swedish iron.

If the native blacksmith were to value his time at only sixpence per diem, from the day on which he first started for the mountains, till the day that he returned from his iron-smelting expedition, he would find that his metal would have cost him rather a high price per hundredweight; and if he were to make the same calculation of the value of time, he would discover that by the time he had completed one axe, he could have purchased ready-made, for one-third the money, an English tool of superior manufacture. This, however, is not their style of calculation. Time has no value, according to their crude ideas; therefore, if they want an article, and can produce it without the actual outlay of cash, no matter how much time is expended, they will prefer that method of obtaining it.

Unfortunately, the expense of transit is so heavy from Newera Ellia to Colombo, that this valuable metal, like the fine timber of the forests, must remain useless.

CHAPTER IV.

Poverty of Soil—Ceylon Sugar—Fatality of Climate—Supposed Fertility of Soil—Native Cultivation—Neglect of Rice Cultivation—Abandoned Reservoirs—Former Prosperity—Ruins of Cities—Pollanarua—The Great Dagoba—Architectural Relics—The Rock Temple—Destruction of Population—Neglected Capabilities—Suggestions for Increasing Population—Progress of Pestilence—Deserted Villages—Difficulties in the Cultivation of Rice—Division of Labour—Native Agriculture.

FROM the foregoing description, the reader will have inferred that Newera Ellia is a delightful place of residence, with a mean temperature of 60° Fahr., abounding with beautiful views of mountain and plain, and of boundless panoramas in the vicinity. He will also have discovered that, in addition to the healthiness of its climate, its natural resources are confined to its timber and mineral productions, as the soil is decidedly poor.

The appearance of the latter has deceived everyone, especially the black soil of the patina, which my bailiff on his first arrival declared to be excellent. Lord Torrington, who is well known as an agriculturist, was equally deceived. He was very confident in the opinion that 'it only required draining to enable it to produce anything.' The real fact is, that it is far inferior to the forest land, and will not pay for the working.

Nevertheless, it is my decided opinion that the generality of the forest land at Newera Ellia and the vicinity is superior to that in other parts of Ceylon.

There are necessarily rich lots every now and then in such a large extent as the surface of the low country; but these usually lie on the banks of rivers which have been subjected to inundations, and they are not fair samples of Ceylon soil. A river's bank or a valley's bottom must be tolerably good even in the poorest country.

The great proof of the general poverty of Ceylon is shown in the failure of every agricultural experiment in which a rich soil is required.

Cinnamon thrives; but why? It delights in a soil of quartz sand, in which nothing else will grow.

Cocoa-nut trees flourish for the same reason; sea air, a sandy soil, and a dry subsoil are all that the cocoa-nut requires.

On the other hand, those tropical productions which require a strong soil invariably prove failures, and sugar, cotton, indigo, hemp, and tobacco, cannot possibly be cultivated with success.

Even on the alluvial soil upon the banks of rivers,

sugar does not pay the proprietor. The only sugar estate in the island that can keep its head above water, is the Peredenia estate, within four miles of Kandy. This, again, lies upon the bank of the Mahawelli river, and it has also the advantage of a home market for its produce, as it supplies the interior of Ceylon at the rate of 23*s*. per cwt. upon the spot.

Any person who thoroughly understands the practical cultivation of the sugar-cane can tell the quality of sugar that will be produced by an examination of the soil. I am convinced that no soil in Ceylon will produce a sample of fine straw-coloured, dry, bright, large crystallized sugar. The finest sample ever produced of Ceylon sugar is a dull grey; and always moist; requiring a very large proportion of lime in the manufacture, without which it could neither be cleansed nor crystallized.

The sugar-cane, to produce *fine* sugar, requires a rich, stiff, and very dry soil. In Ceylon there is no such thing as a *stiff* soil existing. The alluvial soil upon the banks of rivers is adapted for the growth of cotton and tobacco, but not for the sugar-cane. In such light and moist alluvial soil the latter will grow to a great size, and will yield a large quantity of juice in which the saccharometer may stand well; but the degree of strength indicated will proceed from an immense proportion of mucilage, which will give much trouble in the cleansing during boiling; and the sugar produced must be wanting in dryness and fine colour.

There are several rivers in Ceylon whose banks would produce good cotton and tobacco, especially those in the districts of Hambantotte and Batticaloa; such as the 'Wallawé,' the 'Yallé river,' the 'Koombookanaar,' &c.; but even here the good soil is very limited, lying on either bank for only a quarter of a mile in width. In addition to this, the unhealthiness of the climate is so great that I am convinced no European constitution could withstand it. Even the natives are decimated at certain seasons by the most virulent fevers and dysentery.

These diseases generally prevail to the greatest extent during the dry season. This district is particularly subject to severe droughts; months pass away without a drop of rain or a cloud upon the sky. Every pool and tank is dried up; the rivers forsake their banks, and a trifling stream trickles over the sandy bed. Thus all the rotten wood, dead leaves, and putrid vegetation brought down by the torrent during the wet season, are left upon the dried bed to infect the air with miasma.

This deadly climate would be an insurmountable obstacle to the success of estates. Even could managers be found to brave the danger, one season of sickness and death among the coolies would give the estate a name which would deprive it of all future supplies of labour.

Indigo is indigenous to Ceylon; but it is of an inferior quality, and an experiment made in its cultivation was a total failure.

In fact, nothing will permanently succeed in Ceylon soil without abundance of manure, with the exception of cinnamon and cocoa-nuts. Even the native gardens will not produce a tolerable sample of the common sweet potato without manure, a positive proof of the general poverty of the soil.

Nevertheless, Ceylon has had a character for fertility. Bennett, in his work entitled 'Ceylon and its Capabilities,' describes the island in the most florid terms, as 'the most important and valuable of all the insular possessions of the imperial crown.' Again, he speaks of 'its fertile soil, and indigenous vegetable productions,' &c. &c. Again: 'Ceylon, though comparatively but little known, is pre-eminent in natural resources.' All this serves to mislead the public opinion. Agricultural experiments in a tropical country in a little garden highly manured may be very satisfactory and very amusing. Everything must necessarily come to perfection with great rapidity; but these experiments are no proof of what Ceylon will produce, and the popular idea of its fertility has been at length proved a delusion.

It is a dangerous thing for any man to sit down

to '*make*' a book. If he has had personal experience, let him write a description of those subjects which he understands ; but if he attempts to 'make' a book, he must necessarily collect information from hearsay, when he will most probably gather some 'chaff' with his grain.

Can any man, when describing the 'fertility' of Ceylon, be aware that newly-cleared forest land will only produce one crop of the miserable grain called korrakan? Can he understand why the greater portion of Ceylon is covered by dense thorny jungles? It is simply this, that the land is so desperately poor, that it will only produce one crop, and thus an immense acreage is required for the support of a few inhabitants ; thus, from ages past up to the present time, the natives have been continually felling fresh forest and deserting the last clearing, which has accordingly grown into a dense thorny jungle, forming what are termed the 'Chénars' of Ceylon.[1]

So fully aware are the natives of the impossibility of getting more than one crop out of the land, that they plant all that they require at the same time. Thus may be seen in a field of korrakan (a small grain), extensive coracana, Indian corn, millet, and pumpkins,

[1] It has been satisfactorily proved that although the soil of Ceylon is poor, it is nevertheless peculiarly adapted for the growth of wood. Thus such shrubs as coffee, tea, cinnamon, and cinchona, arrive at great perfection.

all growing together, and harvested as they respectively become ripe.

The principal articles of native cultivation are rice, korrakan, Indian corn, betel, areca nuts, pumpkins, onions, garlic, gingelly-oil seed, tobacco, millet, red peppers, curry seeds, and sweet potatoes.

The staple articles of Ceylon production are coffee, cinnamon, and cocoa-nut oil; which are, for the most part, cultivated and manufactured by Europeans.

The chief article of native consumption, 'rice,' should be an export from Ceylon; but there has been an unaccountable neglect on the part of Government regarding the production of this important grain, for the supply of which Ceylon is mainly dependent upon importation. In the hitherto overrated general resources of Ceylon, the cultivation of rice has scarcely been deemed worthy of notice; the all-absorbing subject of coffee cultivation has withdrawn the attention of the Government from that particular article, for the production of which the resources of Ceylon are both naturally and artificially immense.

This neglect is the more extraordinary as the increase of coffee cultivation involves a proportionate increase in the consumption of rice, by the additional influx of cooly labour from the coast of India; therefore the price and supply of rice in Ceylon becomes a question of similar importance to the price of corn in England. This dependence upon a foreign soil for the supply involves the necessary fluctuations in price, caused by uncertain arrivals and precarious harvests; and the importance of an unlimited quantity at an even rate may be imagined, when it is known that every native consumes a bushel of rice per month, when he can obtain it.

Nevertheless, the great capabilities of Ceylon for the cultivation of this all important 'staff of life' are entirely neglected by the Government. The tanks which afforded a supply of water for millions in former ages now lie idle and out of repair; the pelican sails in solitude upon their surface, and the crocodile basks upon their shores; the thousands of acres which formerly produced rice for a dense population are now matted over by a thorny and impenetrable jungle. The wild buffalo descendant from the ancient stock which tilled the ground of a great nation now roams through barren forest, which in olden times was a soil glistening with fertility. The ruins of the mighty cities tower high above the trees, sad monuments of desolation, where all was once flourishing, and where thousands pwelt within their walls.

All are passed away; and in the wreck of former ages we trace the great resources of the country which produced sufficient food to support millions; while for the present comparatively small population, Ceylon is dependent upon imports.

These lakes, or tanks, were works of much art and of immense labour, for the purpose of reservoirs, from the supply of which the requisite amount of land could be irrigated for rice cultivation. A valley of the required extent being selected, the courses of neighbouring or distant rivers were conducted into it, and the exit of the waters was prevented by great causeways, or dams of solid masonry, which extended for some miles across the lower side of the valley thus converted into a lake. The exit of the water was then regulated by means of sluices, from which it was conducted by channels to the rice lands.

These tanks are of various extent, and extremely numerous throughout Ceylon. The largest are those of Minneria, Kandellai, Padavellkiellom, and the Giant's Tank. These are from fifteen to twenty-five miles in circumference; but in former times, when the sluices were in repair and the volume of water at its full height, they must have been much larger.

In those days the existence of a reservoir of water was a certain indication of a populous and flourishing neighbourhood; and the chief cities of the country were accordingly situated in places which were always certain of a supply. So careful were the inhabitants in husbanding those liquid resources upon which their very existence depended, that even the surplus waters of one lake were not allowed to escape unheeded. Channels were cut connecting a chain of tanks of slightly varying elevations, over an extent of sixty or seventy miles of apparently flat country, and the overflow of one tank was thus conducted in succession from lake to lake until they all attained the desired level.

In this manner was the greater portion of Ceylon kept in the highest state of cultivation. From the north to the south, the island was thickly peopled, and the only portions which then remained in the hands of nature were those which are now seen in the state of primeval forest.

Well may Ceylon in those times have deserved the name of the 'Paradise of the East.' The beauties which nature has showered upon the land were heightened by cultivation; the forest-capped mountains rose from a waving sea of green; the valleys teemed with wealth; no thorny jungles gave a barren cast to the interminable prospect, but the golden tints of ripening crops spread to the horizon. Temples stood upon the hill-tops; cities were studded over the land, their lofty dagobas and palaces reflected on the glassy surface of the lakes, from which their millions of inhabitants derived food, wealth, and life.

The remains of these cities sufficiently attest the former amount of population, and the comparative civilisation which existed at that remote era among the progenitors of the present degraded race of barbarians. The ruins of 'Anaradupoora,' which cover 256 square miles of ground, are all that remain of the noble city which stood within its walls in a square of sixteen miles. Some idea of the amount of population may be arrived at, when we consider the present density of inhabitants in all Indian houses and towns. Millions must, therefore, have streamed from the gates of a city, to which our modern London was comparatively a village.

There is a degree of sameness in the ruins of all the ancient cities of Ceylon, which renders a description tedious. Those of 'Anaradupoora' are the largest in extent, and the buildings appear to have been more lofty, the great dagoba having exceeded 400 feet in height; but the ruins do not exhibit the same 'finish' in the style of architecture which is seen in the remains of other towns.

Among these 'Toparé,' anciently called 'Pollanarua,' stands foremost. This city appears to have been laid out with a degree of taste which would have done credit to our modern towns.

Before its principal gate stretched a beautiful

lake of about fifteen miles' circumference (now only nine). The approach to this gate was by a broad road, upon the top of a stone causeway, of between two and three miles in length, which formed a massive dam to the waters of the lake which washed its base. To the right of this dam stretched many miles of cultivation; to the left on the farther shores of the lake, lay park-like grass-lands, studded with forest trees, some of whose mighty descendants still exist in the noble 'tamarind,' rising above all others. Let us return in imagination to Pollanarua as it once stood. Having arrived upon the causeway in the approach to the city, the scene must have been beautiful in the extreme: the silvery lake, like a broad mirror in the midst of a tropical park; the flowering trees shadowing its waters; the groves of tamarinds sheltering its many nooks and bays; the gorgeous blossoms of the pink lotus, resting on its glassy surface; and the carpet-like glades of verdant pasturage, stretching far away upon the opposite shores covered with countless elephants, tamed to complete obedience. Then on the right, below the massive granite steps which form the causeway, the water rushing from the sluice carries fertility among a thousand fields; and countless labourers and cattle till the ground: the sturdy buffaloes straining at the plough, the women laden with golden sheaves of corn, and baskets of fruit, crowding along the palm-shaded road winding towards the city, from whose gate a countless throng are passing and returning. Behold the mighty city! rising like a snow-white cloud from the broad margin of the waters. The groves of cocoa-nuts and palms of every kind, grouped in the inner gardens, throwing a cool shade upon the polished walls; the lofty palaces towering among the stately areca trees, and the gilded domes reflecting a blaze of light from the rays of a mid-day sun. Such let us suppose the exterior of Pollanarua.

The gates are entered, and a broad street, straight as an arrow, lies before us, shaded on either side by rows of palms. Here stand, on either hand, the dwellings of the principal inhabitants, bordering the wide space, which continues its straight and shady course for about four miles in length. In the centre, standing in a spacious circle, rises the great dagoba, forming a grand *coup d'œil,* from the entrance gate. Two hundred and sixty feet from the base, the dagoba rears its lofty summit. Two circular terraces, each of some twenty feet in height, rising one upon the other, with a width of fifty feet, and a diameter at the base of about 250, form the step-like platform upon which the dagoba stands. These are ascended by broad flights of steps, each terrace forming a circular promenade around the dagoba; the whole having the appearance of white marble, being covered with polished stucco, ornamented with figures in bas-relief. The dagoba is a solid mass of brick-work in the shape of a dome, which rises from the upper terrace. The whole is covered with polished stucco, and surmounted by a gilded spire standing upon a square pedestal, highly ornamented with with large figures, also in bas-relief; this pedestal is a cube of about thirty feet, supporting the tall gilded spire, which is surmounted by a golden umbrella.

Around the base of the dagoba on the upper terrace are eight small entrances with highly ornamented exteriors. These are the doors to eight similar chambers of about twelve feet square, in each of which is a small altar and carved golden idol.

This dagoba forms the main centre of the city, from which streets branch off in all directions radiating from the circular space in which it stands.

The main street from the entrance-gate continues to the further extremity of the city, being crossed at right angles in the centre by a similar street, thus forming two great main streets through the city, terminating in four gates or entrances to the town—north, south, east, and west.

Continuing along the main street from the great dagoba for about a mile, we face another dagoba of similar appearance, but of smaller dimensions, also standing in a spacious circle. Near this rises the king's palace, a noble building of great height, edged at the corners by narrow octagon towers.

At the farther extremity of this main street, close to the opposite entrance-gate, is the rock temple, with the massive idols of Buddha flanking the entrance.

This, from the form and position of the existing ruins, we may conceive to have been the appearance of Pollanarua in its days of prosperity. But what remains of its grandeur? It has vanished like 'a tale that is old;' it is passed away like a dream; the palaces are dust; the grassy sod has grown in mounds over the ruins of streets and fallen houses; nature has turfed them in one common grave with their inhabitants. The lofty palms have faded away, and given place to forest trees, whose roots spring from the crumbled ruins; the bear and the leopard crouch in the porches of the temples; the owl roosts in the casements of the palaces; the jackal roams among the ruins in vain; there is not a bone left for him to gnaw of the multitudes which have passed away. There is their handwriting upon the temple wall, upon the granite slab which has mocked at Time; but there is no man to decipher it. There are the gigantic idols before whom millions have bowed; there is the same vacant stare upon their features of rock which gazed upon the multitudes of yore; but they no longer stare upon the pomp of the glorious city, but upon ruin, and rank weeds, and utter desolation. How many suns have risen, and how many nights have darkened the earth since silence has reigned amidst the city, no man can tell. No mortal can say what fate befel those hosts of heathens, nor when they vanished from the earth. Day and night succeed each other, and the shade of the setting sun still falls from the great dagoba; but it is the 'valley of the shadow of death' upon which that shadow falls, like a pall over the corpse of a nation.

The great dagoba now remains a heap of mouldering brickwork, still retaining its form, but shorn of all its beauty. The stucco covering has almost all disappeared, leaving a patch here and there upon the most sheltered portions of the building. Scrubby brushwood and rank grass and lichens have for the most part covered its surface, giving it the appearance rather of a huge mound of earth than of an ancient building. A portion of the palace is also standing, and, although for the most part blocked up with ruins, there is still sufficient to denote its former importance. The bricks, or rather the tiles, of which all the buildings are composed, are of such an imperishable nature, that they still adhere to each other in large masses in spots where portions of the buildings have fallen.

In one portion of the ruins there are a number of

beautiful fluted columns, with carved capitals, still remaining in a perfect state. Among these are the remains of a large flight of steps; near them, again, a stone-lined tank, which was evidently intended as a bath; and everything denotes the original comfort and arrangement of a first-class establishment. There are innumerable relics, all interesting and worthy of individual attention, throughout the ruins over a surface of many miles; but they are mostly overgrown with jungle or covered with rank grass. The apparent undulations of the ground in all directions are simply the remains of fallen streets and buildings overgrown in like manner with tangled vegetation.

The most interesting, as being the most perfect, specimen is the rock temple, which, being hewn out of the solid stone, is still in complete preservation. This is a small chamber in the face of an abrupt rock, which doubtless, being partly a natural cavern, has been enlarged to the present size by the chisel; and the entrance, which may have been originally a mere hole, has been shaped into an arched doorway. The interior is not more than perhaps twenty-five feet by eighteen, and is simply fitted up with an altar and the three figures of Buddha, in the positions in which he is usually represented,—the sitting, the reclining, and the standing postures.

The exterior of the temple is far more interesting. The narrow archway is flanked on either side by two inclined planes, hewn from the face of the rock, about eighteen feet high by twelve in width. These are completely covered with an inscription in the old Pali language, which has never been translated. Upon the left of one plane is a kind of sunken area hewn out of the rock, in which sits a colossal figure of Buddha, about twenty feet in height. On the right of the other plane is a figure in the standing posture about the same height; and still further to the right, likewise hewn from the solid rock, is an immense figure in the recumbent posture, which is about fifty-six feet in length, or, as I measured it, not quite nineteen paces.

These figures are of a far superior class of sculpture to the idols usually seen in Ceylon, especially that in the reclining posture, in which the impression of the head upon the pillow is so well executed that the massive pillow of gneiss rock actually appears yielding to the weight of the head.

This temple is supposed to be coeval with the city, which was founded about 300 years before Christ, and is supposed to have been in ruins for upwards of 600 years. The comparatively recent date of its destruction renders its obscurity the more mysterious, as there is no mention made of its annihilation in any of the Cingalese records, although the city is constantly referred to during the time of its prosperity in the native history of Ceylon. It is my opinion that its destruction was caused by famine.

In those days the kings of Ceylon were perpetually at variance. The Queen of the South, from the great city of Mahagam in the Hambantotte district, made constant war with the kings of Pollanarua. They again made war with the Arabs and Malabars, who had invaded the northern districts of Ceylon; and as in modern warfare the great art consists in cutting off the enemy's supplies, so in those days the first and most decisive blow to be inflicted was the cutting off the 'water.' Thus, by simply turning the course of a river which supplied a principal tank, not only would that tank be exhausted, but the whole of the connected chain of tanks dependent upon the principal would in like manner be deprived of water.

This being the case, the first summer or dry season would lay waste the country. I have myself seen the lake of Minneria, which is twenty-two miles in circumference, evaporate to the small dimensions of four miles circuit during a dry season.

A population of some millions wholly dependent upon the supply of rice for their existence would be thrown into sudden starvation by the withdrawal of the water. Thus have the nations died out, like a fire for lack of fuel.

This cause will account for the decay of the great cities of Ceylon. The population gone, the wind and the rain would howl through the deserted dwellings, the white ants would devour the supporting beams, the elephants would rub their colossal forms against the already tottering houses, and decay would proceed with a rapidity unknown in a cooler clime. As the seed germinates in a few hours in a tropical country, so with equal haste the body of both vegetable and animal decays when life is extinct. A perpetual and hurrying change is visible in all things. A few showers, and the surface of the earth is teeming with verdure, — a few days of drought, and the seeds already formed are falling to the earth, springing in their turn to life at the approach of moisture. The same rapidity of change is exhibited in their decay. The heaps of vegetable putridity upon the banks of rivers, when a swollen torrent has torn the luxuriant plants from the loosened soil, are but the effects of a few hours' change. The tree that arrives at maturity in a few years rots in as short a time when required for durability: thus it is no mystery that either a house or a city should shortly fall to decay when the occupant is gone.

In like manner, and with still greater rapidity, is a change effected in the face of nature. As the flowers usurp the place of weeds under the care of man, so, when his hand is wanting, a few short weeks bury them beneath an overwhelming mass of thorns. In one year a jungle will conceal all signs of recent cultivation. Is it therefore a mystery that Ceylon is covered with such vast tracts of thorny jungle now that her inhabitants are gone?

Throughout the world there is a perpetual war between man and nature; but in no country has the original curse of the earth been carried out to a fuller extent than in Ceylon: 'thorns also and thistles shall it bring forth to thee.' This is indeed exemplified when a few months' neglect of once-cultivated land renders it almost impassable; and where man has vanished from the earth, and thorny jungles have covered the once broad tracts of prosperous cultivation.

A few years will thus produce an almost total ruin throughout a deserted city. The air of desolation created by a solitude of six centuries can be easily imagined. There exists, however, among the ruins of Pollanarua a curious instance of the power of the smallest apparent magnitude to destroy the works of man. At some remote period a bird has dropped the seed of the Banian tree (*Ficus indica*) upon the decaying summit of a dagoba. This, germinating, has struck its roots downwards through the brickwork, and, by the gradual and insinuating progress of its growth, it has split the immense mass of building into two sections; the twisted roots now appearing through the clefts, while the victorious tree waves in exultation above the ruin: an emblem of the silent growth of 'civilization,' which will overturn the immense fabric of heathen superstition.

It is placed beyond a doubt that the rice-growing resources of Ceylon have been suffered to lie dormant since the disappearance of her ancient population; and to these neglected capabilities the attention of Government should be directed.

An experiment might be commenced on a small scale by the repair of one tank,—say Kandellai, which is only twenty-six miles from Trincomalee, on the high road to Kandy. This tank, when the dam and sluices are repaired, would rise to about nine feet above its present level, and would irrigate many thousand acres.

The grand desideratum in the improvement of Ceylon is the increase of the population; all of whom should in some measure be made to increase the revenue.

The Government should therefore hazard this one experiment to induce the emigration of the industrious class of Chinese to the shores of Ceylon. Show them a never-failing supply of water, and land of unlimited extent to be had on easy terms, and the country would soon resume its original prosperity. A tax of five per cent. upon the produce of the land, to commence in the ratio of o per cent. for the first year, three per cent. for the second and third, and the full amount of five for the fourth, would be a fair and easy rent to the settler, and would not only repay the Government for the cost of repairing the tank, but would in a few years become a considerable source of revenue, in addition to the increased value of the land (now worthless) by a system of cultivation.

Should the first experiment succeed, the plan might be continued throughout Ceylon, and the soil of her own shores would produce a supply for the island consumption. The revenue would be derived direct from the land, which now produces nothing but thorny jungle. The import trade of Ceylon would be increased in proportion to the influx of population, and the duties upon enlarged imports would again tend to swell the revenue of the country.

The felling and clearing of the jungle, which cultivation would render necessary, would tend in a great measure to dispel the fevers and malaria always produced by a want of free circulation of air. In a jungle-covered country like Ceylon, diseases of the most malignant character are harboured in those dense and undisturbed tracts, which year after year reap a pestilential harvest from the thinly-scattered population. Cholera, dysentery, fever, and small-pox all appear in their turn, and annually sweep whole villages away. I have frequently hailed with pleasure the distant tope of waving cocoa-nut trees after a long day's journey in a broiling sun, when I have cantered towards these shady warders of cultivation in hopes of a night's halt at a village. But the palms have sighed in the wind over tenantless abodes, and the mouldering dead have lain beneath their shade. Not a living soul remaining; all swept away by pestilence; huts recently fallen to decay, fruits ripening on the trees, and no hand left to gather them; the shaddock and the lime falling to the earth, to be preyed upon by the worm, like their former masters. All dead; not one left to tell the miserable tale.

The decay of the population is still progressing; and the next fifty years will see whole districts left uninhabited, unless something can be done to prevent it. There is little doubt that, if land and water could be obtained from Government in a comparatively healthy and populous neighbourhood, many would migrate to that point from the half-deserted districts, who might assist in the cultivation of the country, instead of rotting in a closing jungle.

One season of pestilence, even in a large village, paves the road for a similar visitation in the succeeding year, for this reason.

Say that a village, comprising 200 men, is reduced by sickness to a population of 100. The remaining 100 cannot keep in cultivation the land formerly open; therefore, the jungle closes over the surface, and rapidly encroaches upon the village. Thus the circulation of air is impeded, and disease again decimates the population. In each successive year the wretched inhabitants are thinned out, and disease becomes the more certain as the jungle continues to advance. At length the miserable few are no longer sufficient to cultivate the rice lands; their numbers will not even suffice for driving their buffaloes. The jungle closes round the village; cholera finishes the scene by sweeping off the remnant; and groves of cocoa-nut trees, towering over the thorny jungle, become monuments sacred to the memory of an exterminated village.

The number of villages which have thus died out is almost incredible. In a day's ride of twenty miles, I have passed the remains of as many as three or four; how many more may have vanished in the depths of the jungle!

Wherever the cocoa-nut trees are still existing, the ruin of the village must have been comparatively recent, as the wild elephants generally overturn the palms in a few years after the disappearance of the inhabitants, browsing upon the succulent tops, and destroying every trace of a former habitation.

There is no doubt that when sickness is annually reducing the population of a district, the inhabitants, and accordingly the produce of the land, must shortly come to an end. In all times of pestilence, the first impulse among the natives is to fly from the neighbourhood; but at present there is no place of refuge. It is, therefore, a matter of certainty that the repair of one of the principal tanks would draw together in thousands the survivors of many half-perished villages, who would otherwise fall victims to succeeding years of sickness.

The successful cultivation of rice at all times requires an extensive population, and large grazing grounds for the support of the buffaloes necessary for the tillage of the land.

The labour of constructing dams and forming water-courses is performed by a general gathering, similar to the American principle of a 'Bee;' and, as 'many hands make light work,' the cultivation proceeds with great rapidity. Thus a large population can bring into tillage a greater individual proportion of ground than a smaller number of labourers, and the rice is accordingly produced at a cheaper rate.

Few people understand the difficulties with which a small village has to contend in the cultivation of rice. The continual repairs of temporary dams, which are nightly trodden down and destroyed by elephants; the filling up of the water-courses from the same cause; the nocturnal attacks upon the crops by elephants and hogs; the devastating attacks of birds as the grain becomes ripe; a scarcity of water at the exact moment that it is required; and other numerous difficulties, which are scarcely felt by a large population.

By the latter the advantage is enjoyed of the

division of labour. The dams are built of permanent material; every work is rapidly completed; the night-fires blaze in the lofty watch-houses, while the shouts of the watchers scare the wild beasts from the crops. Hundreds of children are daily screaming from their high perches to scare away the birds. Rattles worked by long lines extend in every direction, unceasingly pulled by the people in the watch-houses; wind-clackers (similar to our cherry-clackers) are whirling in all places; and by the division of the toil among a multitude, the individual work proceeds without fatigue.

Every native is perfectly aware of this advantage in rice cultivation; and were the supply of water insured to them by the repair of a principal tank, they would gather around its margin. The thorny jungles would soon disappear from the surface of the ground, and a densely-populated and prosperous district would again exist, where all has been a wilderness for 1,000 years.

The system of rice cultivation is exceedingly laborious. The first consideration being a supply of water, the second a perfect level, or series of levels to be irrigated. Thus a hill-side must be terraced out into a succession of platforms or steps; and a plain, however apparently flat, must, by the requisite embankments, be reduced to the most perfect surface.

This being completed, the water is laid on for a certain time, until the soil has become excessively soft and muddy. It is then run off, and the land is ploughed by a simple implement, which, being drawn by two buffaloes, stirs up the soil to a depth of eighteen inches. This finished, the water is again laid on until the mud becomes so soft, that a man will sink knee deep. In this state it is then trodden over by buffaloes, driven backwards and forwards in large gangs, until the mud is so thoroughly mixed, that upon the withdrawal of the water it sinks to a perfect level.

Upon this surface the paddy, having been previously soaked in water, is now sown; and, in the course of a fortnight, it attains a height of about four inches. The water is now again laid on, and continued at intervals, until within a fortnight of the grain becoming ripe. It is then run off; the ground hardens, the ripe crop is harvested by the sickle, and the grain is trodden out by buffaloes. The rice is then separated from the paddy or husk, by being pounded in a wooden mortar.

This is a style of cultivation in which the Cingalese particularly excel; nothing can be more beautifully regular than their flights of green terraces from the bottoms of the valleys to the very summits of the hills; the labour required in their formation must be immense, as they are frequently six feet one above the other. The Cingalese are peculiarly a rice-growing nation ; give them an abundant supply of water and land on easy terms.

CHAPTER V.

Real Cost of Land—Want of Communication—Coffee-planting—Comparison between French and English Settlers—Landslips—Forest Clearing—Manuring—The Coffee Bug—Rats—Fatted Stock—Suggestions for Sheep Farming—Attack of a Leopard—Leopards and Chetahs—Boy Devoured—Traps—Musk Cats, and the Mongoose—Vermin of Ceylon.

WHAT is the Government price of land in Ceylon? and what is the *real cost* of the land? These are two questions which should be considered separately, and with grave attention, by the intending settler or capitalist.

The upset price of Government land is *20s.* per acre; thus, the inexperienced purchaser is very apt to be led away by the apparently low sum per acre into a purchase of great extent. The question of the *real* cost will then be solved at his expense. There are few colonies belonging to Great Britain where the Government price of land is so high, compared to the value of the natural productions of the soil.[1]

The staple commodity of Ceylon being coffee, I will assume that a purchase is concluded with the

[1] It must be remembered that this was twenty years ago.

Government for 1,000 acres of land, at the upset price of 20*s.* per acre. What has the purchaser obtained for this sum?—1,000 acres of dense forest, to which there is no road. The 1,000*l.* passes into the Government chest, and the purchaser is no longer thought of; he is left to shift for himself, and to make the most of his bad bargain.

He is, therefore, in this position. He has parted with 1,000*l.* for a similar number of acres of land, which will not yield him one penny in any shape until he has cleared it from forest. This he immediately commences by giving out contracts, and the forest is cleared, lopped, and burnt. The ground is then planted with coffee, and the planter has to wait three years for a return. By the time of full bearing the whole cost of felling, burning, planting, and cleaning, will be about 8*l.* per acre; this, in addition to the prime cost of the land, and about 2,000*l.* expended in buildings, machinery, &c. &c., will bring the price of the land, when in a yielding condition, to 11*l.* an acre at the lowest calculation. Thus before his land yields him one fraction, he will have invested 11,000*l.*—if he clears the whole of his purchase. Many persons lose sight of this necessary outlay, when first purchasing their land, and subsequently discover to their cost that their capital is insufficient to bring the estate into cultivation.

Then comes the question of a road! The Government will give him no assistance; accordingly, the whole of his crop must be conveyed on coolies' heads along an arduous path to the nearest highway; perhaps fifteen miles distant. Even this rough path of fifteen miles, the planter must form at his own expense.

Considering the risks that are always attendant upon agricultural pursuits, and especially upon coffee-planting, the price of rough land must be acknowledged as absurdly high under the present conditions of sales. There is a great medium to be observed, however, in the sales of crown land; too low a price is even a greater evil than too high a rate, as it is apt to encourage speculators in land, who do much injury to a colony by locking up large tracts in an uncultivated state to take the chance of a future rise in the price.

This evil might easily be avoided by retaining the present *bonâ fide* price of the land per acre, qualified by an arrangement that one half of th: purchase-money should be expended in the formation of roads from the land in question. This would be of immense assistance to the planters, especially in a populous planting neighbourhood, where the purchases of land were large and numerous; in which case the aggregate sum would be sufficient to form a carriage-road to the main highway, which might be kept in repair by a slight toll. An arrangement of this kind is not only fair to the planters, but would be ultimately beneficial to the Government. Every fresh sale of land would ensure either a new road or the improvement of an old one; and the country would be opened up through the most remote districts. This fact of good communication would expedite the sales of crown lands, which are now valueless from their isolated position.

Coffee-planting in Ceylon has passed through the various stages inseparable from every 'mania.'

In the early days of our possession, the Kandian district was little known, and sanguine imaginations painted the hidden prospect in their ideal colours, expecting that a track once opened to the interior would be the road to fortune.

How these golden expectations have been disappointed, the broken fortunes of many enterprising planters can explain.

The protective duty being withdrawn, a competition with foreign coffee at once reduced the splendid prices of olden times to a more moderate standard, and took forty per cent. out of the pockets of the planters. Coffee, which in those days brought from 100*s*. to 140*s*. per cwt., is now reduced to from 60*s*. to 80*s*.

This sudden reduction created an equally sudden panic among the planters, many of whom were men of straw, who had rushed to Ceylon at the first cry of coffee 'fortunes,' and who had embarked on an extensive scale with borrowed capital. These were the first to smash. In those days the expenses of bringing land into cultivation were more than double the present rate; and, the cultivation of coffee not being so well understood, the produce per acre was comparatively small. This combination of untoward circumstances was sufficient cause for the alarm which ensued, and estates were thrust into the market, and knocked down for whatever could be realised. Mercantile houses were dragged down into the general ruin, and a dark cloud settled over the Cinnamon Isle.

As the after effects of a 'hurricane' are a more healthy atmosphere and an increased vigour in all vegetation, so are the usual sequels to a panic in the commercial world. Things are brought down to their real value and level; men of straw are swept away, and affairs are commenced anew upon a sound and steady basis. Capital is invested with caution, and improvements are entered upon step by step, until success is assured.

The reduction in the price of coffee was accordingly met by a corresponding system of expenditure, and by an improved state of cultivation; and at the present time the agricultural prospects of the colony are in a more healthy state than they have ever been since the commencement of coffee cultivation.

There is no longer any doubt that a coffee estate

in a good situation in Ceylon will pay a large interest for the capital invested, and will ultimately enrich the proprietor, provided that he has *his own capital* to work his estate, that he gives his own personal superintendence, and that he *understands* the management. These are the usual conditions of success in most affairs; but a coffee estate is not unfrequently abused for not paying — when it is worked with borrowed capital, at a high rate of interest, under questionable superintendence.

It is a difficult thing to define the amount which constitutes a 'fortune:' that which is enough for one man is a pittance for another; but one thing is certain, that, no matter how small his first capital, the coffee planter hopes to make his 'fortune.'

Now, even allowing a net profit of twenty per cent. per annum on the capital invested, it must take at least ten years to add double the amount to the first capital, allowing no increase to the spare capital required for working the estate. A rapid fortune can never be made by working a coffee estate. Years of patient industry and toil, chequered by many disappointments, may eventally reward the proprietor; but it will be at a time of life when a long residence in the tropics will have given him a distaste for the chilly atmosphere of old England; his early friends will have been scattered abroad, and he will meet few faces to welcome him on his native shores. What cold is so severe as a cold reception?—no thermometer can mark the degree. No fortune, however large, can compensate for the loss of home, and friends, and early associations.

This feeling is peculiarly strong throughout the British nation. You cannot convince an English settler that he will be abroad for an indefinite number of years; the idea would be equivalent to transportation; he consoles himself with the hope that something will turn up to alter the apparent certainty of his exile; and in this hope, with his mind ever fixed upon his return, he does little for posterity in the colony. He rarely even plants a fruit-tree, hoping that his stay will not allow him to gather from it. This accounts for the poverty of the gardens and enclosures around the houses of the English inhabitants, and the general dearth of any fruits worth eating.

How different is the appearance of French colonies, and how different are the feelings of the settler! The word 'Adieu' once spoken, he sighs an eternal farewell to the shores of 'La belle France,' and, with the natural light-heartedness of the nation, he settles cheerfully in a colony as his adopted country. He lays out his grounds with taste, and plants groves of exquisite fruit-trees, whose produce will, he hopes, be tasted by his children and grandchildren. Accordingly, in a French colony there is a tropical beauty in the cultivated trees and flowers, which is seldom seen in our own possessions. The fruits are brought to perfection, as there is the same care taken in pruning and grafting the finest kinds as in our gardens in England.[1]

A Frenchman is necessarily a better settler; everything is arranged for permanency, from the building of a house to the cultivation of an estate. He does not distress his land for immediate profit, but from the very commencement he adopts a system of the highest cultivation.

The latter is now acknowledged as the most remunerative course in all countries; and its good effects are already seen in Ceylon, where, for some years past, much attention has been devoted to manuring on coffee estates.

No crop has served to develop the natural poverty of the soil so much as coffee; and there is no doubt that, were it possible to procure manure in sufficient quantity, the holes should be well filled at the time of planting. This would give an increased vigour to the young plant, that would bring the tree into bearing at an earlier date, as it would the sooner arrive at perfection.

The present system of coffee-planting on a good estate is particularly interesting. It has now been proved that the best elevation in Ceylon to combine

[1] *Vide* Mauritius and Bourbon.

fine quality with large crops, is from 2,500 feet to 4,000. At one time it was considered that the finest sample was produced at the highest range; but the estates at an elevation of 5,000 feet are so long at arriving at perfection, and the crop produced is so small, that the lower elevation is preferred.

In the coffee districts of Ceylon there is little or no level ground to be obtained; and the steep sides of the hills offer many objections to cultivation. The soil, naturally light and poor, is washed by every shower, and the more soluble portions, together with the salts of the manure applied to the trees, are being continually robbed by the heavy rains. Thus it is next to impossible to keep an estate in a high state of cultivation, without an enormous expense in the constant application of manure.

Many estates are peculiarly subject to landslips, which are likewise produced by the violence of the rains. In these cases the destruction is frequently to a large extent; great rocks are detached from the summits of the hills, and sweep off whole lines of trees in their descent.

Wherever landslips are frequent, they may be taken as an evidence of a poor, clay subsoil. The rain soaks through the surface; and not being able to percolate through the clay with sufficient rapidity, it lodges between the two strata, loosening the upper surface, which slides from the greasy clay; launched, as it were, by its own gravity into the valley below.

This is the worst kind of soil for the coffee-tree, whose long tap-root is ever seeking nourishment from beneath. On this soil it is very common to see a young plantation giving great promise; but as the trees increase in growth, the tap-root reaches the clay subsoil, and the plantation immediately falls off. The subsoil is of far more importance to the coffee-tree than the upper surface; the latter may be improved by manure, but if the former is bad, there is no remedy.

The first thing to be considered being the soil, and the planter being satisfied with its quality, there is another item of equal importance to be taken into consideration, when choosing a locality for a coffee estate. This is an extent of grazing land sufficient for the support of the cattle required for producing manure.

In a country with so large a proportion of forest as Ceylon, this is not always practicable; in which case, land should be cleared, and grass planted, as it is now proved that without manure, an estate will never pay the proprietor.

The locality being fixed upon, the clearing of the forest is commenced. The felling is begun from the base of the hills, and the trees being cut nearly half through, are started in sections of about an acre at one fall. This is easily effected by felling some large tree from the top, which, falling upon its half-divided neighbour, carries everything before it, like a pack of cards.

The number of acres required having been felled, the boughs and small branches are all lopped, and, together with the cleared underwood, they form a mass over the surface of the ground impervious to man or beast. This tangled ruin, exposed to a powerful sun, soon becomes sufficiently dry for burning, and the time of a brisk breeze being selected, the torch is applied.

The magnificent sight of so extensive a fire is succeeded by the desolate appearance of blackened stumps and smouldering trunks of trees; the whole of the branches and underwood having been swept away by the mighty blaze, the land is comparatively clear.

Holes two feet square are now dug in parallel lines at a distance of from six to eight feet apart throughout the estate; and advantage being taken of the wet season, they are planted with young coffee-trees of about twelve inches high. Nothing is now required but to keep the land clean until the trees attain the height of about four feet, and come into bearing. This, at an elevation of 3,000 feet, they generally do in two years and a half. The stem is then topped, to prevent its higher growth, and to produce a large supply of lateral shoots.

The system of pruning is the same as with all fruit-trees; the old wood being kept down to induce fruit-bearing shoots, whose number must be proportioned to the strength of the tree.

The whole success of the estate now depends upon constant cleaning, plentiful manuring, and careful pruning, with a due regard to a frugal expenditure, and care in the up-keep of buildings, &c. &c. Much attentión is also required in the management of the cattle on the estate; for without a proper system, the amount of manure produced will be proportionately small. They should be bedded up every night hock deep with fresh litter, and the manure thus formed should be allowed to remain in the shed until it is between two or three feet deep. It should then be treated on a 'Geoffrey' pit (named after its inventor).

This is the simplest and most perfect method for working up the weeds from an estate, and effectually destroying their seeds, at the same time that they are converted into manure:—

A water-tight platform is formed of stucco—say forty feet square—surrounded by a wall two feet high, so as to form a tank. Below this is a sunken cistern —say eight feet square—into which the drainage would be conducted from the upper platform. In this cistern, half filled with a solution of saltpetre and sal-ammoniac, a force-pump is fitted.

A layer of weeds and rubbish is now laid upon the platform for a depth of three feet, surmounted by a stratum of good dung from the cattle-sheds, one foot thick. These layers are continued alternately in the proportion of three to one of weeds, until the mass is piled to a height of twenty feet; the last layer being good dung. Upon this mass the contents of the cistern are pumped and evenly distributed by means of a spreader.

This mixture promotes the most rapid decomposition of vegetable matter, and, combining with the juices of the weeds and the salts of the dung, it drains evenly through the whole mass, forming a most perfect compost. The surplus moisture, upon reaching the bottom of the heap, drains from the slightly inclined platform into the receiving cistern, and is again pumped over the mass.

This is the cheapest and best way of making manure upon an estate, the cattle sheds and pits being arranged in the different localities most suitable for reducing the labour of transport.

The coffee-berry, when ripe, is about the size of a cherry, and is shaped like a laurel-berry. The flesh has a sweet but vapid taste, and encloses two seeds of coffee. These are carefully packed by nature in a double skin.

The cherry coffee is gathered by coolies at the rate of two bushels each per diem, and is cleared from the flesh by passing through a pulper, a machine consisting of cylindrical copper graters, which tear the flesh from the berry and leave the coffee in its second covering of parchment. It is then exposed to a partial fermentation by being piled for some hours in a large heap. This has the effect of loosening the fleshy particles, which, by washing in a cistern of running water, are detached from the berry. It is then rendered perfectly dry in the sun, or by means of artificially heated air; and, being packed in bags, it is forwarded to Colombo. Here it is unpacked and sent to the mill, which, by means of heavy rollers, detaches the parchment and under silver skin, and leaves the greyish blue berry in a state for market. The injured grains are sorted out by women, and the coffee is packed for the last time and shipped to England.

A good and well managed estate should produce an average crop of ten hundredweight per acre, leaving a nett profit of fifteen shillings per hundredweight under favourable circumstances. Unfortunately it is next to impossible to make definite calculations in all agricultural pursuits; the inclemency of seasons and the attacks of vermin are constantly marring the planter's expectations. Among the latter plagues the 'bug' stands foremost. This is a minute and gregarious insect, which lives upon the juices of the coffee-tree, and accordingly is most destructive to an estate. It attacks a variety of plants, but more particularly the tribe of jessamine; thus the common jessamine, the 'Gardenia' (Cape jessamine), and the coffee (*Jasminum arabicum*) are more especially subject to its ravages.

The dwelling of this insect is frequently confounded with the living creature itself. This is in shape and appearance like the back shell of a tortoise, or, still more, like a 'limpet;' it is attached to the stem of the tree in the same manner that the latter adheres to a rock. This is the nest or house, which, although no larger than a split hempseed, contains some hundreds of the 'bug.' As thousands of these scaly nests exist upon one tree, myriads of insects must be feeding upon its juices.

The effect produced upon the tree is a blackened and sooty appearance, like a London shrub; the branches look withered, and the berries do not plump out to their full size, but, for the most part, fall to the ground unripened. This attack is usually of about two years' duration, after which the tree loses its blackened appearance; this peels off the surface of the leaves like gold-beaters' skin, and they appear in their natural colour. Coffee plants of young growth are liable to complete destruction if severely attacked by 'bug.'

Rats are also very destructive to an estate; they are great adepts at pruning, and completely strip the trees of their young shoots, thus utterly destroying a crop. These vermin are more easily guarded against than the insect tribe, and should be destroyed by poison. Hog's lard, ground cocoa-nut, and phosphorus, form the most certain bait and poison combined.

These are some of the drawbacks to coffee-planting, to say nothing of bad seasons and fluctuating prices, which, if properly calculated, considerably lessen the average profits of an estate, as it must be remembered that while a crop is reduced in quantity, the expenses continue, and are severely felt when consecutive years bring no produce to meet them.

Were it not for the poverty of the soil, the stock of cattle required on a coffee estate for the purpose of manure might be made extremely profitable, and the gain upon fatted stock would pay for the expense of manuring the estate. This would be the first and most reasonable idea to occur to an agriculturist—'buy poor cattle at a low price, fatten them for the butcher, and they give both profit and manure.'

Unfortunately, the natural pasturage is not sufficiently good to fatten beasts indiscriminately. There are some few out of a herd of a hundred who will grow fat upon anything; but the generality will not improve to any great degree. This accounts for the scarcity of fine meat throughout Ceylon. Were the soil only tolerably good, so that oats, vetches, turnips, and mangel wurtzel could be grown on virgin land without manure, beasts might be stall-fed; the manure would be doubled by that method, and a profit made on the animals. Pigs are now kept extensively on coffee estates for the sake of their manure, and being fed on Mauritius grass (a coarse description of gigantic 'couch') and a liberal allowance of cocoa-nut oil-cake ('Poonac'), are found to succeed, although the manure is somewhat costly.

English or Australian sheep have hitherto been untried—for what reason I cannot imagine, unless from the expense of their prime cost, which is about 2*l.* per head. These thrive to such perfection at Newera Ellia, and also in Kandy, that they should succeed in a high degree in the medium altitudes of the coffee estates. There are immense tracts of country peculiarly adapted for sheep farming throughout the highlands of Ceylon, especially in the neighbourhood of the coffee estates. There are two enemies, however, against which they would have to contend,—viz., 'leopards' and 'leeches.' The former are so destructive, that the shepherd could never lose sight of his flock without great risk; but the latter, although troublesome, are not to be so much dreaded as people suppose. They are very small, and the quantity of blood drawn by their bite is so trifling that no injury could possibly follow—unless from the flies, which would be apt to attack the sheep on the smell of blood. These are drawbacks which might be easily avoided by common precaution; and I feel thoroughly convinced that sheep farming upon the highland pasturage would be a valuable adjunct to a coffee estate, both as productive of manure and profit. I have heard the same opinion expressed by an experienced Australian sheep farmer.

This might be experimented upon in the 'down' country of Ouva with great hopes of success, and by a commencement upon a small scale the risk would be trifling. Here there is an immense tract of country, with a peculiar short grass in every way adapted for sheep pasturage, and with the additional advantage of being nearly free from leopards. Should sheep succeed on an extensive scale, the advantage to the farmer and to the colony would be mutual.

The depredations of leopards among cattle are no inconsiderable causes of loss. At Newera Ellia hardly a week passes without some casualty among the stock of different proprietors. Here the leopards are particularly daring, and cases have frequently occurred where they have effected their entrance to a cattle shed by scratching a hole through the thatched roof. They then commit a wholesale slaughter among sheep and cattle. Sometimes, however, they catch a 'Tartar.' The native cattle are small, but very active, and the cows are particularly savage when the calf is with them.

About three years ago a leopard took it into his head to try the beefsteaks of a very savage and sharp-horned cow, who with her calf was the property of the blacksmith. It was a dark rainy night, the blacksmith and his wife were in bed, and the cow and her calf were nestled in the warm straw in the cattle-shed. The door was locked, and all was apparently secure, when the hungry leopard prowled stealthily round the cow-house, sniffing the prey within. The strong smell of the leopard at once alarmed the keen senses of the cow, made doubly acute by her anxiety for her little charge, and she stood ready for the danger, as the leopard, having mounted on the roof, commenced scratching his way through the thatch.

Down he sprang!—but at the same instant, with a splendid charge, the cow pinned him against the wall, and a battle ensued which can easily be imagined. A cooly slept in the corner of the cattle-shed, whose wandering senses were completely scattered when he found himself the unwilling umpire of the fight.

He rushed out and shut the door. In a few minutes he succeeded in awakening the blacksmith, who struck a light, and proceeded to load a pistol, the only weapon that he possessed. During the whole of this time the bellowing of the cow, the roars of the leopard, and the thumping, trampling, and shuffling which proceeded from the cattle-shed, explained the savage nature of the fight.

The blacksmith, who was no sportsman, shortly found himself with a lanthorn in one hand, a pistol in the other, and no idea what he meant to do. He waited, therefore, at the cattle-shed door, and holding the light so as to shine through the numerous small apertures in the shed, he looked in.

The leopard no longer growled; but the cow was mad with fury. She alternately threw a large dark mass above her head, then quickly pinned it to the ground on its descent, then bored it against the wall, as it crawled helplessly towards a corner of the shed. This was the 'beefeater' in reduced circumstances! The gallant little cow had nearly killed him, and was giving him the finishing strokes. The blacksmith perceived the leopard's helpless state, and, boldly opening the door, he discharged his pistol, and the next moment was bolting as hard as he could run with the warlike cow after him! She was regularly 'up,' and was ready for any thing or any body. However, she was at length pacified, and the dying leopard was put out of his misery.

There are two distinct species of the leopard in Ceylon, viz., the 'chetah,' and the 'leopard' or 'panther.' There have been many opinions on the subject, but I have taken particular notice of the two animals, and nothing can be more clear than the distinction.[1]

The 'chetah' is much smaller than the leopard, seldom exceeding seven feet from the nose to the end of the tail. He is covered with round black '*spots*' of the size of a shilling, and his weight rarely exceeds ninety pounds.

The leopard varies from eight to nine feet in length, and has been known to reach even ten feet. His body is covered with black '*rings*,' with a rich brown centre—his muzzle and legs are speckled with black '*spots*,' and his weight is from 110 to 170 pounds. There is little or no distinction between the leopard and the panther, they are synonymous terms for a variety of species in different countries.

In Ceylon all leopards are termed 'chetahs'; which proceeds from the general ignorance of the presence of the two species.

The power of the animal is wonderful in proportion to its weight. I have seen a full-grown bullock with its neck broken by a leopard. It is the popular belief that the effect is produced by a blow of the paw; this is not the case; it is not simply the blow, but it is the combination of the

[1] The chetah is the general name for the small species, but it is totally distinct from the well-known chetah or *hunting leopard*, which does not exist in Ceylon.

weight, the muscular power, and the momentum of the spring, which render the effects of a leopard's attack so surprising.

Few leopards rush boldly upon their prey like a dog; they stalk their game, and advance crouchingly, making use of every object that will afford them cover until they are within a few bounds of their victim. Then the immense power of muscle is displayed in the concentrated energy of the spring; he flies through the air, and settles on the throat, usually throwing his own body over the animal, while his teeth and claws are fixed on the neck: this is the manner in which the spine of an animal is broken, by a sudden twist, and not simply by a blow.

The blow from the paw is nevertheless immensely powerful, and at one stroke will rip open a bullock like a knife; but the after effects of the wound are still more to be dreaded than the force of the stroke. There is a peculiar poison in the claw, which is highly dangerous. This is caused by the putrid flesh which they are constantly tearing, and which is apt to cause gangrene by inoculation.

It is a prevalent idea that a leopard will not eat putrid meat, but that he forsakes a rotten carcase and seeks fresh prey. There is no doubt that a natural love of slaughter induces him to a constant search for prey, but it has nothing to do with the daintiness of his appetite. A leopard will eat any stinking offal that offers, and I once had a melancholy proof of this.

I was returning from a morning's hunting; it was a bitter day, the rain was pouring in torrents, the wind was blowing a gale, and sweeping the water in sheets along the earth. The hounds were following at my horse's heels, with their ears and sterns down, looking very miserable, and altogether it was a day when man and beast should have been at home. Presently upon turning a corner of the road, I saw a Malabar boy of about sixteen years of age, squatted shivering by the road-side. His only covering being a scanty cloth round his loins, I told him to get up, and go on, or he would be starved with cold. He said something in reply, which I could not understand, and, repeating my first warning, I rode on. It was only two miles to my house, but upon arrival I could not help thinking that the boy must be ill, and having watched the gate for some time, to see if he passed by, I determined to send for him.

Accordingly I started off a couple of men with orders to carry him up if he were sick.

They returned in little more than an hour, but the poor boy was dead! sitting crouched in the same position in which I had seen him. He must have died of cold and starvation; he was a mere skeleton.

I sent men to the spot and had him buried by the road-side, and a few days after I rode down to see where they had laid him.

A quantity of fresh-turned earth lay scattered about, mingled with fragments of rags. Bones much gnawed lay here and there on the road, and a putrid skull had rolled from a shapeless hole among a confused and horrible heap. The leopards had scratched him up and then devoured him; their footprints were still fresh upon the damp ground.

Both leopards and chetahs are frequently caught at Newera Ellia. The common trap is nothing more or less in principle than an old-fashioned mouse-trap, with a falling door on a large scale; this is baited with a live kid or sheep; but the leopard is naturally so wary that he frequently refuses to enter the ominous-looking building, although he would not hesitate to break into an ordinary shed. The best kind of snare is a gun set with a line, and the bait placed so that the line must be touched as the animal advances towards it. This is certain destruction to the leopard; but it is extremely dangerous, in case any stranger should happen to be in the neighbourhood who might inadvertently touch the cord.

Leopards are particularly fond of stealing dogs, and have frequently taken them from the very verandahs of the houses at Newera Ellia in the dusk of the evening. Two or three cases have occurred within the last two years where they have actually sprung out upon dogs who have been accompanying their owners upon the high road in broad daylight. Their destruction should be encouraged by a Government reward of one pound per head, in which case their number would be materially decreased in a few years.

The best traps for chetahs would be very powerful vermin-gins, made expressly of great size and strength, so as to lie one foot square when open. Even a common jackal-trap would hold a leopard, provided the chain was fastened to an elastic bough, so that it would yield slightly to his spring; but if it were secured to a post, or to anything that would enable him to get a dead pull against it, something would most likely give way. I have constantly set these gins for them, but always without success, as some other kind of vermin is nearly certain to spring the trap before the chetah's arrival. Among the variety of small animals thus caught I have frequently taken the civet cat. This is a very pretty and curious creature, about forty inches long from nose to tip of tail. The fur is ash-grey, mottled with black spots, and the tail is divided by numerous black rings. It is of the genus *Viverra*, and is exceedingly fierce when attacked. It preys chiefly upon fowls, hares, rats, &c. Its great peculiarity is the musk-bag or gland, situated nearly under the tail; this is a projecting and valved gland, which secretes the musk, and is used medicinally by the Cingalese, on which account it is valued at about six shillings a pod. The smell is very powerful, and in my opinion very offensive when the animal is alive; but when a pod of musk is extracted and dried, it has nothing more than the well-known scent used by perfumers. The latter is more frequently the production of the musk deer, although the scent is possessed by many animals, and also insects, as the musk ox, the musk deer, the civet or musk cat, the musk rat, the musk beetle, &c.

Of these, the musk rat is a terrible plague, as he perfumes every thing that he passes over, rendering fruit, cakes, bread, &c., perfectly uneatable, and (it is said) even flavouring bottled wine by running over the bottles. This, however, requires a little explanation, although it is the popular belief that he taints the wine through the glass. The fact is, he taints the cork, and the flavour of musk is communicated to the wine during the process of uncorking the bottle.

There are a great variety of rats in Ceylon, from the tiny shrew to the large 'bandicoot.' This is a most destructive creature in all gardens, particularly among potato crops, whole rows of which he digs out and devours. He is a perfect rat in appearance, but he would rather astonish one of our English tom cats if encountered during his rambles in search of rats, as the 'bandicoot' is about the same size as the cat.

There is an immense variety of vermin throughout Ceylon, including many of that useful species the ichneumon, who in courage and strength stands first of his tribe. The destruction of snakes by this animal renders him particularly respected, and no person ever thinks of destroying one. No matter how venomous the snake, the ichneumon, or mongoose, goes straight at him, and never gives up the contest until the snake is vanquished.

It is the popular belief that the mongoose eats some herb which has the property of counteracting the effects of a venomous bite; but this has been proved to be a fallacy, as pitched battles have been witnessed between a mongoose and the most poisonous snakes in a closed room, where there was no possibility of his procuring the antidote. His power consists in his vigilance and activity; he avoids the dart of the snake, and adroitly pins him by the back of the neck. Here he maintains his hold, in spite of the contortions and convulsive writhing of the snake, until he succeeds in breaking the spine. A mongose is about three feet long from the nose to the tip of the tail, and is of the same genus as the civet cat. Unfortunately he does not confine his destruction to vermin, but now and then pays a visit to a hen-roost, and sometimes, poor fellow, he puts his foot in the traps.

Ceylon can produce an enticing catalogue of attractions, from the smallest to the largest of the enemies to the human race. Ticks, bugs, fleas, tarantulas, centipedes, scorpions, leeches, snakes, lizards, crocodiles, &c.,—of which, more hereafter.

CHAPTER VI.

'Game Eyes' for Wild Sports—Enjoyments of Wild Life—Cruelty of Sports—Native Hunters—Moormen Traders—Their wretched Guns —Rifles and Smooth Bores—Heavy Balls and Heavy Metal—Beattie's Rifles—Balls and Patches—Experiments—The Double-Groove—Power of Heavy Metal—Curious Shot at a Bull Elephant—African and Ceylon Elephants—Structure of Skull—Lack of Trophies —Boar Spears and Hunting Knives—Bertram—A Boar-hunt—Fatal Cut.

IN travelling through Ceylon, the remark is often made by the tourist that 'he sees so little game.' From the accounts generally written of its birds and beasts, a stranger would naturally expect to come upon them at every turn, instead of which, it is a well-known fact that 100 miles of the wildest country may be traversed without seeing a single head of game, and the uninitiated might become sceptical as to its existence.

This is accounted for by the immense proportion of forest and jungle, compared to the open country. The nature of wild animals is to seek cover at sunrise, and to come forth at sunset; therefore it is not surprising that so few are casually seen by the passing traveller. But there is another reason, that would frequently apply even in an open country. Unless the traveller is well accustomed to wild sports, he has not his 'game eye' open; in fact, he either passes animals without observing them, or they see him and retreat from view before he remarks them.

It is well known that the colour of most animals is adapted by nature to the general tint of the country which they inhabit. Thus, having no contrast, the animal matches with surrounding objects, and is difficult to be distinguished.

It may appear ridiculous to say that an elephant is very difficult to be seen!—he would be plain enough certainly on the snow, or on a bright green meadow in England, where the contrasted colours would make him at once a striking object; but in a dense jungle his skin matches so completely with the dead sticks and dry leaves, and his legs compare so well with the surrounding tree-stems, that he is generally unperceived by a stranger, even when pointed out to him. I have actually been taking aim at an elephant within seven or eight paces, when he has been perfectly unseen by a friend at my elbow, who was peering through the bushes in quest of him.

Quickness of eye is an indispensable quality in sportsmen, the possession of which constitutes one of their little vanities. Nothing is so conducive to the perfection of all the senses as the constant practice in wild and dangerous sports. The eye and the ear become habituated to watchfulness, and their powers are increased in the same proportion as the muscles of the body are by exercise. Not only is an animal immediately observed, but anything out of the common among surrounding objects instantly strikes the attention; the waving of one bough in particular when all are moving in the breeze; the twitching of a deer's ear above the long grass; the slight rustling of an animal moving in the jungle. The senses are regularly tuned up, and the limbs are in the same condition from continual exercise.

There is a peculiar delight which passes all description, in feeling thoroughly well strung, mentally and physically, with a good rifle in your hand, and a trusty gun-bearer behind you with another; thus stalking quietly through a fine country, on the look-out for '*anything*'—no matter what. There is a delightful feeling of calm excitement, if I might so express it, which nothing but wild sports will give. There is no time when a man knows himself so thoroughly as when he depends upon himself, and this forms his excitement. With a thorough confidence in the rifle, and a bright look-out, he stalks noiselessly along the open glades, picking out the softest places, avoiding the loose stones or anything that would betray his steps; now piercing the deep shadows of the jungles, now scanning the distant plains, leaving neither nook nor hollow unsearched by his vigilant gaze. The fresh breakage of a branch, the barking of a tree-stem, the lately nibbled grass, with the sap still oozing from the delicate blade, the disturbed surface of a pool; everything is noted, even to the alarmed chatter of a bird: nothing is passed unheeded by an experienced hunter.

To quiet steady-going people in England, there is an idea of cruelty inseparable from the pursuit of large game; people talk of 'unoffending elephants,' 'poor buffaloes,' 'pretty deer,' and a variety of nonsense about things which they cannot possibly understand. Besides, the very person who abuses wild sports on the plea of cruelty indulges personally in conventional cruelties which are positive tortures. His appetite is not destroyed by the knowledge that his cook has skinned the eels alive, or that the lobsters were plunged into boiling water to be cooked. He should remember that a small animal has the same feeling as the largest, and if he condemns any sport as cruel, he must condemn all.

There is no doubt whatever that a certain amount of cruelty pervades all sports. But in 'wild sports' the animals are for the most part large, dangerous, and mischievous, and they are pursued and killed in the most speedy, and therefore in the most merciful manner.

The Government reward for the destruction of elephants in Ceylon was formerly ten shillings per tail; it is now reduced to seven shillings in some districts, and is altogether abolished in others, as the number killed was so great that the Government imagine they cannot afford the annual outlay.

Although the number of these animals is still so immense in Ceylon, they must nevertheless have been much reduced within the last twenty years.[1] In those days the country was overrun with them, and some idea of their numbers may be gathered from the fact, that three first-rate shots in three days bagged 104 elephants. This was told to me by one of the parties concerned, and it throws our modern shooting into the shade. In those days, however, the elephants were comparatively undisturbed, and they were accordingly more easy to approach. One of the oldest native hunters has assured me that he has seen the elephants, when attacked, recklessly expose themselves to the shots, and endeavour to raise their dead comrades. This was at a time when guns were first heard in the interior of Ceylon, and the animals had never been shot at. Since that time the decrease in the game of Ceylon has been immense. Every year increases the number of guns in the possession of the natives, and accordingly diminishes the number of animals. From the change which has come over many

[1] Since this was written, twenty years ago, game laws have been established in Ceylon, as both the elephants and other animals were rapidly diminished in numbers.

parts of the country within my experience of the last eight years, I am of opinion that the next ten years will see the deer-shooting in Ceylon completely spoiled, and the elephants very much reduced. There are now very few herds of elephants in Ceylon, that have not been shot at by either Europeans or natives, and it is a common occurrence to kill elephants with numerous marks of old bullet wounds. Thus the animals are constantly on the '*qui vive*,' and at the report of a gun, every herd within hearing starts off for the densest jungles.

A native can now obtain a gun for thirty shillings; and with two shillings' worth of ammunition, he starts on a hunting trip. Five elephants, at a reward of seven shillings per tail, more than pay the prime cost of his gun; to say nothing of the deer and other game that he has bagged in the interim.

Some, although very few, of the natives are good sportsmen in a *potting* way. They get close to their game, and usually bag it. This is a terrible system of destruction, and the more so as it is unceasing. There is no rest for the animals; in the daytime they are tracked up, and on moonlight nights the drinking places are watched, and an unremitting warfare is carried on. This is sweeping both deer and buffalo from the country, and must eventually almost annihilate them.

The Moormen are the best hunters, and they

very general), but rather let him say '*I cannot carry a heavy gun*,' and '*I cannot shoot with a rifle*.'

There is a vast difference between shooting at a target and shooting at live game. Many men who are capital shots at target practice cannot touch a deer, and cannot even use the rifle at live game, but actually knock the sights out, and use it as a smooth bore. This is not the fault of the weapon, it is the fault of the man. It is a common saying in Ceylon, and also in India, that you cannot shoot quick enough with the rifle, because you cannot get the proper sight in an instant.

Whoever makes use of this argument must certainly be in the habit of very random shooting with a smooth bore. How can he possibly get a correct aim with 'ball,' even out of a smooth bore, without squinting along the barrel and taking the muzzle sight accurately? The fact is that many persons fire so hastily at game, that they take no sight at all, as though they were snipe shooting with many hundred grains of shot in the charge. This will never do for ball practice; and when the rifle is placed in such hands, the breech sights naturally bother the eye which is not accustomed to recognise any sight, and while the person is vainly endeavouring to get his aim correctly upon a moving object, the animal is increasing his distance. By way of cutting the Gordian knot, he therefore knocks his sight out, and accordingly spoils the shooting of the rifle altogether.

Put a rifle in the hands of a man who knows how to handle it, and let him shoot against the mutilated weapon deprived of its sight, and laugh at the trial. Why a man might as well take the rudder off a ship because he could not steer, and then abuse the vessel for not keeping her course!

My idea of guns and rifles is this, that the former should be used for what their makers intended them, viz., shot shooting, and that no ball should be fired from any but the rifle. Of course it is just as easy and as certain to kill an elephant with a smooth bore as with a rifle, as he is seldom fired at until within ten or twelve paces; but a man, when armed for wild sport, should be provided with a weapon which is fit for any kind of ball shooting at any reasonable range, and his battery should be perfect for the distance at which he is supposed to aim.

I have never seen any rifles which combine the requisites for Ceylon shooting to such a degree as my four double-barrelled No. 10, which I had made to order. Then some persons exclaim against their weight, which is fifteen pounds per gun. But a word upon that subject.

No person who understands anything about a rifle would select a light gun, with a large bore, any more than he would have a heavy carriage for a small horse.

If the man objects to the weight of the rifle, let him content himself with a smaller bore, but do not rob the barrels of their good metal for the sake of a heavy ball. The more metal that the barrel possesses in proportion to the diameter of the bore the better will the rifle carry, nine times out of ten. Observe the Swiss rifles for accurate target practice; again, remark the American pea rifle; in both the thickness of metal is immense in proportion to the size of the ball, which in great measure accounts for the precision with which they carry.

In a light barrel there is a vibration or jar at the time of explosion, which takes a certain effect upon the direction of the ball. This is necessarily increased by the use of a heavy charge of powder; and it is frequently seen that a rifle which carries accurately enough with a very small charge, shoots wide of the mark when the charge is increased. This arises from several causes, generally from the jar of the barrel in the stock, proceeding either from the want of metal in the rifle or from improper workmanship in the fittings.

To avoid this, a rifle should be made with double bolts, and a silver plate should always be let into the stock under the breech; without which the woodwork will imperceptibly wear, and the barrels will become loose in the stock, and jar when fired.[1]

[1] My rifles were made with such success upon this plan, by Mr.

There is another reason for the necessity of heavy barrels, especially for two-grooved rifles. Unless the grooves be tolerably deep, they will not hold the ball when a heavy charge is behind it; it quits the grooves, strips its belt, and flies out as though fired from a smooth bore.

A large-bored rifle is a useless incumbrance, unless it is so constructed that it will bear a proportionate charge of powder, and shoot as accurately with its proof charge as with a single drachm. The object in having a large bore is to possess an extra powerful weapon, therefore the charge of powder must be increased in proportion to the weight of the ball, or the extra power is not obtained. Nevertheless most of the heavy rifles that I have met with will not carry an adequate charge of powder, and they are accordingly no more powerful than guns of lighter bore which carry their proportionate charge—the powder has more than its fair amount of work.

Great care should be therefore taken in making rifles for heavy game. There cannot be a better calibre than No. 10; it is large enough for any animal in the world, and a double-barrelled rifle of this bore without a ramrod is not the least cumber-

Beattie, of 205, Regent Street, that they are as sound and unshaken at the present moment as they were when they left his shop; although they have been tried by many years of hard work, and heavy charges of powder. This has been a satisfactory proof of first-class workmanship.

some, even at the weight of fifteen pounds. A ramrod is not required to be in the gun for Ceylon shooting, as there is always a man behind with a spare rifle, who carries a loading rod; and were a ramrod fitted to a rifle of this size it would render it very unhandy, and would also weaken the stock.

The sights should be of platinum at the muzzle, and blue steel with a platinum strip with a broad and deep letter V cut in the breech sights. In a gloomy forest it is frequently difficult to catch the muzzle sight, unless it is of some bright metal, such as silver or platinum; and a broad cut in the breech sights, if shaped as described, allows a rapid aim, and may be taken fine or coarse, at option.

The charge of powder must necessarily depend upon its strength. For elephant shooting, I always use six drachms of the best fine-grain powder for the No. 10 rifles, and four drachms as the minimum charge for deer and general shooting; the larger charge is then unnecessary, it both wastes ammunition and alarms the country by the loudness of the report.

There are several minutiæ to be attended to in the sports of Ceylon. The caps should always be carried in a shot charger (one of the common spring-lid chargers) and never be kept loose in the pocket. The heat is so intense, that the perspiration soaks through everything, and so injures the caps, that the very best will frequently miss fire.

The powder should be dried for a few minutes in the sun before it is put into the flask, and it should be well shaken and stirred to break any lumps that may be in it. One of these, by obstructing the passage in the flask, may cause much trouble in loading quickly, especially when a wounded elephant is regaining his feet. In such a case you must keep your eyes on the animal while loading, and should the passage of the powder flask be stopped by a lump, you may fancy the gun is loaded when in fact not a grain of powder has entered it.

The patches should be of silk, soaked in a mixture of one part of beeswax and two of fresh hog's lard, free from salt. If they are spread with pure grease, it melts out of them in a hot country, and they become dry. Silk is better than linen, as it is not so liable to be cut by the sharp grooves of the rifle. It is also thinner than linen or calico, and the ball is therefore more easily rammed down.

All balls should be made of pure lead without any hardening mixture. It was formerly the fashion to use zinc balls, and lead with a mixture of tin, &c., in elephant shooting. This was not only unnecessary, but the balls, from a loss of weight by admixture with lighter metals, lost force in a proportionate degree. Lead may be a soft metal, but it is much harder than any animal's skull, and if a tallow candle can be shot through a deal board, surely a leaden bullet is hard enough for an elephant's head.

I once tried a very conclusive experiment on the power of balls of various metals propelled by an equal charge of powder.

I had a piece of wrought iron five-eighths of an inch thick, and six feet high by two in breadth. I fired at this at 170 yards with my two-grooved four-ounce rifle with a reduced charge of six drachms of powder, and a ball of pure lead. It bulged the iron like a piece of putty, and split the centre of the bulged spot into a star, through the crevice of which I could pass a pen-blade.

A ball composed of half zinc and half lead, fired from the same distance, hardly produced a perceptible effect upon the iron target. It just slightly indented it.

I then tried a ball of one-third zinc and two-thirds lead, but there was no perceptible difference in the effect.

I subsequently tried a tin ball, and again a zinc ball, but neither of them produced any other effect than slightly to indent the iron.

I tried all these experiments again at fifty yards' range, with the same advantage in favour of the pure lead; and at this reduced distance a double-barrelled No. 16 smooth bore, with a large charge of four drachms of powder and a lead ball, also bulged and split the iron into a star. This gun, with a hard tin ball and the same charge of powder, did not produce any other effect than an almost imperceptible indentation.

If a person wishes to harden a ball for any purpose, it should be done by an admixture of quicksilver to the lead while the latter is in a state of fusion, a few seconds before the ball is cast. The mixture must be then quickly stirred with an iron rod, and formed into the moulds without loss of time, as at this high temperature the quicksilver will evaporate. Quicksilver is heavier than lead, and makes a ball excessively hard; so much so that it would very soon spoil a rifle. Altogether, the hardening of a ball has been shown to be perfectly unnecessary, and the latter receipt would be found very expensive.

If a wonderful effect is required, the steel-tipped conical ball should be used. I once shot through fourteen elm planks, each one inch thick, with a four-ounce steel-tipped cone, with the small charge (for that rifle) of four drachms of powder. The proper charge for that gun is one-fourth the weight of the ball, or one ounce of powder, with which it carries with great nicety and terrific effect, owing to its great weight of metal (twenty-one pounds); but it is a small piece of artillery, which tries the shoulder very severely in the recoil.

I have frequently watched a party of soldiers winding along a pass, with their white trousers, red coats, white cross-belts, and brass plates, at about 400 yards, and thought what a raking that rifle would give a body of troops in such colours for a mark. A ball of that weight, with an ounce of powder, would knock down six or eight men in a row. A dozen of such weapons well handled on board a ship would create an astonishing effect; but for most purposes, the weight of the ammunition is a serious objection.

There is a great difference of opinion among sportsmen regarding the grooves of a rifle; some prefer the two-groove and belted ball; others give preference to the eight- or twelve-groove and smooth ball. There are good arguments on both sides.

There is no doubt that the two-groove is the hardest hitter and the longest ranger; it also has the advantage of not fouling so quickly as the many grooved. On the other hand, the many grooved is much easier to load; it hits quite hard enough; and it ranges truly much farther than any person would think of firing at an animal. Therefore, for sporting purposes, the only advantage which the two-groove possesses is the keeping clean; while the many grooved claims the advantage of quick loading.

The latter is by far the more important recommendation, especially as the many grooved can be loaded without the assistance of the eye, as the ball, being smooth and round, can only follow the right road down the barrel. The two-grooved rifle, when new, is particularly difficult to load, as the ball must be tight to avoid windage, and it requires some nicety in fitting and pressing the belt of the bullet into the groove in such a manner, that it shall start straight upon the pressure of the loading rod. If it gives a slight heel to one side at the commencement, it is certain to stick in its course, and it then occupies much time and trouble in being rammed home. Neither will it shoot with accuracy, as, from the amount of ramming to get the ball to its place, it has become so misshapen, that it is a mere lump of lead, and no longer a rifle-ball.

My double-barrelled No. 10 rifles are two-grooved; and they gave much trouble during the first two years. I have sometimes given my whole weight to the loading rod, when a ball stuck half-way down the barrel, while wounded elephants lay struggling upon the ground expected every moment to rise. From constant use and repeated cleaning, they have now become so perfect, that they load with the greatest ease; but guns of their age are not fair samples of their class, and for rifles in general for sporting purposes, I should give a decided preference to the many grooved. I have a long two-ounce rifle of the latter class, which I have shot with for many years, and it certainly is not so hard a hitter as the two-grooved No. 10's; but it hits uncommonly hard too; and if I do not bag with it it is always my fault, and no blame can be attached to the rifle.

For heavy game shooting, I do not think there can be a much fairer standard for the charge of powder than one-fifth the weight of the ball for all bores. Some persons do not use so much as this; but I am always an advocate for strong guns and plenty of powder.[1]

A heavy charge will reach the brain of an elephant, no matter in what position he may stand, provided a proper angle is taken for attaining it. A trifling amount of powder is sufficient, if the elephant offers a front shot, or the temple at right angles, or the ear shot; but if a man pretend to a knowledge of elephant shooting, he should think of nothing but the brain, and his acquaintance with the anatomy of the elephant's head should be such, that he can direct a straight line to this mark from any position. He then

[1] When this was written, twenty years ago, no one but myself advocated heavy charges of powder for rifles. It is curious to observe the advance made in our knowledge of rifle-shooting within that comparatively short interval. The world has now discovered the value of heavy charges; and the *small-bore* of the present day is loaded with as much as five or six drachms. After great experience through many years in Africa since this book was written, I adhere to my original opinion, that a No. 10 rifle is the best size for general hunting among heavy and dangerous game. This should carry ten drachms of No. 6 grain powder.

requires a rifle of such power that the ball will crash through every obstacle along the course directed. To effect this he must not be stingy of the powder.

I have frequently killed elephants by curious shots with the heavy rifles in this manner; but I once killed a bull elephant by one shot in the upper *jaw*, which will exemplify the advantage of a powerful rifle in taking the angle for the brain.

My friend Palliser and I were out shooting on the day previous, and we had spent some hours in vainly endeavouring to track up a single bull elephant. I forget what we bagged, but I recollect well that we were unlucky in finding our legitimate game. That night at dinner, we heard elephants roaring in the Yallé river, upon the banks of which our tent was pitched in fine open forest. For about an hour the roaring was continued, apparently on both sides the river, and we immediately surmised that our gentleman friend on our side of the stream was answering the call of the ladies of some herd on the opposite bank. We went to sleep with the intention of waking at dawn of day, and then strolling quietly along with only two gun-bearers each, who were to carry my four double No. 10's, while we each carried a single barrel for deer.

The earliest grey tint of morning saw us dressed and ready; the rifles loaded; a preliminary cup of hot chocolate swallowed, and we were off while the forest was still gloomy; the night seemed to hang about it, although the sky was rapidly clearing above.

A noble piece of Nature's handiwork is that same Yallé forest. The river flows sluggishly through its centre in a breadth of perhaps ninety yards, and the immense forest trees extend their giant arms from the high banks above the stream, throwing dark shadows upon its surface, enlivened by the silvery glitter of the fish as they dart against the current. Little glades of rank grass occasionally break the monotony of the dark forest; sandy gullies, in deep beds formed by the torrents of the rainy season, cut through the crumbling soil, and drain towards the river. Thick brushwood now and then forms an opposing barrier, but generally the forest is beautifully open, consisting of towering trees, the leviathans of their race, sheltering the scanty saplings which had sprung from their fallen seeds. For a few hundred yards on either side of the river, the forest extends in a ribbon-like strip of lofty vegetation, in the surrounding sea of low scrubby jungle. The animals leave the low jungle at night, passing through the forest on their way to the river to bathe and drink; they return to the low and thick bush at break of day, and we hoped to meet some of the satiated elephants on their way to their dense habitations.

We almost made sure of finding our friend of yesterday's track, and we accordingly kept close to

CURIOUS SHOT AT A BULL ELEPHANT

the edge of the river, keeping a sharp eye for footprints upon the sandy bed below.

We had strolled for about a mile along the high bank of the river, without seeing a sign of an elephant, when I presently heard a rustle in the branches before me, and upon looking up, I saw a lot of monkeys gamboling in the trees. I was carrying my long two-ounce rifle, and I was passing beneath the monkey-covered boughs, when I suddenly observed a young tree of the thickness of a man's thigh, shaking violently just before me.

It happened that the jungle was a little thicker in this spot, and at the same moment that I observed the tree shaking almost over me, I passed the immense stem of one of those smooth barked trees which grow to such an enormous size on the banks of rivers. At the same moment that I passed it, I was almost under the trunk of a single bull elephant, who was barking the stem with his tushes [1] as high as he could reach, with his head thrown back. I saw in an instant that the only road to his brain lay through his upper jaw, in the position in which he was standing; and knowing that he would discover me in another moment, I took the direct line for his brain, and fired upwards through his jaw. He fell stone

[1] There are very few elephants with regular tusks in Ceylon, and their very small ivories are called 'tushes.'

dead, with the silk patch of the rifle smoking in the wound.

Now in this position no light gun could have killed that elephant; the ball had to pass through the roots of the upper grinders, and keep its course through hard bones and tough membranes for about two feet before it could reach the brain; but the line was all right, and the heavy metal and charge of powder kept the ball to its work.

This is the power which every elephant gun should possess: it should have an elephant's head under complete command in every attitude.

There is another advantage in heavy metal; a heavy ball will frequently stun a vicious elephant when in full charge, when a light bullet would not check him; his quietus is then soon arranged by another barrel. Some persons, however, place too much confidence in the weight of the metal, and forget that it is necessary to hold a powerful rifle as straight as the smallest gun. It is then very common during a chase of a herd to see the elephants falling tolerably well to the shots; but on a return for their tails, it is found that the stunned brutes have recovered and decamped.

Conical balls should never be used for elephants; they are more apt to glance, and the concussion is not so great as that produced by a round ball. In fact, there is nothing more perfect for sporting purposes than a good rifle from a first-rate maker, with a plain ball of from No. 12 to No. 10. There can be no improvement upon such a weapon for the range generally required by a good shot.

I am very confident that the African elephant would be killed by the brain shot by Ceylon sportsmen with as much ease as the Indian species. The shape of the head has nothing whatever to do with the shooting, provided the guns are powerful, and the hunter knows where the brain lies.[1]

When I arrived in Ceylon, one of my first visits was to the museum at Colombo. Here I carefully observed the transverse sections of an elephant's skull, until perfectly acquainted with its details. From the museum I went straight to the elephant stables, and thoroughly examined the head of the living animal; comparing it in my own mind with the skull, until I was thoroughly certain of the position of the brain, and the possibility of reaching it from any position.

An African sportsman would be a long time in

[1] I have since proved that I was partly in error when I expressed this opinion. The skull of the African elephant is totally different to that of the Indian species. The forehead or front shot, which is so fatal in Ceylon, is seldom effective against an African elephant. This much enhances the danger, as the sportsman is almost helpless should the elephant charge. Although the front shot is unsatisfactory, I have killed African elephants by a shot behind the ear, or at right angles through the temples, with the same immediate effect as produced on the Indian species.

killing a Ceylon elephant, if he fired at the long range described by most writers; in fact, he would not kill one out of twenty that he fired at in such a jungle-covered country as Ceylon, where in most cases everything depends upon the success of the first barrel.

It is the fashion in Ceylon to get as close as possible to an elephant before firing; this is usually at about ten yards' distance, at which range nearly every shot must be fatal. In Africa, according to all accounts, elephants are fired at at thirty, forty, and even at sixty yards. It is no wonder, therefore, that African sportsmen take the shoulder shot, as the hitting of the brain would be a most difficult feat at such a distance, seeing that the even and dusky colour of an elephant's head offers no peculiar mark for a delicate aim.

The first thing that a good sportsman considers with every animal is the point at which to aim so as to bag him as speedily as possible. It is well known that all animals, from the smallest to the largest, sink into instant death when shot through the brain; and that a wound through the lungs or heart is equally fatal, though not so instantaneous. These are accordingly the points for aim, the brain from its small size being the most difficult to hit. Nevertheless in a jungle country elephants must be shot through the brain, otherwise they would not be bagged, as they would retreat with a mortal wound into such dense jungle that no man could follow. Seeing how easily they are dropped by the brain shot, if approached sufficiently near to ensure the correctness of the aim, no one would ever think of firing at the shoulder who had been accustomed to aim at the head.

A Ceylon sportsman arriving in Africa would naturally examine the skull of the African elephant, and when once certain of the position of the brain, he would require no further information. Leave him alone for hitting it if he knew where it was.

What a sight for a Ceylon elephant hunter would be the first view of a herd of African elephants—all tuskers! In Ceylon a 'tusker' is a kind of spectre, to be talked of by a few who have had the good luck to see one. And when he is seen by a good sportsman, it is an evil hour for him,—he is followed till he gives up his tusks.

It is a singular thing that Ceylon is the only part of the world where the male elephant has no tusks; they have miserable little grubbers projecting two or three inches from the upper jaw, and inclining downwards. Thus a man may kill some hundred elephants without having a pair of tusks in his possession. The largest that I have seen in Ceylon were about six feet long, and five inches in diameter in the thickest part. These would be considered rather below the average in Africa, although in Ceylon they were thought magnificent.[1]

Nothing produces either ivory or horn in fine specimens throughout Ceylon. Although some of the buffaloes have tolerably fine heads, they will not bear a comparison with those of other countries. The horns of the native cattle are not above four inches in length. The elk and the spotted deer's antlers are small compared with deer of their size on the continent of India. This is the more singular, as it is evident from the geological formation that at some remote period Ceylon was not an island, but formed a portion of the main land, from which it is now only separated by a shallow and rocky channel of some few miles. In India the bull elephants have tusks, and the cattle and buffaloes have very large horns. My opinion is that there are elements wanting in the Ceylon pasturage (which is generally poor) for the formation of both horn and ivory. Thus many years of hunting and shooting are rewarded by few trophies of the chase. So great is the natural inactivity of the natives, that no one understands the preparation of the skins; thus all the elk and deer hides are simply dried in the sun, and the hair soon rots and falls off. In India the skin of the Samber deer (the Ceylon elk)

[1] These, I have since discovered, would be rather *above* the average of African bull elephants' tusks, although they are often found of much larger size.

is prized above all others, and is manufactured into gaiters, belts, pouches, coats, breeches, &c.; but in Ceylon these things are entirely neglected by the miserable and indolent population, whose whole thoughts are concentrated upon their daily bread, or rather their curry and rice.

At Newera Ellia the immense number of elk that I have killed would have formed a valuable collection of skins, had they been properly prepared, instead of which the hair has been singed from them, and they have been boiled up for dogs' meat.

Boars' hides have shared the same fate. These are far thicker than those of the tame species, and should make excellent saddles. So tough are they upon the live animal, that it requires a very sharp-pointed knife to penetrate them, and too much care cannot be bestowed upon the manufacture of a blade for this style of hunting, as the boar is one of the fiercest and most dangerous of animals.

Living in the thickest jungles, he rambles out at night in search of roots, fruits, large earthworms, or anything else that he can find, being, like his domesticated brethren, omnivorous. He is a terrible enemy to the pack, and has cost me several good dogs within the last few years. Without first-rate seizers it would be impossible to kill him with the knife without being ripped, as he invariably turns to bay, after a short run, in the thickest jungle he can find. There is no doubt that a good stout boar spear, with a broad blade and strong handle, is the proper weapon for the attack; but a spear is very unhandy, and even dangerous, to carry in such a hilly country as the neighbourhood of Newera Ellia. The forests are full of steep ravines, and such tangled underwood, that following the hounds is always an arduous task, but with a spear in the hand it is still more difficult, and the point is almost certain to get injured by striking against the numerous rocks, in which case it is perfectly useless, when perhaps most required. I never carry a spear for these reasons, but am content with the knife, as in my opinion, any animal that can beat off good hounds and their master deserves to escape.

My knife was made to my own pattern by Paget of Piccadilly. The blade is one foot in length, and two inches broad in the widest part, and slightly concave in the middle. The steel is of the most exquisite quality, and the entire knife weighs three pounds. The peculiar shape, added to the weight of the blade, gives an extraordinary force to a blow; being double edged for three inches from the point, it inflicts a fearful wound: altogether it is a very desperate weapon, and admirably adapted for this kind of sport.

A feat is frequently performed by the Nepaulese by cutting off a buffalo's head at one blow of a sabre or tulwal. The blade of this weapon is peculiar, being concave, and the extremity is far heavier than the hilt; the animal's neck is tied down to a post, so as to produce a tension on the muscles, without which, the blow, however great, would have a comparatively small effect.

The accounts of this feat always appeared very marvellous to my mind, until I one day unintentionally performed something similar on a small scale with the hunting knife.

I was out hunting in the Elk Plains, and having drawn several jungles blank, I ascended the mountains which wall in the western side of the patinas (grass plains) making sure of finding an elk near the summit. It was a lovely day, perfectly calm and cloudless; in which weather the elk, especially the large bucks, are in the habit of lying high up the mountains.

I had nine couple of hounds out, among which were some splendid seizers, 'Bertram,' 'Killbuck,' 'Hecate,' 'Bran,' 'Lucifer,' and 'Lena,' the first three being the progeny of the departed hero, old 'Smut,' who had been killed by a boar a short time before. They were then just twelve months old, and 'Bertram' stood twenty-eight and a half inches high at the shoulder. To him his sire's valour had descended untarnished, and for a dog of his young age, he was the most courageous that I have ever seen. In appearance he was a tall Manilla bloodhound, with the strength of a young lion; very affectionate in disposition, and a general favourite, having won golden opinions in every contest. Whenever a big buck was at bay, and punishing the leading hounds, he was the first to get his hold; no matter how great the danger, he never waited, but recklessly dashed in. 'There goes Bertram! Look at Bertram! Well done, Bertram!'—were the constant exclamations of a crowd of excited spectators when a powerful buck was brought to bay. He was a wonderful dog, but I prophesied an early grave for him, as no hound in the world could long escape death that rushed so recklessly upon his dangerous game.[1] His sister, 'Hecate,' was more careful, and she is alive at this moment, and a capital seizer of great strength, combined with speed, having derived the latter from her dam, 'Lena,' an Australian greyhound, than whom a better or truer bitch never lived. 'Old Bran,' and his beautiful son, 'Lucifer,' were fine specimens of greyhound and deerhound, and as good as gold.

There was not a single elk track the whole of the way up the mountain, and upon arriving at the top, I gave up all hope of finding for that day, and I enjoyed the beautiful view over the vast valley of forest, which lay below, spangled with green plains, and bounded by the towering summit of Adam's Peak, at

[1] Speared through the body by the horns of a buck elk, and killed shortly after this was written.

about twenty-five miles distance. The coffee estates of Dimboola lay far beneath upon the right, and the high mountains of Kirigallapotta, and Totapella bounded the view upon the left.

There is a good path along the narrow ridge, on the summit of the Elk Plain hills, which has been made by elephants. This runs along the very top of the knife-like ridge, commanding a view of the whole country to the right and left. The range is terminated abruptly by a high peak, which descends in a sheer precipice at the extremity.

I strolled along the elephant path, intending to gain the extreme end of the range for the sake of the view, when I suddenly came upon the track of a 'boar,' in the middle of the path. It was perfectly fresh, as were also the ploughings in the ground close by, and the water of a small pool was still curling with clouds of mud, showing most plainly that he had been disturbed from his wallowing by my noise in ascending the mountain side.

There was no avoiding the find; and away went 'Bluebeard,' 'Ploughboy,' 'Gaylass,' and all the leading hounds, followed by the whole pack, in full chorus straight along the path at top speed. Presently they turned sharp to the left into the thick jungle, dashing down the hill side as though off to the Elk Plains below. At this pace I knew the hunt would not last long, and from my elevated stand I waited impatiently for the first sounds of the bay. Round they turned again, up the steep hill side, and the music slackened a little, as the hounds had enough to do in bursting through the tangled bamboo upon the hill.

Presently I heard the rush of the boar in the jungle, coming straight up the hill towards the spot where I was standing; and, fearing that he might top the ridge and make down the other side towards Dimboola, I gave him a halloo to head him back. Hark, for-r-rard to him! yoick! yo-o-ick! to him!

Such a yell, right in his road, astonished him, and, as I expected, he headed sharp back. Up came the pack, going like race horses, and wheeling off where the game had turned, a few seconds running along the side of the mountain, and then, such a burst of music! such a bay! The boar had turned sharp round, and had met the hounds on a level platform on the top of a ridge.

'Lucifer' never leaves my side until we are close up to the bay; and plunging and tearing through the bamboo grass and tangled nillho for a few hundred yards, I at length approached the spot, and I heard Lord Bacon grunting and roaring loud above the din of the hounds.

Bertram has him for a guinea! Hold him, good lad! and away dashed 'Lucifer' from my side at the halloo.

In another moment I was close up, and with my

WILD BOAR HUNT

knife ready I broke through the dense jungle, and was immediately in the open space cleared by the struggles of the boar and pack. Unluckily I had appeared full in the boar's front, and though five or six of the large seizers had got their holds, he made a sudden charge at me that shook them all off, except 'Bertram' and 'Lena.'

It was the work of an instant, as I jumped quickly on one side, and instinctively made a downward cut at him in passing. He fell all of a heap, to the complete astonishment of myself and the furious pack.

He was dead! killed by one blow with the hunting knife. I had struck him across the back just behind the shoulders, and the wound was so immense, that he had the appearance of being nearly half divided. Not only was the spine severed, but the blade had cut deep into his vitals and produced instant death.

One of the dogs was hanging on his hind quarters when he charged, and as the boar was rushing forward, the muscles of the back were accordingly stretched tight, and thus the effect of the cut was increased to this extraordinary degree. He was a middling sized boar, as near as I could guess, about two and a half hundredweight.

Fortunately none of the pack were seriously hurt, although his tusks were as sharp as a knife. This was owing to the short duration of the fight, and also to the presence of so many seizers, who backed each other up without delay.

There is no saying to what size a wild boar grows. I have never killed them with the hounds above four hundredweight; but I have seen solitary boars in the low country that must have weighed nearly double.

I believe the flesh is very good; by the natives it is highly prized; but I have so strong a prejudice against it from the sights I have seen of their feasting upon putrid elephants, that I never touch it.

The numbers of wild hogs in the low country is surprising, and they are most useful in cleaning up the carcases of dead animals, and destroying vermin. I seldom or never fire at a pig in those districts, as their number is so great, that there is no sport in shooting them. They travel about in herds of one or two hundred, and even more. These are composed of sows and young boars; as the latter leave the herd when arrived at maturity.

CHAPTER VII.

Curious Phenomenon—Panorama of Ouva—South-west Monsoon—Hunting Followers—Fort M'Donald River—Jungle Paths—Dangerous Locality—Great Waterfall—Start for Hunting—The Find—A Gallant Stag—'Bran' and 'Lucifer'—'Phrenzy's' Death—Buck at Bay—The Cave Hunting-box—'Madcap's' Dive—Elk Soup—Former Inundation—'Bluebeard' Leads Off—'Hecate's' Course—The Elk's Leap—Variety of Deer—The Axis—Ceylon Bears—Variety of Vermin—Trials for Hounds—Hounds and their Masters—A Sportsman 'Shut Up'—A Corporal and Centipede.

FROM June to November, the south-west monsoon brings wind and mist across the Newera Ellia mountains.

Clouds of white fog boil up from the Dimboola valley, like the steam from a huge cauldron, and invade the Newera Ellia plain through the gaps in the mountains to the westward.

The wind howls over the high ridges, cutting the jungle with its keen edge, so that it remains as stunted brushwood, and the opaque screen of driving fog and drizzling rain is so dense, that one feels convinced there is no sun visible within at least 100 miles.

There is a curious phenomenon, however, in this locality. When the weather described prevails at Newera Ellia, there is actually not one drop of rain within four miles of my house in the direction of Badulla. Dusty roads, a cloudless sky, and dazzling sunshine astonish the thoroughly soaked traveller, who rides out of the rain and mist into a genial climate, as though he passed through a curtain. The wet weather terminates at a mountain called Hackgalla (or more properly Yakkadagalla, or Iron Rock). This bold rock, whose summit is about 6,500 feet above the sea, breasts the driving wind, and seems to command the storm. The rushing clouds halt in their mad course upon its crest, and curl in sudden impotence around the craggy summits. The deep ravine formed by an opposite mountain is filled with the vanquished mist, which sinks powerless in its dark gorge; and the bright sun, shining from the east, spreads a perpetual rainbow upon the gauze-like cloud of fog which settles in the deep hollow.

This is exceedingly beautiful. The perfect circle of the rainbow stands like a fairy spell in the giddy depth of the hollow, and seems to forbid the advance of the monsoon. All before is bright and cloudless: the lovely panorama of the Ouva country spreads before the eye for many miles beneath the feet. All behind is dark and stormy; the wind is howling, the forests are groaning, the rain is pelting upon the hills.

The change appears impossible; but there it is, ever the same, season after season, year after year, the rugged top of Hackgalla struggles with the storms, and ever victorious the cliffs smile in the sunshine on the eastern side; the rainbow re-appears with the monsoon, and its vivid circle remains like the guardian spirit of the valley.

It is impossible to do justice to the extraordinary appearance of this scene by description. The panoramic view in itself is celebrated; but as the point in the road is reached where the termination of the monsoon dissolves the cloud and rain into a thin veil of mist, the panorama seen through the gauze-like atmosphere has the exact appearance of a dissolving view: the depth, height, and distance of every object, all great in reality, are magnified by the dim and unnatural appearance; and by a few steps onward the veil gradually fades away, and the distant prospect lies before the eye with a glassy clearness made doubly striking by the sudden contrast.

The road winds along about midway up the mountain, bounded on the right by the towering cliffs and sloping forest of Hackgalla, and on the left by the almost precipitous descent of nearly 1,000 feet, the sides of which are clothed by alternate forest and waving grass. At the bottom flows a torrent, whose roar ascending from the hidden depth, increases the gloomy mystery of the scene.

On the north, east and south-east of Newera Ellia, the sunshine is perpetual during the reign of the misty atmosphere, which the south-west monsoon drives upon the western side of the mountains. Thus, there is always an escape open from the wet season at Newera Ellia, by a short walk of three or four miles.

A long line of dark cloud is then seen, terminated by a bright blue sky. So abrupt is the line, and the cessation of the rain, that it is difficult to imagine how the moisture is absorbed.

This sudden termination of the cloud-capped mountain gives rise to a violent wind in the sunny valleys and bare hills beneath. The chilled air of Newera Ellia pours down into the sun-warmed atmosphere below, and creates a gale that sweeps across the grassy hill-tops with great force, giving the sturdy rhododendrons an inclination to the north-east, which clearly marks the steadiness of the monsoon.

It is not to be supposed, however, that Newera Ellia lies in unbroken gloom for months together. One month generally brings a share of uninterrupted bad weather; this is from the middle of June to the middle of July. This is the commencement of the south-west monsoon, which usually sets in with great violence. The remaining portion of what is called the wet season, till the end of November, is about as uncertain as the climate of England, some days fine, others wet, and every now and then a week of rain at one bout.

A thoroughly saturated soil, with a cold wind, and driving rain, and forests as full of water as sponges, are certain destroyers of scent;—therefore, hunting at Newera Ellia is out of the question during such weather. The hounds would get sadly out of condition, were it not for the fine weather in the vicinity, which then invites a trip.

I have frequently walked ten miles to my hunting ground, starting before day-break, and then, after a good day's sport up and down the steep mountains, I have returned home in the evening. But this is twelve hours' work, and it is game thrown away, as there is no possibility of getting the dead elk home. An animal that weighs between 400 and 450 pounds without his inside, is not a very easy creature to move at any time, especially in such a steep mountainous country as the neighbourhood of Newera Ellia. As previously described, at the base of the mountains are cultivated rice lands, generally known as paddy fields, where numerous villages have sprung up, from the facility with which a supply of water is obtained from the wild mountains above them. I have so frequently given the people elk and hogs, which I have killed on the heights above their paddy fields, that they are always on the alert at the sound of the bugle, and a few blasts from the mountain top immediately creates a race up from the villages, some two or three thousand feet below. Like vultures scenting carrion, they know that an elk is killed, and they start off to the well-known sound like trained hounds.

Being thorough mountaineers, they are extraordinary fellows for climbing the steep grassy sides. With a light stick about six feet long in one hand, they will start from the base of the mountains and clamber up the hill sides in a surprisingly short space of time; such as would soon take the conceit out of a 'would-be pedestrian.' This is owing to the natural advantages of naked feet, and no inexpressibles.

Whenever an elk has given a long run in the direction of this country, and after a persevering and arduous chase of many hours, I have at length killed him on the grassy heights above the villages. I always take a delight in watching the tiny specks issuing from the green strips of paddy as the natives start off at the sound of the horn.

At this altitude, it requires a sharp eye to discern a man; but at length they are seen scrambling up the ravines and gullies, and breasting the sharp pitches, until at last the first man arrives thoroughly 'used up;' and a string of fellows of lesser wind come in, in sections, all completely blown.

However, the first man in, never gets the lion's share, as the poor old men, with willing spirits and weak flesh, always bring up the rear, and I insist upon a fair division between the old and young, always giving an extra piece to a man who happens to know a little English. This is a sort of reward for acquirements, equivalent to a university degree, and he is considered a literary character by his fellows.

There is nothing that these people appreciate so much as elk and hog's flesh. Living generally upon boiled rice, and curry composed of pumpkins and sweet potatoes, they have no opportunities of tasting meat, unless upon these occasions.

During the very wet weather at Newera Ellia, I sometimes take the pack and bivouac for a fortnight in the fine-weather country. About a week previous, I send down word to the village people of my intention; but upon these occasions I never *give* them the elk. I always insist upon their bringing rice, &c., for the dogs and myself, in exchange for venison, otherwise I should have some hundreds of noisy idle vagabonds flocking up to me like carrion crows.

Of course I give them splendid bargains, as I barter simply on the principle that no man shall come for nothing. Thus if a man assists in building the kennel, or carrying a load, or cutting bed grass, or searching for lost hounds, he gets a share of meat. The others bring rice, coffee, fowls, eggs, plantains, vegetables, &c., which I take at ridiculous rates—a bushel of rice for a full-grown elk, &c. The latter being worth a couple of pounds, and the rice about seven shillings. Thus the hounds keep themselves in rice, and supply me with every thing that I require during the trip, at the same time gratifying the natives.

The direct route to this country was unknown to Europeans at Newera Ellia, until I discovered it one day accidentally in following the hounds.

A large tract of jungle-covered hill stretches away from the Moon Plains at Newera Ellia towards the east, forming a Hog's Back of about three and a half miles in length. Upon the north side this shelves into a deep gorge, at the bottom of which, flows, or rather tumbles, Fort M'Donald river, on its way to the low country, through forest-covered hills and perpendicular cliffs, until it reaches the precipitous patina mountains, when, in a succession of large cataracts, it reaches the paddy fields in the first village of Péréwellé (guava paddy field). Thus the river in the gorge below runs parallel to the long Hog's Back of mountain. This is bordered on the other side by another ravine and smaller torrent, to which the Badulla road runs parallel, until it reaches the mountain of Hackgalla, at which place, the ravine deepens into the misty gorge already described.

At one time, if an elk crossed the Badulla road,

and gained the Hog's Back jungle, both he and the hounds were lost, as no one could follow through such impenetrable forest without knowing either the distance or direction.

'They are gone to Fort M'Donald river!'—this was the despairing exclamation at all times when the pack crossed the road, and we seldom saw the hounds again until late that night, or on the following day. Many never returned,—and Fort M'Donald river became a by-word as a locality to be always dreaded.

After a long run one day, the pack having gone off in this fatal direction; I was determined at any price to hunt them up; and accordingly, I went some miles down the Badulla road to the limestone quarries, which are five miles from the Newera Ellia plain. From this point I left the road, and struck down into the deep grassy valley, crossing the river (the same which runs by the road higher up), and continuing along the side of the slope, until I ascended the opposite range of hills. Descending the precipitous hollow, I at length reached the paddy fields in the low country, which were watered by Fort M'Donald river, and I looked up to the lofty range, formed by the Hog's Back hill, now about 3,000 feet above me. Thus I had gained the opposite side of the Hog's Back, and, after a stiff pull up the mountain, I returned home by a good path, which I had formerly discovered along the course of the river through the forest to Newera Ellia, viâ Rest and be Thankful Bottom and the Barrack Plains; I had thus made a circuit of about twenty-five miles, and become thoroughly conversant with all the localities. I immediately determined to have a path cut from the Badulla road across the Hog's Back jungle to the patinas, which looked down upon Fort M'Donald on the other side, and up which I had ascended on my return. I judged the distance would not exceed two miles across, and I chose the point of junction with the Badulla road, two miles and a half from my house. My reason for this was, that the elk invariably took to the jungle at this spot, which proved it to be the easiest route.

This road, on completion, answered every expectation, connecting the two sides of the Hog's Back by an excellent path of about two miles, and debouching on the opposite side on a high patina peak, which commanded an extensive view. Thus was the whole country opened up by this single path; and should an elk play his old trick, and be off across the Hog's Back to Fort M'Donald river, I could be there nearly as soon as he could, and also keep within hearing of the hounds throughout the run.

I was determined to take the tent, and regularly hunt up the whole country on the other side of the Hog's Back, as the weather was very bad at Newera

Ellia, while in this spot it was beautifully fine, although very windy.

I therefore sent on the tent, kennel-troughs, and pots, and all the paraphernalia indispensable for the jungle; and on the 31st May, 1852, I started, having two companions, Captain Pelly, 37th Regiment, who was then Commandant of Newera Ellia, and his brother on a visit.

It was not more than an hour and a half's good walking from my house to the high patina peak upon which I pitched the tent; but the country and climate are so totally distinct from anything at Newera Ellia, that it gives everyone the idea of being fifty miles away.

We hewed out a spacious arbour at the edge of the jungle, and in this I had the tent pitched to protect it from the wind, which it did effectually, as well as the kennel, which was near the same spot. The servants made a good kitchen, and the encampment was soon complete.

There could not have been a more romantic or beautiful spot for a bivouac. To the right lay the distant view of the low country, stretching into an undefined distance, until the land and sky appeared to melt together. Below, at a depth of about 3,000 feet, the river boiled through the rocky gorge until it reached the village of Péréwellé at the base of the line of mountains, whose cultivated paddy fields looked no larger than the squares upon a chess-board. On the opposite side of the river, rose a precipitous and impassable mountain even to a greater altitude than the facing ridge upon which I stood, forming as grand a foreground as the eye could desire. Above, below, around, there was the bellowing sound of heavy cataracts echoed upon all sides.

Certainly this country is very magnificent; but it is an awful locality for hunting, as the elk has too great an advantage over both hounds and hunters. Mountainous patinas, of the steepest inclination, broken here and there by abrupt precipices, and with occasional level platforms of waving grass, descend to the river's bed. These patina mountains are crowned by extensive forests, and narrow belts of jungle descend from the summit to the base, clothing the numerous ravines which furrow the mountain's side. Thus the entire surface of the mountains forms a series of rugged grass lands, so steep as to be ascended with the greatest difficulty, and the elk lie in the forests on the summits, and also in the narrow belts which cover the ravines.

The whole country forms a gorge, like a gigantic letter V. At the bottom roars the dreaded torrent Fort M'Donald river, in a succession of foaming cataracts, all of which, however grand individually, are completely eclipsed by its last great plunge of

300 feet perpendicular depth into a dark and narrow chasm of wall-bound cliffs.

The bed of the river is the most frightful place that can be conceived, being choked by enormous fragments of rock, amidst which, the irresistible torrent howls with a fury that it is impossible to describe.

The river is confined on either side by rugged cliffs of gneiss rock, from which these fragments have from time to time become detached, and have accordingly fallen into the torrent, choking up the bed, and throwing the obstructed waters into frightful commotion. Here they lie piled one upon the other, like so many inverted cottages; now forming dripping caverns; then resembling walls of slippery rock, over which the water falls in thundering volumes into pools, black from their mysterious depth, and from which there is no visible means of exit. These dark and dangerous pools are walled in by hoary-looking rocks, beneath which the pent-up water dives and boils in subterranean caverns, until it at length escapes through secret channels, and reappears on the opposite side of its prison walls. Lashing itself into foam in its mad frenzy, it forms rapids of giddy velocity through the rocky bounds; now flying through a narrowed gorge, and leaping, striving, and wrestling with unnumbered obstructions, it at length meets with the mighty fall, like death in a madman's course.

One plunge! without a single shelf to break the fall, and down, down it sheets; at first like glass, then like the broken avalanche of snow, and lastly!—we cannot see more—the mist boils from the ruin of shattered waters, and conceals the bottom of the fall. The roar vibrates like thunder in the rocky mountain, and forces the grandeur of the scene through every nerve.

No animal or man, once in those mysterious pools, could ever escape without assistance. Thus in years past, when elk were not followed up in this locality, the poor beast being hard pressed by the hounds, might have come to bay in one of these fatal basins, in which case both he and every hound who entered the trap, found sure destruction.

The hard work, and the danger to both man and hound in this country, may be easily imagined, when it is explained, that the nature of the elk prompts him to seek for water as his place of refuge when hunted; thus he makes off down the mountain for the river, in which he stands at bay. Now the mountain itself is steep enough, but within a short distance of the bottom, the river is in many places guarded by precipices of several hundred feet in depth. A few difficult passes alone give access to the torrent; but the descent requires great caution.

Altogether this forms the wildest and most arduous country that can be imagined for hunting ; but it abounds with elk.

The morning was barely grey, when I woke up the servants, and ordered coffee, and made the usual preparations for a start. At last, thank goodness ! the boots are laced. This is the troublesome part of dressing before broad daylight, and nevertheless laced ankle boots must be worn as a protection against sprains and bruises in such a country. Never mind the trouble of lacing them, they are on now, and there is a good day's work in store for them.

It was the 30th May, 1853, a lovely hunting morning, and a fine dew on the patinas ; *rather* too windy, but that could not be helped.

Quiet now !—down, Bluebeard !—back, will you, Lucifer ! Here's a smash ! there goes the jungle kennel ! the pack squeezing out of it in every direction, as they hear the preparations for departure.

Now we are all right, ten couple out, and all good ones. 'Come along, yo-o-i, along here ;' and a note on the horn brings the pack close together as we enter the forest on the very summit of the ridge. Thus the start was completed just as the first tinge of gold spread along the eastern horizon, about ten minutes before sunrise.

The jungles were tolerably good, but there were not as many elk tracks as I had expected ; probably, the high wind on the ridge had driven them lower down for shelter; accordingly I struck an oblique direction downwards, and I was not long before I discovered a fresh track; fresh enough, certainly, as the thick moss which covered the ground showed a distinct path where the animal had been recently feeding.

Every hound had stolen away; even the greyhounds buried their noses in the broad track of the buck, so fresh was the scent; and I waited quietly for 'the find.' The greyhounds stood round me with their ears cocked, and glistening eyes, intently listening for the expected sound.

There they are!—all together, such a burst! They must have stolen away mute, and have found on the other side the ridge, for they were now coming down at full speed from the very summit of the mountain.

From the amount of music, I knew they had a good start; but I had no idea that the buck would stand to such a pack at the very commencement of the hunt. Nevertheless, there was a sudden bay within a few hundred yards of me, and the elk had already turned to fight. I knew that he was an immense fellow from his track, and I at once saw that he would show fine sport.

Just as I was running through the jungle towards the spot, the bay broke, and the buck had evidently gone off straight away, as I heard the pack in full cry rapidly increasing their distance, and going off down the mountain.

Sharp following was now the order of the day, and away we went. The mountain was so steep that it was necessary, every now and then, to check the momentum of a rapid descent by clinging to the tough saplings. Sometimes a branch would give way, and a considerable spill would be the consequence. However, I soon got out on the patina, about one-third of the way down the mountain, and here I met one of the natives, who was well posted. Not a sound of the pack was now to be heard; but this man declared most positively that the elk had suddenly changed his course, and, instead of keeping down the hill, had struck off to his left, along the side of the mountain. Accordingly, off I started as hard as I could go, with several natives, who all agreed as to the direction.

After running for about a mile along the patinas, in the line which I judged the pack had taken, I heard one hound at bay in a narrow jungle, high up on my left. It was only the halt of an instant, for the next moment I heard the same hound's voice evidently running on the other side of the strip of jungle, and taking off down the mountain straight for the dreaded river. Here was a day's work cut out as neatly as could be!

Running towards the spot, I found the buck's

track leading in that direction, and I gave two or three view halloos at the top of my voice, to bring the rest of the pack down upon it. They were close at hand, but the high wind had prevented me from hearing them, and away they came from the jungle, rushing down upon the scent like a flock of birds. I stepped off the track to let them pass as they swept by, and 'For-r-r-a-r-d to him! For-r-r-ard!' was the word the moment they had passed, as I gave them a halloo down the hill. It was a bad look-out for the elk now; every hound knew their master was close up, and they went like demons.

The 'Tamby'[1] was the only man up, and he and I immediately followed in chase down the precipitous patinas; running when we could, scrambling, and sliding on our hams, when it was too steep to stand, and keeping good hold of the long tufts of grass, lest we should gain too great an impetus, and slide to the bottom.

After about half a mile passed in this manner, I heard the bay, and I saw the buck far beneath, standing upon a level grassy platform, within 300 yards of the river. The whole pack was around him except the greyhounds, who were with me; but not a hound had a chance with him, and he repeatedly charged in among them, and regularly drove them before him,

[1] An exceedingly active Moorman, who was my great ally in hunting.

sending any single hound spinning whenever he came within his range. But the pack quickly re-united, and always returned with fresh vigour to the attack. There was a narrow wooded ravine between me and them, and with caution and speed combined, I made towards the spot down the precipitous mountain, followed by the greyhounds, 'Bran' and 'Lucifer.'

I soon arrived on a level with the bay, and, plunging into the ravine, I swung myself down from tree to tree, and then climbed up the opposite side. I broke cover within a few yards of him. What a splendid fellow he looked!—he was about thirteen hands high, and carried the most beautiful head of horns that I had ever seen upon an elk. His mane was bristled up, his nostril was distended, and, turning from the pack, he surveyed me, as though taking the measure of his new antagonist. Not seeming satisfied, he deliberately turned, and, descending from the level space, he carefully picked his way. Down narrow elk runs along the steep precipices, and at a slow walk, with the whole pack in single file at his heels, he clambered down towards the river. I followed on his track over places which I would not pass in cold blood; and I shortly halted above a cataract of some eighty feet in depth, about 100 paces above the great waterfall.

It was extremely grand; the roar of the falls so entirely hushed all other sounds, that the voices of the hounds were perfectly inaudible, although within a few yards of me, as I looked down upon them from a rock that overhung the river.

The elk stood upon the brink of the swollen torrent; he could not retreat, as the wall of rock was behind him, with the small step-like path by which he had descended: this was now occupied by the yelling pack.

The hounds knew the danger of the place; but the buck, accustomed to these haunts from his birth, suddenly leapt across the boiling rapids, and, springing from rock to rock along the verge of the cataract, he gained the opposite side. Here he had mistaken his landing place, as a shelving crag upon which he had alighted, was so steep, that he could not retain his footing, and he gradually slid down towards the river.

At this moment, to my horror, both 'Bran' and 'Lucifer' dashed across the torrent, and bounding from rock to rock, they sprang at the already tottering elk,, and in another moment both he and they rolled over in a confused mass into the boiling torrent! One more instant, and they re-appeared; the buck gallantly stemming the current, which his great length of limb and weight enabled him to do; the dogs, overwhelmed in the foam of the rapids, were swept down towards the fall, in spite of their frantic exertions to gain the bank. They were not fifteen feet from the edge of the fall, and I saw them spun round and round in the whirlpools, being hurried towards certain destruction. The poor dogs seemed aware of the danger, and made the most extraordinary efforts to avoid their fate. They were my two favourites of the pack, and I screamed out words of encouragement to them, although the voice of a cannon could not have been heard among the roar of waters. They had nearly gained the bank, on the very verge of the fall, when a few tufts of lemon grass concealed them from my view. I thought they were over; and I could not restrain a cry of despair at their horrible fate. I felt sick with the idea. But the next moment I was shouting hurrah! they are all right; thank goodness, they were saved. I saw them struggling up the steep bank, through the same lemon grass, which had for a moment obscured their fate. They were thoroughly exhausted, and half drowned.

In the meantime, the elk had manfully breasted the rapids, carefully choosing the shallow places; and the whole pack, being mad with excitement, had plunged into the water, regardless of the danger. I thought every hound would have been lost. For an instant they looked like a flock of ducks, but a few moments afterwards they were scattered in the boiling eddies, hurrying with fatal speed towards the dreadful cataract. Poor 'Phrenzy,' round she spun in the giddy vortex; nearer and nearer she approached the verge—her struggles were unavailing—over she went! and was of course never heard of afterwards.

This was a terrible style of hunting; rather too much so to be pleasant.

I clambered down to the edge of the river just in time to see the elk climbing as nimbly as a cat up the precipitous bank on the opposite side, threading his way at a slow walk under the overhanging rocks, and scrambling up the steep mountain with a long string of hounds at his heels in single file. 'Valiant,' 'Tiptoe,' and 'Ploughboy,' were close to him, and I counted the other hounds in the line, fully expecting to miss half of them. To my surprise and delight, only one was absent; this was 'Phrenzy.' The others had all managed to save themselves. I now crossed the river by leaping from rock to rock with some difficulty, and with hands and knees I climbed the opposite bank. This was about sixty feet high, from the top of which the mountain commenced its ascent; although very precipitous, the air was so covered with long lemon grass, that it was easy enough to climb. I looked behind me, and there was the Tamby, all right, within a few paces.

The elk was no longer in sight, and the roar of the water was so great that it was impossible to hear the hounds. However, I determined to crawl along his track which was plainly discernible, the high grass being broken into a regular lane which skirted the precipice of the great waterfall in the direction of the villages.

We were now about a hundred feet above, and on one side of the great fall, looking into the deep chasm into which the river leapt, forming a cloud of mist below. The lemon grass was so high in tufts among the rocks that we could not see a foot before us, and we knew not whether the next step would land us on firm footing, or deposit us some hundred feet below. Clutching fast to the long grass, therefore, we crept carefully on for about a quarter of a mile, now climbing the face of the rocks, now descending by means of their irregular surfaces, but still skirting the dark gorge down which the river fell.

At length, having left the fall some considerable distance behind us, the ear was somewhat relieved from the bewildering noise of water, and I distinctly heard the pack at bay not very far in advance. In another moment I saw the elk standing on a platform of rock about a hundred yards ahead, on a lower shelf of the mountain, and the whole pack at bay. This platform was the top of a cliff which overhung the deep gorge; the river flowing in the bottom after its great fall, and both the elk and hounds appeared to be in 'a fix.' The descent had been made to this point by leaping down places which he could not possibly re-ascend, and there was only one narrow outlet, which was covered by the hounds. Should he charge through the hounds to force this passage, half a dozen of them must be knocked over the precipice.

However, I carefully descended, and soon reached the platform. This was not more than twenty feet square, and it looked down into the gorge of about three hundred feet. The first seventy of this depth were perpendicular, as the top of the rock overhung; after which, the side of the cliff was marked by great fissures and natural steps formed by the detachment from time to time of masses of rock which had fallen into the river below. Bushes and rank grass filled the interstices of the rocks, and an old deserted water-course lay exactly beneath the platform, being cut and built out of the side of the cliff.

It was a magnificent sight in such grand scenery to see the buck at bay when we arrived upon the platform. He was a dare-devil fellow, and feared neither hounds nor man; every now and then he charged through the pack, and came almost within reach of the Tamby's spear. It was difficult to kill him. I was afraid to go in at him, lest in his struggles he should drag the hounds over the precipice, and I would not cheer the seizers on for the same reason. Indeed, they seemed well aware of the danger, and every now and then retreated to me, as

THE ELK'S LEAP

though to induce the elk to make a move to some better ground.

However, the buck very soon decided the question. I made up my mind to halloo the hounds on, and to ham-string the elk, to prevent him from nearing the precipice; I gave a shout, and the pack rushed at him. Not a dog could touch him; he was too quick with his horns and fore-feet. He made a dash into the pack, and then regained his position close to the verge of the precipice. He then turned his back to the hounds, looked down over the edge, and, to the astonishment of all, he plunged into the abyss below! A dull crash sounded from beneath, and then nothing was heard but the roaring of the waters as before. The hounds looked over the edge, and yelled with a mixture of fear and despair. Their game was gone!

By making a circuit of about half a mile among these frightful precipices and gorges, we at length arrived at the foot of the cliff down which the buck had leapt. Here we of course found him lying dead, as he had broken most of his bones. He was in very fine condition; but it was impossible to move him from such a spot. I therefore cut off his head, as his antlers were the finest that I have ever killed before or since.

To regain the tent, I had a pull for it, having to descend into the village of Pérėwellé, and then to re-ascend the opposite mountain of 3,000 feet; but even this I thought preferable to returning in cold blood by the dangerous route I had come.

Tugging up such a mountain was no fun after a hard morning's work, and I resolved to move the encampment to a large cave, some 800 feet lower down the mountain. Accordingly, I struck the tent, and after breakfast we took up our quarters in a cavern worthy of Robin Hood. This had been formed by a couple of large rocks, the size of a moderate house, which had been detached from the overhanging cliff above, and had fallen together. There was a smaller cavern within, which made a capital kennel; rather more substantial than the rickety building of yesterday.

Some of the village people, hearing that the buck was killed and lying in the old watercourse, went in a gang to cut him up. What was their surprise on reaching the spot to find the carcase removed. It had evidently been dragged along the watercourse, as the trail was distinct in the high grass, and upon following it up, away went two fine leopards bounding along the rocks to their adjacent cave. They had consumed a large portion of the flesh; but the villagers did not leave them much for another meal. Skin, hoofs, and in fact every vestige of an elk is consumed by these people.

For my own part, I no not think much of elk venison, unless it be very fat, which is rarely the case. It is at all times more like beef than any other meat, for which it is a very good substitute. The marrow-bones are the '*bonne bouche*,' being peculiarly rich and delicate. Few animals can have a larger proportion of marrow than the elk, as the bones are more hollow than those of most quadrupeds. This cylindrical formation enables them to sustain the severe shocks in descending rough mountains at full speed. It is perfectly wonderful to see an animal of near 600 pounds' weight bounding down a hill-side over rocks and ruts and every conceivable difficulty of ground, at a pace which will completely distance the best hound; and even at this desperate speed, the elk will never make a false step; sure-footed as a goat, he will still fly on through bogs, ravines, tangled jungles, and rocky rivers, ever certain of his footing.

The foregoing description of an elk hunt will give the reader a good idea of the power of this animal in stemming rapids and climbing dangerous precipices; but even an elk is not proof against the dangers of Fort M'Donald river, an example of which we had on the following morning.

The hounds found a doe, who broke cover close to me in a small patina, and made straight running for the river. She had no sooner reached it than I heard her cry out, and as she was closely followed I thought she was seized. However, the whole pack shortly returned, evidently thrown out, and I began to abuse them pretty roundly, thinking that they had lost their game in the river. So they had; but in an excusable manner; the poor doe had been washed down a rapid, and had broken her thigh. We found her dead under a hollow rock in the middle of the river.

Here we had a fine exemplification of the danger of the mysterious pools.

While I was opening the elk, with the pack all round me, licking their lips in expectation, old 'Madcap' was jostled by one of the greyhounds, and slipped into a basin among the rocks which formed an edge of about two feet above the surface.

The opposite side of the pool was hemmed in by rocks about six feet high, and the direction of the under current was at once shown by poor old 'Madcap' being swept up against this high wall of rock, where she remained paddling with all her might in an upright position.

I saw the poor beast would be sucked under, and yet I could not save her. However, I did my best, at the risk of falling in myself.

I took off my handkerchief and made a slip knot,

and, begging Pelly to lie down on the top of the rock, I took his hand while I clung to the face of the wall as I best could by a little ledge of about two inches' width. With great difficulty I succeeded in hooking the bitch's head in the slip knot, but in my awkward position I could not use sufficient strength to draw her out. I could only support her head above the water, which I could distinctly feel was drawing her from me. Presently she gave a convulsive struggle, which freed her head from the loop, and in an instant she disappeared.

I could not help going round the rock to see if her body should be washed out when the torrent reappeared, when, to my astonishment, she popped up all right, not being more than half drowned by her subterranean excursion, and we soon helped her safe ashore. Fortunately for her, the passage had been sufficiently large to admit her, although I have no doubt a man would have been held fast and drowned.

There was so much water in the river that I determined to move from this locality as too dangerous for hunting. I, therefore, ordered the village people to assemble on the following morning to carry the loads and tent. In the meantime I sent for the dead elk.

There could not be a better place for a hunting box than that cave. We soon had a glorious fire roaring round the kennel pot, which, having been well scoured with sand and water, was to make the soup. Such soup!—shades of gourmands, if ye only smelt that cookery! The pot held six gallons, and the *whole elk*, except a few steaks, was cut up and alternately boiled down in sections. The flesh was then cut up small for the pack; the marrow bones reserved for 'master,' and the soup was then boiled until it had evaporated to the quantity required. A few green chillies, onion in slices fried, and a little lime juice, salt, black pepper and mushroom ketchup, and,—in fact, there is no use thinking of it, as the soup is not to be had again. The fire crackled and blazed as the logs were heaped upon it as night grew near, and lit up all the nooks and corners of the old cave. Three beds in a row contained three sleepy mortals. The hounds snored, and growled, and then snored again. The servants jabbered, chewed betel, spit, then jabbered a little more, and at last every thing and every body was fast asleep within the cave.

The next morning we had an early breakfast and started; the village people marching off in good spirits with the loads. I was now *en route* for Bertram's patinas, which lay exactly over the mountain on the opposite side of the river. This being perpendicular, I was obliged to make a great circuit by keeping the old Newera Ellia path along the river for two or three miles, and then, turning off at right angles, I knew an old native trace over the ridge. Altogether it was a round of about six miles, although the patinas were not a mile from the cave in a straight line.

The path, in fact, terminates upon the high peak, exactly opposite the cave, looking down upon my hunting-ground of the day before, and on the other side of the ridge, lie Bertram's patinas.

The extreme point which I had now gained forms one end of a horseshoe or amphitheatre; the other extremity is a high mountain exactly opposite, at about two miles' distance. The bend of the horseshoe forms a circuit of about six miles, the rim of which is a wall of precipices and steep patina mountains which are about 600 or 700 feet above the basin or the bottom of the amphitheatre. The tops of the mountains are covered with good open forest, and ribbon-like strips descend to the base. The base forms an uneven shelf of great extent, about 2,000 feet above the villages. This shelf or valley appears to have suffered at some remote period from a terrible inundation. Landslips of great size and innumerable deep gorges and ravines furrow the bottom of the basin, until at length a principal fissure carries away the united streams to the paddy fields below.

The cause of this inundation is plain enough. The basin has been the receptacle for the drainage of an extensive surface of mountain. This drainage has been effected by innumerable small torrents, which have united in one general channel through the valley. The exit of this stream is through a narrow gorge, by which it descends to the low country. During the period of heavy rains, a landslip has evidently choked up this passage, and the exit of the water being thus obstructed, the whole area of the valley has become a lake. The accumulated water has suddenly burst through the obstruction and swept everything before it. The elk are very fond of lying under the precipices in the strips of jungle already mentioned. When found they are accordingly forced to take to the open country and come down to the basin below, as they cannot possibly ascend the mountain except by one or two remote deer runs. Thus the whole hunt from the find to the death is generally in view.

From every point of this beautiful locality there is a boundless and unbroken panorama of the low country.

Unfortunately, although the weather was perfectly fine, it was the windy season, and a gale swept across the mountains, that rendered ears of little use, as a hound's voice was annihilated in such a hurricane. This was sadly against sport, as the main body of the pack would have no chance of joining the finding hound.

However, the hounds were unkennelled at break

of day, and, the tent being pitched at the bottom of the basin, we commenced a pull up the steep patinas, hoping to find somewhere on the edge of the jungles.

'There's scent to a certainty!—look at old Bluebeard's nose upon the ground, and the excited wagging of his stern. Ploughboy notices it; now Gaylass—they'll hit it off presently to a certainty, though it's as cold as charity. That elk was feeding here early in the night; the scent is four hours old if a minute. There they go into the jungle, and we shall lose the elk ten to one, as not another hound in the pack will work it up. It can't be helped; if any three hounds will rouse him out, those are the three.'

For a couple of hours we had sat behind a rock sheltered from the wind watching the immense prospect before us. The whole pack were lying around us, except the three missing hounds, of whom we had seen nothing since they stole away upon the cold scent.

That elk must have gone up to the top of the mountains after feeding, and a pretty run he must be having, very likely off to Matturatta Plains; if so, good-bye to all sport for to-day, and the best hounds will be dead tired for to-morrow.

I was just beginning to despair, when I observed a fine large buck at about half a mile distance cantering easily towards us across an extensive flat of table-land. This surface was a fine sward, on the same level with the point upon which we sat, but separated from us by two small wooded ravines, with a strip of patina between them. I at once surmised that this was the hunted elk, although as yet no hounds were visible.

On arrival at the first ravine, he immediately descended, and shortly after he reappeared on the small patina between the two ravines, within 300 yards of us. Here, the strong gale gave him our scent. It was a beautiful sight to see him halt in an instant, and, drawing up to his full height, sniff the warning breeze and wind the enemy before him.

Just at this moment I heard old 'Bluebeard's' deep note swelling in the distance, and I saw him leading across the table-land as true as gold upon the track; 'Ploughboy' and 'Gaylass' were both with him, but they were running mute.

The buck heard the hounds as well as we did, and I was afraid that the whole pack would also catch the sound, and, by hurrying towards it, would head the elk and turn him from his course. Up to the present time they had not observed him.

Still the buck stood in an attitude of acute suspense. He winded an enemy before him, and he heard another behind, which was rapidly closing up, and, as though doubting his own power of scent, he gave preference to that of hearing, and gallantly continued his course and entered the second ravine just beneath our feet.

I immediately jumped up, and, exciting the hounds in a subdued voice, I waved my cap at the spot, and directed a native to run at full speed to the jungle, to endeavour to meet the elk, as I knew the hounds would then follow him. This they did; and they all entered the jungle with the man, except the three greyhounds, 'Lucifer,' 'Bran,' and 'Hecate,' who remained with me.

A short time passed in breathless suspense; during which the voices of the three following hounds rapidly approached as they steadily persevered in the long chase; when suddenly, as I had expected, the main body of the pack met the elk in the strip of jungle.

Joyful must have been the burst of music to the ears of old 'Bluebeard' after his long run. Out crashed the buck upon the patinas near the spot where the pack had entered, and away he went over the grassy hills, at a pace which soon left the hounds behind. The greyhounds will stretch his legs for him. Yo-i-ck to him, Lucifer! For-r-r-ard to him, Hecate!

Off dashed the three greyhounds from my side at a railway pace; but, as the buck was above them and had a start of about 200 yards, in such an uphill race, both Bran and Lucifer managed to lose sight of him in the undulations.

Now was the time for Hecate's enormous power of loin and thigh to tell, and, never losing a moment's view of her game, she sped up the steep mountain side, and was soon after seen within fifty yards of the buck all alone, but going like a rocket.

Now she has turned him!—that pace could not last up hill, and round the elk doubled, and came flying down the mountain side.

From the point of the hill upon which we stood we had a splendid view of the course; the bitch gained upon him at every bound, and there was a pitiless dash in her style of going that boded little mercy to her game. What alarmed me, however, was the direction that the buck was taking. An abrupt precipice of about 250 feet was lying exactly in his path; this sunk sheer down to a lower series of grass lands.

At the tremendous pace at which they were going I feared lest their own impetus should carry both elk and dog to destruction before they could see the danger.

Down they flew with unabated speed; they neared the precipice, and a few more seconds would bring them to the verge.

The stride of the buck was no match for the bound of the greyhound: the bitch was at his flanks! and he pressed along at flying speed.

He was close to the danger! and it was still unseen! a moment more, and 'Hecate' sprang at his ear. Fortunately, she lost her hold as the ear split. This check saved her. I shouted 'he'll be over!' and the next instant he was flying through the air to headlong destruction!

Bounding from a projecting rock upon which he struck, he flew outwards, and, with frightfully increasing momentum, he spun round and round in his descent, until the centrifugal motion drew out his legs and neck as straight as a line. A few seconds of this multiplying velocity, and . . . . crash!

It was all over. The bitch had pulled up on the very brink of the precipice, but it was a narrow escape.

Sportsmen are contradictory creatures. If that buck had come to bay, I should have known no better sport than going in at him with the knife to the assistance of the pack; but I now felt a great amount of compassion for the poor brute who had met so terrible a fate. It did not seem *fair*; and yet I would not have missed such a sight for anything. Nothing can be conceived more terribly grand than the rush of so large an animal through the air; and it was a curious circumstance, that within a few days no less than two bucks had gone over precipices, although I had never witnessed such an accident more than once before.

Upon reaching the fatal spot I of course found him lying stone dead. He had fallen at least 250 feet, to the base of the precipice; and the ground being covered with detached fragments of rock, he had broken most of his bones, besides bursting his paunch and smashing in the face. However, we cut him up and cleaned him, and, with the native followers heavily laden, we reached the tent.

The following morning I killed another fine buck after a good run on the patinas, where he was coursed and pulled down by the greyhounds; but the wind was so very high, that it destroyed the pleasure of hunting. I therefore determined on another move,—to the Matturatta Plains, within three miles of my present hunting ground.

After hunting four days at the Matturatta Plains, I moved on to the Elephant Plains; and from thence returned home, after twelve days' absence, having killed twelve elk and two red deer.

The animal known as the 'red deer' in Ceylon is a very different creature to his splendid namesake in Scotland; he is particularly unlike a deer in the disproportionate size of his carcass to his length of leg. He stands about twenty-six inches high at the shoulder, and weighs (live weight) from forty-five to fifty pounds. He has two sharp tusks in the upper jaw, projecting about an inch and a half from the gum. These are exactly like the lower-jaw tusks of a boar; but they incline in the contrary direction, viz., downwards, and they are used as weapons of defence.

The horns of the red deer seldom exceed eight inches in length, and have no more than two points upon each antler, formed by a fork-like termination. This kind of deer has no brow antler. They are very fast, and excel especially in going up hill; in which ground they frequently escape from the best greyhounds.

There is no doubt that the red-deer venison is the best in Ceylon; but the animal itself is not generally sought after for sport. He gives a most uninteresting run; never going straight away like a deer, but doubling about over fifty acres of ground like a hare, until he is at last run into and killed. They exist in extraordinary numbers throughout every portion of Ceylon, but are never seen in herds.

Next to the red deer is the still more tiny species, the 'mouse deer.' This animal seldom exceeds twelve inches in height, and has the same characteristic as the red deer in the heavy proportion of body to its small length of limb. The skin is a mottled ash-grey, covered with dark spots. The upper jaw is furnished with sharp tusks similar to the red deer; but the head is free from horns.

The skull is perfectly unlike the head of a deer, and is closely allied to the rat; which it would exactly resemble, were it not for the difference in the teeth. The mouse deer lives principally upon berries and fruits; but I have seldom found much herbage upon examination of the paunch. Some people consider the flesh very good; but my ideas perhaps give it a '*ratty*' flavour that makes it unpalatable.

These little deer make for some well-known retreat the moment that they are disturbed by dogs, and they are usually found after a short run safely ensconced in a hollow tree.

It is a very singular thing, that none of the deer tribe in Ceylon have more than six points on their horns, viz., three upon each. These are, the brow antler point, and the two which form the extremity of each horn. I have seen them occasionally with more; but these were deformities in the antlers.

A stranger is always disappointed in a Ceylon elk's antlers; and very naturally, for they are quite out of proportion to the great size of the animal. A very large Scotch red deer is not more than two-thirds the size of a moderately fine elk, and yet he carries a better head of horns.

In fact, so rare are fine antlers in Ceylon, that I could not pick out more than a dozen of really handsome elk horns out of the great numbers that I have killed.

A handsome pair of antlers is a grand addition to the beauty of a fine buck, and gives a majesty to his bearing which is greatly missed when a fine animal breaks cover with only a puny head. There is as great a difference in his appearance as there would be in a life-guardsman in full uniform or in his shirt.

The antlers of the axis, or spotted deer, are generally longer than those of the elk; they are also more slender and graceful. Altogether the spotted deer is about the handsomest of that beautiful tribe. A fine stag is the perfection of elegance, colour, strength, courage, and speed. He has a proud and thorough-bred way of carrying his head, which is set upon his neck with a peculiar grace. Nothing can surpass the beauty of his full black eye. His hide is as sleek as satin; a rich brown, slightly tinged with red, and spotted as though mottled with flakes of snow. His weight is about 250 pounds (alive).

It is a difficult thing to judge of a deer's weight with any great accuracy; but I do not think I am far out in my estimation of their average, as I tried the experiment by weighing a dead elk. I had always considered that a mountain elk, which is smaller than those of the low country, weighed about 400 pounds when cleaned, or 550 pounds live weight. I happened one day to kill an average sized buck, though with very small horns, close to the road, so, having cleaned him, I sent a cart for his carcass on my return home. This elk I weighed whole, minus his inside, and he was 411 pounds. Many hours had elapsed since his death, so that the carcass must have lost much weight by drying; this, with the loss of blood and offal, must have been at least 150 pounds, which would have made his live weight 561 pounds.

Of the five different species of deer in Ceylon the spotted deer is alone seen upon the plains. No climate can be too hot for his exotic constitution, and he is never found at a higher elevation than 3,000 feet. In the low country, when the mid-day sun has driven every other beast to the shelter of the densest jungles, the sultan of the herd and his lovely mates are sometimes contented with the shade of an isolated tree, or the simple border of the jungle; where they drowsily pass the day, flapping their long ears in listless idleness until the hotter hours have passed away. At about four in the afternoon they stroll upon the open plains, bucks, does, and fawns, in beautiful herds; when undisturbed, as many as a hundred together. This is the only species of deer in Ceylon that is gregarious.

Neither the spotted deer, nor the bear or buffalo, is to be found at Newera Ellia. The axis and the buffalo, being the usual denizens of the hottest countries, are not expected to exist in their natural state in so low a temperature; but it is extraordinary that the bear, who in most countries inhabits the mountains, should in Ceylon adhere exclusively to the low country.

The Ceylon bear is of that species which is to be seen in the Zoological Gardens, as the 'sloth bear;' an ill-bred-looking fellow with a long-haired black coat and a grey face.

A Ceylon bear's skin is not worth preserving ; there is no fur upon it, but it simply consists of rather a stingy allowance of black hairs. This is the natural effect of his perpetual residence in a hot country, where the coat adapts itself to the climate. He is desperately savage, and is more feared by the natives than any other animal, as he is in the constant habit of attacking people without the slightest provocation. His mode of attack increases the danger, as there is a great want of fair play in his method of fighting. Lying in wait, either behind a rock or in a thick bush, he makes a sudden spring upon the unwary wanderer, and in a moment he attacks the face with teeth and claws. The latter are about *two inches* long, and the former are much larger than a leopard's ; hence it may easily be imagined how even a few seconds of biting and clawing might alter the most handsome expression of countenance.

Bears have frequently been known to tear off a man's face like a mask, leaving nothing but the bones of a skull.

The quadrupeds of Newera Ellia and the adjacent highlands are confined to the following classes :—The elephant, hog, leopard, chetah, elk, red deer, mouse deer, hare, otter, jackal, civet cat, mongoose, and two others (varieties of the species), black squirrel, grey squirrel, Wanderoo monkey (the largest species in Ceylon), the porcupine, and a great variety of rats.

Imagine the difficulty of breaking in a young hound for elk hunting, when the jungles are swarming with such a list of vermin! The better the pup, the more he will persevere in hunting everything that he can possibly find; and with such a variety of animals, some of which have the most enticing scent, it is a source of endless trouble in teaching a young hound what to hunt and what to avoid.

It is curious to witness the sagacity of the old hounds, in joining or despising the opening note of a new comer.

The jungles are fearfully thick, and it requires great exertion on the part of a dog to force his way through from a distance at a pace that will enable him to join the finding hound; thus he feels considerable disappointment, if upon arrival he finds the scent of a monkey, or a cat, instead of his legitimate game. An old hound soon marks the inexperienced voice of the babbler, and after the cry of 'wolf' has been again repeated, nothing will induce him to join the false finder.

Again, it is exceedingly interesting to observe the quickness of all hounds in acknowledging their leader. Only let them catch the sound of old 'Bluebeard's' voice, and see the dash with which they rush through the jungle to join him. They know the old fellow's note is true to an elk or hog, and, with implicit confidence in his 'find,' they never hesitate to join.

There are numerous obstacles to the breaking and training of dogs of all kinds in such a country. A hound when once in the jungle is his own master. He obeys the sound of the halloo or the horn, or not, as he thinks proper. It is impossible to correct him, as he is out of sight.

Now, the very fact of having one or two *first-rate* finders in a pack, will very likely be the cause of spoiling the other hounds. After repeated experience, their instinct soon shows them that, no matter how the whole pack may hunt, the 'find' will be achieved by one of the first-rate hounds, and gradually they give up hunting, and take to *listening* for the opening note of the favourite. Of course in an open country they would be kept to their work by the whip; but at Newera Ellia this is impossible. This accounts for the extreme paucity of first-rate 'finders.'

Hunting in a wild country is a far more difficult task for hounds than the ordinary chase at home. Wherever a country is cultivated, it must be enclosed. Thus, should a flock of sheep have thrown the hounds out by crossing the scent, a cast round the fences must soon hit it off again, if the fox has left the field. But in elk hunting it is scarcely possible to assist the hounds; a dozen different animals, or even a disturbed elk, may cross the scent in parts of the jungle where the cry of the hounds is even out of hearing. Again, an elk has a constant habit of running or swimming down a river, his instinct prompting him to drown his own scent, and thus throw off his pursuers. Here is a trial for the hounds!—the elk has waded or swum down the stream, and the baffled pack arrive upon the bank; their cheering music has ceased; the elk has kept the water for perhaps a quarter of a mile, or he may have landed several times during that distance, and again have taken to water.

Now the young hounds dash thoughtlessly across the river, thinking of nothing but a straight course, and they are thrown out on the barren bank on the other side. Back they come again, wind about the last track for a few minutes, and then they are forced to give it up;—they are thrown out altogether.

Mark the staunch old hounds!—one has crossed the river; there is no scent, but he strikes down the bank with his nose close to the ground, and away he goes along the edge of the river casting for a scent. Now mark old 'Bluebeard,' swimming steadily down the stream; he knowns the habits of his game as well as I do, and two to one that he will find, although 'Ploughboy' has just started along the near bank; so, that both sides of the river are being hunted.

This is what I call difficult hunting; bad enough if the huntsman be up to assist his hounds, but nine times out of ten this happens in the middle of a run without a soul within a mile.

The only way to train hounds in this style of country is to accustom them to complete obedience from puppyhood. This is easily effected by taking them out for exercise upon a road, coupled to old hounds. A good walk every morning, accompanied by the horn and the whip, and they soon fall into such a habit of obedience that they may be taken out without the couples.

The great desideratum, then, is to gain their affection and confidence, otherwise they will obey upon the road, and laugh at you when in the jungle. Now 'affection' is a difficult feeling to instil into a fox-hound, and can only be partially attained by the exercise of cupboard love; thus a few pieces of dry liver or bread, kept in the pocket to be given to a young hound who has sharply answered to his call, will do more good than a month of scolding and rating.

'Confidence,' or the want of it, in a hound, depends entirely upon the character of his master. There is an old adage of 'like master, like man;' and this is strongly displayed in the hound. The very best seizer would be spoiled if his master were a *leetle* slow in going in with the knife; and, on the other hand, dogs naturally shy of danger turn into good seizers where their master invariably leads them in.

Not only is their confidence required and gained at these times, but they learn to place implicit reliance upon their master's knowledge of hunting, in the same manner that they acknowledge the superiority of a particular hound. This induces them to obey beyond any method of training, as they feel a certain dependence upon the man, and they answer his halloo or the horn without a moment's hesitation.

Nothing is so likely to destroy the character of a pack as a certain amount of laziness or incapacity upon the master's part in following them up. This is natural enough, as the best hounds, if repeatedly left unassisted for hours when at bay with their game, until they are regularly beaten off, will lose their relish for the sport. On the other hand, perseverance on the huntsman's part will ensure a corresponding amount in the hound's; they will become so accustomed to the certain appearance of their master at the bay at some time or other, that they will stick to their game till night. I have frequently killed elk at two or three o'clock in the afternoon that have been found at six in the morning. Sometimes I have killed them even later than this, when, after wandering fruitlessly the whole day in every direction but the right one, my ears have at length been gladdened by the distant sound of the bay. The particular moment when hope and certainty combined, reward the day's toil, is the very quintessence of joy and delight. Nothing in the shape of enjoyment can come near it. What a strange power has that helpless looking mass—the brain! One moment, and the limbs are fagged, the shins are tender with breaking all the day through the densest jungles, the feet are worn with unrequited labour, and hark!! The bay! —no doubt of it—the bay! There is the magic spell which, acting on the brain, flies through every nerve. New legs, new feet, new everything, in a moment! fresh as though just out of bed; here we go tearing through the jungle like a buffalo, and as happy as though we had just come in for a fortune—happier a great deal.

Nevertheless, elk hunting is not a general taste, as people have not opportunities of enjoying it constantly. Accordingly, they are out of condition, and soon become distressed, and of necessity 'shut up' (a vulgar but expressive term). This must be fine fun for a total stranger rather inclined to corpulency, who has dauntlessly persevered in keeping up with the huntsman although at some personal inconvenience. There is a limit to all endurance, and he is obliged to stop; quite blown, completely done. He loses all sounds of hounds, and huntsman, and everything connected with the hunt. Where is he? How horrible the idea that flashes across his mind! he has no idea where he is, except that he is quite certain that he is in some jungle in Ceylon.

Distraction! Ceylon is nearly all jungle, 280 miles long, and he is in this—somewhere. He tries to recollect by what route he has come. Impossible! He has been up one mountain, and then he turned to the right, and got into a ravine; he recollects the ravine, for he fell on his head, with the end of a dead stick in his stomach just as he got to the bottom; he forgets every other part of his route, simply having an idea that he went down a great many ravines, and up a number of hills, and turned to the right and left several times. He gives it up; he finds himself 'lost,' and, if he is sensible, he will sit down and wait till someone comes to look for him, when he will start with joy at the glad sound of the horn. But should he attempt to find his way alone through those pathless jungles, he will only increase his distance from the right course.

One great advantage in Newera Ellia is the comparative freedom from poisonous vermin. There are three varieties of snakes, only one of which is hurtful, and all are very minute. The venomous species is the 'carrawellé,' whose bite is generally fatal; but this is not often met with. There are neither ticks, bugs, leeches, scorpions, white ants, wasps, nor mosquitoes; in fact, there is nothing venomous except the snake alluded to, and a small species of centipede. Fleas there are certainly; indeed, a fair sprinkling of fleas; but they are not troublesome, except in houses which are unoccupied during a portion of the year. There is a peculiarity of a Ceylon flea—he is a great colonist; and should a house be untenanted for a few months, so sure will it be occupied by these 'settlers.' Even a grass hut built for a night's bivouac in the jungle, without a flea in the neighbourhood, will literally swarm with them if deserted for a couple of months. Fleas have a great fancy for settling upon anything white; thus a person with white trowsers will be blackened with them, while a man in darker colours will be comparatively free. I at first supposed that they appeared in larger numbers on the white ground because they were more easily distinguished; but I tried the experiment of putting a sheet of writing-paper and a piece of brown talipot leaf in the midst of fleas, the paper was covered with them, while only two or three were on the talipot.

The bite of the small species of centipede alluded to is not very severe, being about equivalent to a wasp's sting. I have been bitten myself, and I have seen another person suffering from the bite, which was ludicrous enough.

The sufferer was Corporal Phinn, of H.M. 15th Regiment. At that time he was one of Lieutenant

De Montenach's servants, and had accompanied his master on a hunting trip to the Horton Plains.

Now Phinn was an Irishman; an excellent fellow, a dead hand at tramping a bog, and killing a snipe; but (without the slightest intention of impugning his veracity) Phinn's ideality was largely developed. He was never by himself for five minutes in the jungle, without having seen something wonderful before his return: this he was sure to relate in a rich brogue with great facetiousness.

However, we had just finished dinner one night, and Phinn had then taken his master's vacant place (there being only one room) to commence his own meal, when up he jumped like a madman spluttering the food out of his mouth, and shouting and skipping about the room with both hands clutched tightly to the hinder part of his inexpressibles. 'Och, by Jasus! help, sir, help! I've a reptile or some divil up my breeches! Och! bad luck to him, he's biting me! Och! Och! it's sure a sarpint that's stinging me! quick, sir, or he'll be the death o' me!'

Phinn was frantic, and upon lowering his inexpressibles we found the centipede about four inches long which had bitten him. A little brandy rubbed on the part soon relieved the pain.

CHAPTER VIII.

Observations on Nature in the Tropics—The Dung Beetle—The Mason Fly—Spiders—Luminous Insects—Efforts of a Naturalist—Dogs Worried by Leeches—Tropical Diseases—Malaria—Causes of Infection—Disappearance of the 'Mina'—Poisonous Water—Well-digging Elephants.

How little can the inhabitant of a cold or temperate climate appreciate the vast amount of 'life' in a tropical country! The combined action of light, heat, and moisture, calls into existence myriads of creeping things, the offspring of the decay of vegetation. 'Life' appears to emanate from 'death'—the destruction of one material seems to multiply the existence of another,—the whole surface of the earth seems busied in one vast system of giving birth.

An animal dies—a solitary beast—and before his unit life has vanished for one week, how many millions of living creatures owe their birth to his death? What countless swarms of insects have risen from that one carcass; creatures which never could have been brought into existence were it not for the presence of one dead body which has received and hatched the deposited eggs of millions that otherwise would have remained unvivified !

Not a tree falls, not a withered flower droops to the ground, not a fruit drops from the exhausted bough, but it is instantly attacked by the class of insect prepared by Nature for its destruction. The white ant scans a lofty tree whose iron-like timber and giant stem would seem to mock at his puny efforts; but it is rotten at the core, and not a leaf adorns its branches, and in less than a year it will have fallen to the earth a mere shell;—the whole of the wood will have been devoured.

Rottenness of all kinds is soon carried from the face of the land by the wise arrangements of Nature for preserving the world from plagues and diseases, which the decaying and unconsumed bodies of animals and vegetables would otherwise engender.

How beautiful are all the laws of Nature; how perfect in their details! Allow that the great duty of the insect tribe is to cleanse the earth and atmosphere from countless impurities noxious to the human race—how great a plague would our benefactors themselves become, were it not for the various classes of carnivorous insects which prey upon them, and are in their turn the prey of others! It is a grand principle of continual strife which keeps all and each down to their required level.

A feast for an observant mind is afforded in a tropical country. The variety and the multitude of living things are so great that a person of only ordinary observation cannot help acquiring a tolerable knowledge of the habits of some of the most interesting classes. In the common routine of daily life, they are continually in his view, and even should he have no taste for the study of Nature and her productions, still one prevailing characteristic of the insect tribe must impress itself upon his mind. It is the natural instinct not simply of procreating their species, but of laying by a *provision* for their expected offspring. What a lesson to mankind! what an example to the nurtured mind of man from one of the lowest classes of living things!

Here we see no rash matrimonial engagements; no penniless lovers, selfishly and indissolubly linked together to propagate large families of starving children. All the arrangements of the insect tribe, though prompted by sheer instinct, are conducted with a degree of rationality that in some cases raises the mere instinct of the creeping thing above the assumed 'reason' of man.

The bird builds her nest, and carefully provides for the comfort of her young long ere she lays her fragile egg. Even look at that vulgar-looking beetle, whose coarse form would banish the idea of any rational feeling existing in its brain—the Billingsgate fish-woman of its tribe, in coarseness and rudeness of exterior (*Scarabæus carnifex*)—see with what quickness she is running backwards, raised almost upon her head, while with her hind legs she trundles a large ball—herself no bigger than a nutmeg, the ball is four times the size. There she goes along the smooth road. The ball she has just manufactured from some fresh-dropped horsedung; it is as round as though turned by a lathe, and, although the dung has not lain an hour upon the ground, she and her confederates have portioned out the spoil, and each has started off with her separate ball. Not a particle of horsedung remains upon the road. Now she has rolled the ball away from the hard road, and upon the soft sandy border she has stopped to rest. No great amount of rest; she plunges her head into the ground, and with that shovel-like projection of stout horn, she mines her way below: she has disappeared even in these few seconds!

Presently the apparently deserted ball begins to move, as though acted upon by some subterranean force; gradually it sinks to the earth, and it vanishes altogether.

Some persons might imagine that the beetle feeds upon the ordure, and that she has buried her store as a dog hides a bone; but this is not the case: she has formed a receptacle for her eggs, which she deposits in the ball of dung, the warmth of which assists in bringing the larvæ into life, which then feed upon the manure.

It is wonderful to observe with what rapidity all kinds of dung are removed by these beetles. This is effected by the active process of rolling the loads instead of carrying, by which method a large mass is transported at once.

The mason fly is also a ball maker; but she carries her load, and builds an elaborate nest. This insect belongs to the order Hymenoptera, and is of the Ichneumon tribe, being a variety of upwards of four hundred species of that interesting fly.

The whole tribe of Ichneumon are celebrated for their courage; a small fly will not hesitate to attack the largest cockroach, who evinces the greatest terror at sight of his well-known enemy; but the greatest proof of valour in a fly is displayed in the war of the Ichneumon against the spider.

There is a great variety of this insect in Ceylon, from the large black species, the size of the hornet, down to the minute tinsel-green fly, no bigger than a gnat; but every one of these different species wages perpetual war against the arch-enemy of flies.

In very dry weather in some districts when most pools and water holes are dried up, a pail of water thrown upon the ground will as assuredly attract a host of mason flies as carrion will bring together 'blow flies.' They will be then seen in excessive activity upon the wet earth, forming balls of mud, by rolling the earth between their fore feet until they have manufactured each a pill. With this they fly away to build their nests, and immediately return for a further supply.

The arrangement of the nest is a matter of much consideration, as the shape depends entirely upon the locality in which it is built: it may be in the corner of a room, or in a hole in a wall, or in the hollow of a bamboo; but wherever it is, the principle is the same, although the shape of the nest may vary. Every thing is to be hermetically sealed.

The mason fly commences by flattening the first pill of clay upon the intended site (say the corner of a room); she then spreads it in a thin layer over a surface of about two inches, and retires for another ball of cement. This she dabs upon the plastic foundation, and continues the apparently rude operation until some twenty or thirty pills of clay are adhering at equal distances. She then forms these into a number of neat oval-shaped cells, about the size of a wren's egg; and in each cell she deposits one egg. She then flies off in search of spiders, which are to be laid up in stores within the cells as food for the young larvæ when hatched.

Now the transition from the larva to the fly takes place in the cell, and occupies about six weeks from the time the egg is first laid; thus, as the egg itself is not vivified for some weeks after it is deposited, the spiders have to be preserved in a sound and fresh state during that interval until the larva is in such an advanced stage as to require food.

In a tropical country every one knows that a very few hours occasion the putrefaction of all dead animal substances; nevertheless these spiders are to be kept fresh and good, like our tins of preserved meats, to be eaten when required.

One, two, or even three spiders, according to their size, the mason fly deposits in each cell, and then closes it hermetically with clay. The spiders she has pounced upon while sunning themselves in the centre of their delicate nets, and they are hurried off in a panic to be converted into preserved provisions. Each cell being closed, the whole nest is cemented over with a thick covering of clay. In due time the young family hatch, eat their allowance of spiders, undergo their torpid change, and emerge from their clay mansion complete mason flies.

Every variety of Ichneumon, however minute (in Ceylon), chooses the spider as the food for its young. It is not at all uncommon to find a gun well loaded with spiders, clay, and grubs, some mason fly having chosen the barrel for his location. A bunch of keys will invite a settlement of one of the smaller species, who will make its nest in the tube of a key, which it also fills with minute spiders.

In attacking the spider, the mason fly has a choice of his antagonist, and he takes good care to have a preponderance of weight on his own side. His reason for choosing this in preference to other insects for a preserved store may be, that the spider is naturally juicy, plump, and compact; combining advantages both for keeping and packing closely.

There are great varieties of spiders in Ceylon, one of which is of such enormous size as to resemble the *Aranea avicularia* of America. This species stands on an area of about three inches, and never spins a web, but wanders about and lives in holes; his length of limb, breadth of thorax and powerful jaws, give him a most formidable appearance. There is another species of a large-sized spider who spins a web of about two and a half feet in diameter. This is composed of a strong yellow silky fibre, and so powerful is the texture that a moderate-sized walking cane thrown into the web will be retained by it. This spider is about two inches long, the colour black, with a large yellow spot upon the back, and the body nearly free from hair.

Some years ago an experiment was made in France of substituting the thread of the spider for the silk of the silkworm; several pairs of stockings and various articles were manufactured with tolerable success in this new material; but the fibre was generally considered as too fragile.

A sample of such thread as is spun by the spider described could not have failed to produce the desired result, as its strength is so great that it can be wound upon a card without the slightest care required in the operation. The texture is far more silky than the fibre commonly produced by spiders, which has more generally the character of cotton than of silk.

Should this ever be experimented on, a question might arise of much interest to entomologists, whether a difference in the food of the spider would affect the quality of the thread, as is well known to be the case with the common silkworm.

A Ceylon night after a heavy shower of rain is a brilliant sight when the whole atmosphere is teeming with moving lights; bright as the stars themselves, waving around the tree tops in fiery circles, now threading like distant lamps through the intricate branches and lighting up the dark recesses of the foliage, then rushing like a shower of sparks around the glittering boughs. Myriads of bright fire flies in these wild dances meet their destiny, being entangled in opposing spiders' webs, where they hang like fairy lamps, their own light directing the path of the destroyer and assisting in their destruction.

There are many varieties of luminous insects in Ceylon. That which affords the greatest volume of light is a large white grub about two inches in length. This is a fat sluggish animal, whose light is far more brilliant than could be supposed to emanate from such a form.

The light of a common fire fly will enable a person to distinguish the hour on a dial in a dark night, but the glow from the grub described will render the smallest print so legible that a page may be read with ease. I once tried the experiment of killing the grub, but the light was not extinguished with life, and by opening the tail, I squeezed out a quantity of glutinous fluid, which was so highly phosphorescent, that it brilliantly illumined the page of a book which I had been reading by its light for a trial.

All phosphorescent substances require friction to produce their full volume of light; this is exemplified at sea during a calm tropical night, when the ocean sleeps in utter darkness and quietude, and not a ripple disturbs the broad surface of the waters. Then the prow of the advancing steamer cuts through the dreary waste of darkness, and awakens into fiery life the spray which dashes from her sides. A broad stream of light illumines the sea in her wake, and she appears to plough up fire in her rush through the darkened water.

The simple friction of the moving mass agitates the millions of luminous animalcules contained in the water; in the same manner a fish darting through the sea is distinctly seen by the fiery course which is created by his own velocity.

All luminous insects are provided with a certain amount of phosphorescent fluid, which can be set in action at pleasure by the agitation of a number of nerves and muscles situated in the region of the fluid, and especially adapted to that purpose. It is a common belief that the light of the glow-worm is used as a lamp of love, to assist in nocturnal meetings; but there can be little doubt that the insect makes use of its natural brilliancy without any specific intention. It is as natural for the fire fly to glitter by night, as for the coloured butterfly to be gaudy by day.

The variety of beautiful and interesting insects is so great in Ceylon, that an entomologist would consider it a temporary elysium; neither would he have much trouble in collecting a host of different species, who will exhibit themselves without the necessity of a laborious search. Thus, while he may be engaged in pinning out some rare specimen, a thousand minute 'eye flies' will be dancing so close to his eyeballs, that seeing is out of the question. These little creatures, which are no larger than pins' heads, are among the greatest plagues in some parts of the jungle; and what increases the annoyance, is the knowledge of the fact that they dance almost into your eyes out of sheer vanity. They are simply admiring their own reflection in the mirror of the eye; or, may be, some mistake their own reflected forms for other flies performing the part of a 'vis-à-vis' in their unwearying quadrille.

A cigar is a specific against these small plagues, and we will allow that the patient entomologist has just succeeded in putting them to flight, and has resumed the occupation of setting out his specimen. Ha! see him spring out of his chair as though electrified. Watch how, regardless of the laws of buttons, he frantically tears his trowsers from his limbs;—he has him!—no, he hasn't—yes, he has,—no—no, positively he cannot get him off. It is a tick, no bigger than a grain of sand, but his bite is like a red-hot needle boring into the skin. If all the royal family had been present, he could not have refrained from tearing off his trowsers.

The naturalist has been out the whole morning *collecting*, and a pretty collection he has got,—a perfect fortune upon his legs alone. There are about one hundred ticks who have not yet commenced to feed upon him; there are also several fine specimens of the large flat buffalo tick; three or four leeches are enjoying themselves on the juices of the naturalist; these he had not felt, although they had bitten him half an hour before; a fine black ant has also escaped during the recent confusion, fortunately without using his sting.

Oil is the only means of loosening the hold of a tick; this suffocates him, and he dies; but he leaves an amount of inflammation in the wound which is perfectly surprising in so minute an insect. The bite of the smallest species is far more severe than that of the large buffalo or the deer tick, both of which are varieties.

Although the leeches in Ceylon are excessively annoying, and numerous among the dead leaves of the jungle and the high grass, they are easily guarded against by means of leech gaiters: these are wide stockings, made of drill or some other light and close material, which are drawn over the foot and trowsers up to the knee, under which they are securely tied. There are three varieties of the leech: the small jungle leech, the common leech, and the stone leech. The latter will frequently creep up the nostrils of a dog while he is drinking in a stream, and, unlike the other species, it does not drop off when satiated, but continues to live in the dog's nostril. I have known a leech of this kind to have lived more than two months in the nose of one of my hounds; he was so high up, that I could only see his tail occasionally when he relaxed to his full length, and injections of salt and water had no effect upon him. Thus I could not relieve the dog till one day when the leech descended, and I observed the tail working in and out of the nostril; I then extracted him in the usual way with the finger and thumb and the tail of the coat.

I should be trespassing too much upon the province of the naturalist, and attempting more than I could accomplish, were I to enter into the details of the entomology of Ceylon ; I have simply mentioned a few of those insects most common to the every-day observer, and I leave the description of the endless varieties of classes to those who make entomology a study.

It may no doubt appear very enticing to the lovers of such things, to hear of the gorgeous colours and prodigious size of butterflies, moths, and beetles ; the varieties of reptiles, the flying foxes, the gigantic crocodiles ; the countless species of waterfowl, &c. ; but one very serious fact is apt to escape the observation of the general reader, that, wherever insect and reptile life is most abundant, so sure is that locality full of malaria and disease.

Ceylon does not condescend to second-class diseases : there is no such thing as influenza ; hooping-cough, measles, scarlatina, &c., are rarely, if ever, heard of ; we ring the changes upon four first-class ailments—four scourges, which alternately ascend the throne of pestilence and annually reduce the circle of our friends—cholera, dysentery, small-pox, and fever. This year (1854) there has been some dispute as to the routine of succession ; they have accordingly all raged at one time.

The cause of infection in disease has long been a

subject of controversy among medical men; but there can be little doubt that, whatever is the origin of the disease, the same is the element of infection. The question is, therefore, reduced to the prime cause of the disease itself.

A theory that animalcules are the cause of the various contagious and infectious disorders has created much discussion; and although this opinion is not generally entertained by the faculty, the idea is so feasible, and so many rational arguments can be brought forward in its support, that I cannot help touching upon a topic so generally interesting.

In the first place, nearly all infectious diseases predominate in localities which are hot, damp, swampy, abounding in stagnant pools, and excluded from a free circulation of air. In a tropical country, a residence in such a situation would be certain death to a human being, but the same locality will be found to swarm with insects and reptiles of all classes.

Thus, what is inimical to human life is propitious to the insect tribe. This is the first step in favour of the argument. Therefore, whatever shall tend to the increase of insect life must in an inverse ratio war with human existence.

When we examine a drop of impure water, and discover by the microscope the thousands of living beings which not only are invisible to the naked eye, but some of whom are barely discoverable even by the strongest magnifying power, it certainly leads to the inference, that if one drop of impure fluid contains countless atoms endowed with vitality the same amount of impure air may be equally tenanted with its myriads of invisible inhabitants.

It is well known that, different mixtures, which are at first pure, and apparently free from all insect life will, in the course of their fermentation and subsequent impurity, generate peculiar species of animalcules. Thus all water, and vegetable or animal matter, in a state of stagnation and decay, gives birth to insect life; likewise all substances of every denomination which are subjected to putrid fermentation. Unclean sewers, filthy hovels, unswept streets, unwashed clothes, are therefore breeders of animalcules, many of which are perfectly visible without microscopic aid.

Now, if some are discernible by the naked eye, and others are detected in such varying sizes, that some can only just be distinguished by the most powerful lens, is it not rational to conclude, that the *smallest* discernible to human intelligence is but the medium of a countless race? that millions of others still exist, which are too minute for any observation?

Observe the particular quarters of a city which suffer most severely during the prevalence of an epidemic. In all dirty narrow streets, where the inhabitants are naturally of a low and uncleanly class, the cases will be tenfold. Thus, filth is admitted to have at least the power of attracting disease, and we know that it not only attracts, but generates animalcules; therefore filth, insects, and disease are ever to be seen closely linked together.

Now the common preventives against infection are such as are peculiarly inimical to every kind of insect: camphor, chloride of lime, tobacco-smoke, and powerful scents and smokes of any kind. The first impulse on the appearance of an infectious disease is to purify every thing as much as possible, and, by extra cleanliness and fumigations, to endeavour to arrest its progress. The great purifier of Nature is a violent wind, which usually terminates an epidemic immediately; this would naturally carry before it all insect life with which the atmosphere might be impregnated, and the disease disappears at the same moment. It will be well remembered, that the plague of locusts inflicted upon Pharaoh was relieved in the same manner:—

'And the Lord turned a mighty strong west wind, which took away the locusts, and cast them into the Red Sea; there remained not one locust in all the coasts of Egypt.'

Every person is aware that unwholesome air is quite as poisonous to the human system as impure water; and seeing that the noxious qualities of the latter are caused by animalcules, and that the methods used for purifying infected air are those most generally destructive to insect life, it is not irrational to conclude, that the poisonous qualities of bad water and bad air arise from the same cause.

Man is being constantly preyed upon by insects; and were it not for ordinary cleanliness, he would become a mass of vermin; even this does not protect him from the rapacity of ticks, mosquitoes, fleas, and many others. Intestinal worms feed on him within, and, unseen, use their slow efforts for his destruction.

The knowledge of so many classes which actually prey upon the human system naturally leads to the belief that many others endowed with the same propensities exist, of which we have at present no conception. Thus, different infectious disorders might proceed from peculiar species of animalcules, which at given periods are wafted into certain countries, carrying pestilence and death in their invisible course.

A curious phenomenon has recently occurred at Mauritius, where that terrific scourge, the cholera, has been raging with desolating effect.

There is a bird in that island called the 'Martin,' but it is more properly the 'Mina.' This bird is about the size of the starling, whose habits it possesses in a great degree. It exists in immense numbers, and is a grand destroyer of all insects. On this account it is seldom or never shot at, especially as it is a great comforter to all cattle, whose hides it entirely cleans from ticks and other vermin, remaining for many hours perched upon the back of one animal, while its bill is actively employed in searching out and destroying every insect.

During the prevalence of the cholera at Mauritius, these birds disappeared. Such a circumstance had never before occurred, and the real cause of their departure is still a mystery.

May it not have been, that some species of insect upon which they fed had likewise migrated, and that certain noxious animalcules, which had been kept down by this class, had thus multiplied within the atmosphere, until their numbers caused disease? All suppositions on such a subject must, however, remain in obscurity, as no proof can be adduced of their correctness. The time may arrive when science may successfully grapple with all human ailments; but hitherto that king of pestilence, the 'cholera,' has reduced the highest medical skill to miserable uncertainty.[1]

[1] The germ theory of Professor Tyndall is generally accepted; every disease may be propagated by its germ. There are also many

Upon reconsidering the dangers of fevers, dysentery, &c., in the swampy and confined districts described, the naturalist may become somewhat less ardent in following his favourite pursuit. Of one fact I can assure him, that, no matter how great the natural strength of his constitution, the repeated exposure to the intense heat of the sun, the unhealthy districts that he will visit, the nights redolent of malaria, and the horrible water that he must occasionally drink, will gradually undermine the power of the strongest man. Both sportsman and naturalist in this must share alike.

No one who has not actually suffered from the effect, can appreciate the misery of bad water in a tropical country, or the blessings of a cool pure draught. I have been in districts of Ceylon where, for sixteen or twenty miles, not a drop of water is to be obtained fit for an animal to drink; nor a tree to throw a few yards of shade upon the parching ground; nothing but stunted thorny jungles and sandy barren plains far as the eye can reach; the yellow leaves crisp upon the withered branches, the wild fruits hardened for want of sap; all moisture robbed from vegetation by the pitiless drought of several months.

A day's work in such a country is hard indeed,

complaints that are the result of noxious insects—*vide Trichinæ spiralis*, Guinea-worm, &c.

—carrying a heavy rifle for some five and twenty miles, sometimes in deep sand, sometimes on good ground, but always exposed to the intensity of that blaze, added to the reflection from the sandy soil, and the total want of fresh air and water. All Nature seems stagnated; a distant pool is seen, and a general rush takes place towards the cheering sight. The water is thicker than pease soup, a green scum floats upon it, and the temperature is upwards of 130° Fahr. All kinds of insects are swarming in the putrid fluid, and a saltish bitter adds to its nauseating flavour. I have seen the exhausted coolies spread their dirty cloths upon the surface, and form them into filters by sucking the water through them. Oh, for a glass of Newera Ellia water, the purest and best that ever flows, as it sparkles out of the rocks on the mountain tops! what pleasure so perfect as a long, deep, and undisturbed draught of such cold clear nectar, when the throat is parched with unquenchable thirst!

In some parts of Ceylon, especially in the neighbourhood of the coast, where the land is flat and sandy, the water is always brackish, even during the rainy season, and in the dry months it is undrinkable.

The natives then make use of a berry for cleansing it, and precipitating the impurities. I know the shrub well; but it has no English denomination. The berries are about the size of a very large pea, and grow in clusters of from ten to fifteen together, and one is said to be sufficient to cleanse a gallon of water. The method of using them is curious, although simple. The vessel which is intended to contain the water, which is generally an earthen chatty, is well rubbed in the inside with a berry, until the latter, which is of a horny consistency, like vegetable ivory, is completely worn away. The chatty is then filled with the muddy water, and allowed to stand for about an hour or more, until all the impurities have precipitated to the bottom, and the water remains clear.

I have constantly used this ; but I certainly cannot say that the water has ever been rendered perfectly clear ; it has been vastly improved, and what was totally undrinkable before, has been rendered fit for use ; but it has at the best been only comparatively good ; and although the berry has produced a decided effect, the native accounts of its properties are greatly exaggerated.[1]

During the prolonged droughts, many rivers of considerable magnitude are completely exhausted, and nothing remains but a dry bed of sand between

[1] There are many fruits that will produce this effect, especially those which are rich in tannin. The albuminous impurities of the water coagulate, and are precipitated to the bottom. A dozen common almonds, if pounded in a paste and mixed with a glass of water, stirred with the muddy fluid, will in a few hours cleanse and render it wholesome.

lofty banks. At these seasons, the elephants, being hard pressed for water, make use of their wonderful instinct by digging holes in the dry sand of the river's bed ; this they perform with the horny toes of their fore feet, and frequently work to a depth of three feet before they discover the liquid treasure beneath. This process of well-digging almost oversteps the boundaries of instinct, and strongly savours of reason, the two powers being so nearly connected, that it is difficult in some cases to define the distinction. There are so many interesting cases of the wonderful display of both these attributes in animals, that I shall notice some features of this subject in a separate chapter.

CHAPTER IX.

Instinct and Reason—Tailor Birds and Grosbeaks—The White Ant—Black Ants at War—Wanderoo Monkeys—Habits of Elephants—Elephants in the Lake—Herd of Elephants Bathing—Elephant Shooting—The Rencontre—The Charge—Caught by the Tail—Horse Gored by a Buffalo—Sagacity of Dogs—'Bluebeard'—His Hunt—A True Hound.

THERE can be no doubt that man is not the only animal endowed with reasoning powers: he possesses that faculty to an immense extent, but although the amount of the same power possessed by animals may be infinitely small, nevertheless it is *their share* of reason, which they occasionally use apart from mere instinct.

Although instinct and reason appear to be closely allied, they are easily separated and defined.

Instinct is the faculty with which Nature has endowed all animals for the preservation and continuation of their own species. This is accordingly exhibited in various features, as circumstances may call forth the operation of the power; but so wonderful are the attributes of Nature, that the details of her arrangements throughout the animal and insect creation give to every class an amount of sense, which in many instances surmounts the narrow bounds of simple instinct.

The great characteristic of sheer instinct is its want of progression; it never increases, or improves. It is possessed now in the nineteenth century by every race of living creatures in no larger proportion than was bestowed upon them at the Creation.

In general, knowledge increases like a rolling snowball; a certain amount forms a base for extra improvement, and upon successive foundations of increasing altitude, the eminence has been attained of the present era. This is the effect of 'reason;' but 'instinct,' although beautiful in its original construction, remains, like the blossom of a tree, ever the same; a limited effect produced by a given cause; an unchangeable law of Nature that certain living beings shall perform certain functions which require a certain amount of intelligence; this amount is supplied by Nature for the performance of the duties required —this is instinct.

Thus, according to the requirements necessitated by the habits of certain living creatures, to an equivalent amount is their share of instinct.

Reason differs from instinct, as combining the effects of thought and reflection; this being a proof of *consideration*; while instinct is simply a direct emanation from the brain, confined to an *impulse*.

In our observations of Nature, especially in tropical countries, we see numberless exemplifications of these powers, in some of which the efforts of common instinct halt upon the extreme boundary, and have almost a tinge of reason.

What can be more curious than the nest of the 'tailor bird?'—a selection of tough leaves neatly sewn one over the other to form a waterproof exterior to the comfortable little dwelling within. Where does the needle and thread come from? The first is the delicate bill of the bird itself, and the latter is the strong fibre of the bark of a tree, with which the bird sews every leaf, lapping one over the other, in the same manner that slates are laid upon a roof.[1]

Nevertheless this is simple instinct; the tailor bird in the days of Adam constructed her nest in a similar manner, which will be continued without improvement till the end of time.

The grosbeak almost rivals the tailor bird in the beautiful formation of its nest. These birds build in company, twenty or thirty nests being common upon one tree.[2] Their apparent intention in the peculiar construction of their nests is to avoid the attacks of snakes and lizards. These nests are about two feet long, composed of beautifully woven grass, shaped

[1] This bird never makes a mistake in overlapping, so as to admit the rain.

[2] Sometimes there are hundreds upon the same tree.

like an elongated pear. They are attached like fruit to the extreme end of a stalk or branch, from which they wave to and fro in the wind, as though hung out to dry. The bird enters a funnel-like aperture in the bottom, and by this arrangement the young are effectually protected from reptiles.

All nests, whether of birds or insects, are particularly interesting, as they explain the domestic habits of the occupants; but, however wonderful the arrangement and the beauty of the work, as exhibited among birds, bees, wasps, &c., still it is the simple effect of instinct, on the principle that they never vary.

The white ant—that grand destroyer of all timber—always works under cover; he builds as he progresses in his work of destruction, and runs a long gallery of fine clay in the direction of his operations; beneath this, his devastation proceeds until he has penetrated to the interior of the beam, the centre of which he entirely demolishes, leaving a thin shell in the form of the original log, encrusted over the exterior with numerous galleries.

There is less interest in the habits of these destructive wretches than in all other of the ant tribe; they build stupendous nests it is true, but their interior economy is less active and thrifty than that of many other species of ants, among which there is a greater appearance of the display of reasoning powers than in most animals of a superior class.

On a fine sunny morning it is not uncommon to see ants busily engaged in bringing out all the eggs from the nest, and laying them in the sun until they become thoroughly warmed; after which, they carry them all back again, and lay them in their respective places. This looks very like a power of reasoning, as it is decidedly beyond instinct. If they were to carry out the eggs every morning, wet or dry, it would be an effort of instinct to the detriment of the eggs; but as the weather is uncertain, it is an effort of reason on the part of the ants to bring out the eggs to the sun, especially as it is not an every-day occurrence, even in fine weather.

In Mauritius the negroes have a custom of turning the reasoning powers of the large black ant to advantage.

White ants are frequently seen passing in and out of a small hole, from underneath a building, in which case their ravages could only be prevented by taking up the flooring and destroying the nest.

The negroes avoid this by their knowledge of the habits of the black ant, who is a sworn enemy to the white.

They accordingly pour a little treacle on the ground within a yard of the hole occupied by the white ants. The smell of the treacle shortly attracts some of the black species, who on their arrival are not long in observing their old enemies passing in and out of the hole. Some of them leave the treacle; these are evidently messengers, as in the course of the day a whole army of black ants will be seen advancing in a narrow line of many yards in length, to storm the stronghold of the white ants. They enter the hole, and they destroy every white ant in the building. Resistance there can be none, as the plethoric slow-going white ant is as a mouse to a cat in the encounter with his active enemy, added to which the black ant is furnished with a most venomous sting, in addition to a powerful pair of mandibles. I have seen the black ants returning from their work of destruction, each carrying a slaughtered white ant in his mouth, which he devours at leisure. This is again a decided effort of reason, as the black ant arrives at the treacle without a thought of the white ant in his mind, but, upon seeing his antagonist, he despatches messengers for reinforcements, who eventually bring up the army to the 'rendezvous.'

Numerous instances might be cited of the presence of reasoning powers among the insect classes; but this faculty becomes of increased interest when seen in the larger animals.

The power of education is both a proof and a promoter of reason in all animals. This removes them from their natural or instinctive position, and brings forth the full development of the mental powers. This is exhibited in the performances of well-trained dogs, especially among pointers and setters. Again, in the feats performed by educated animals in the circus, where the elephant has lately endeavoured to prove a want of common sense, by standing on his head.[1] Nevertheless, however absurd the tricks which man may teach the animal to perform, the very fact of their performance substantiates an amount of reason in the animal.

Monkeys, elephants, and dogs are naturally endowed with a larger share of the reasoning power than other animals, which is frequently increased to a wonderful extent by education. The former, even in their wild state, are so little inferior to some natives, either in their habits or appearance, that I should feel some reluctance in denying them an almost equal share of reason. The want of speech certainly places them below the Veddahs, but the monkeys on the other hand might assert a superiority by a show of tails.

Monkeys vary in intelligence according to their species, and may be taught to do almost anything. There are several varieties in Ceylon, among which the great black wanderoo, with white whiskers, is the nearest in appearance to the human race. This monkey stands upwards of three feet high, and weighs about eighty pounds. He possesses immense

[1] A tame elephant had recently been exhibiting in this fashion.

muscular power, and he has also a great peculiarity in the formation of the skull, which is closely allied to that of a human being; the lower jaw and the upper being in a straight line with the forehead. In monkeys the jaws usually project. This species exists in most parts of Ceylon, but I have seen it of a larger size at Newera Ellia than in any of the low country districts.

Elephants are proverbially sagacious, both in their wild state and when domesticated. I have previously described the building of a dam by a tame elephant, which was an exhibition of reason hardly to be expected in any animal. They are likewise wonderfully clever in a wild state in preserving themselves from accidents, to which, from their bulk and immense weight, they would be particularly liable, such as the crumbling of the verge of a precipice, the insecurity of a bridge, or the suffocating depth of mud in a lake.

It is the popular opinion, and I have seen it expressed in many works, that the elephant shuns rough and rocky ground, over which he moves with difficulty, and that he delights in level plains, &c. &c. This may be the case in Africa, where his favourite food, the mimosa, grows upon the plain; but in Ceylon it is directly the contrary. In this country the elephant delights in the most rugged localities; he rambles about rocky hills and mountains with a nimbleness that no one can understand without personal experience. So partial are elephants to rocky and uneven ground, that should the ruins of a mountain exist in rugged fragments among a plain of low thorny jungle, five chances to one would be in favour of tracking the herd to this very spot, where they would most likely be found, standing among the alleys formed by the fragments heaped around them. It is surprising to witness the dexterity of elephants in traversing ground over which a man can pass with difficulty. I have seen places on the mountains in the neighbourhood of Newera Ellia bearing the unmistakable marks of elephants where I could not have conceived it possible for such an animal to stand. On the precipitous sides of jungle-covered mountains, where the ground is so steep that a man is forced to cling to the underwood for support, the elephants still plough their irresistible course. In descending or ascending these places, the elephant *always describes a zigzag*, and thus lessens the abruptness of the inclination. Their immense weight acting on their broad feet, bordered by sharp horny toes, cuts away the side of the hill at every stride, and forms a level step; thus they are enabled to skirt the sides of precipitous hills and banks with comparative ease. The trunk is the wonderful monitor of all danger to an elephant, from whatever cause it may proceed. This may arise from the approach of man, or from the character of the country: in either case the trunk exerts its power; in one by the acute sense of smell, in the other by the combination of the sense of scent and touch. In dense jungles, where the elephant cannot see a yard before him, the sensitive trunk feels the hidden way, and when the roaring of waterfalls admonishes him of the presence of ravines and precipices, the never-failing trunk lowered upon the ground keeps him advised of every inch of his path.

Nothing is more difficult than to induce a tame elephant to cross a bridge which his sagacity assures him is insecure; he will sound it with his trunk, and press upon it with one foot, but he will not trust his weight if he can perceive the slightest vibration.

Their power of determining whether bogs or the mud at the bottom of tanks are deep or shallow is beyond my comprehension. Although I have seen elephants in nearly every position, I have never seen one inextricably fixed in a swamp. This is the more extraordinary as their habits induce them to frequent the most extensive morasses, deep lakes, muddy tanks, and estuaries, and yet I have never seen even a young one get into a scrape by being overwhelmed. There appears to be a natural instinct which warns them in their choice of ground, the same as that which influences the buffalo, and in like manner guides him through his swampy haunts.

It is a grand sight to see a large herd of elephants

feeding in a fine lake in broad daylight. This is seldom witnessed in these days, as the number of guns have so disturbed the elephants in Ceylon that they rarely come out to drink until late in the evening or during the night; but some time ago I had a fine view of a grand herd in a lake in the middle of the day.

I was out shooting with a great friend of mine, who is a brother in arms against the game of Ceylon, and than whom a better sportsman does not breathe, and we had arrived at a wild and miserable place while *en route* home after a jungle trip. Neither of us was feeling well; we had been for some weeks in the most unhealthy part of the country, and I was just recovering from a touch of dysentery: altogether we were looking forward with pleasure to our return to comfortable quarters, and for the time we were tired of jungle life. However, we arrived at a little village about sixty miles south of Batticaloa, called 'Gollagangwellɘ́wevé' (pronunciation requires practice), and a very long name it was for so small a place; but the natives insisted that a great number of elephants were in the neighbourhood.

They also declared that the elephants infested the neighbouring tank even during the forenoon, and that they nightly destroyed their embankments, and would not be driven away, as there was not a single gun possessed by the village with which to scare them. This looked all right; so we loaded the guns and started without loss of time, as it was then 1 P.M., and the natives described the tank as a mile distant. Being perfectly conversant with the vague idea of space described by a Cingalese mile, we mounted our horses, and, accompanied by about five and twenty villagers, twenty of whom I wished at Jericho, we started. By the by, I have quite forgotten to describe who '*we*' are,—F. H. Palliser, Esq., and myself.

Whether or not it was because I did not feel in brisk health, I do not know, but somehow or other, I had a presentiment that the natives had misled us, and that we should not find the elephants in the tank, but that, as usual, we should be led up to some dense thorny jungle, and told that the elephants were somewhere in that direction. Not being very sanguine, I had accordingly taken no trouble about my gun-bearers, and I saw several of my rifles in the hands of the villagers, and only one of my regular gun-bearers had followed me; the rest, having already had a morning's march, were glad of an excuse to remain behind.

Our route lay for about a quarter of a mile through deserted paddy land and low jungle, after which we entered fine open jungle. Unfortunately, the recent heavy rains had filled the tank, which had overflowed the broken dam and partially flooded the forest. This was in all parts within 200 yards from the dam a couple of feet deep in water, with a proportionate amount of sticky mud beneath, and through this we splashed until the dam appeared about fifty yards on our right. It was a simple earthen mound, which rose about ten feet from the level of the forest, and was studded with immense trees, apparently the growth of ages. We knew that the tank lay on the opposite side; but we continued our course parallel with the dam until we had ridden about a mile from the village, the natives for a wonder having truly described the distance.

Here our guide, having motioned us to stop, ran quickly up the dam to take a look out on the opposite side. He almost immediately beckoned us to come up. This we did without loss of time, and knowing that the game was in view, I ordered the horses to retire for about a quarter of a mile.

On our arrival on the dam there was a fine sight. The lake was about five miles round, and was quite full of water, the surface of which was covered with a scanty, but tall, rushy, grass. In the lake, browsing upon the grass, we counted twenty-three elephants, and there were many little ones, no doubt, that we could not distinguish in such rank vegetation. Five large elephants were not more than 120 paces distant; the remaining eighteen were in a long line, about a quarter of a mile from the shore, feeding in deep water.

We were well concealed by the various trees which grew upon the dam, and we passed half an hour in watching the manœuvres of the great beasts as they bathed and sported in the cool water. However, this was not elephant shooting, and the question was, how to get at them. The natives had no idea of the sport, as they seemed to think it very odd that we did not fire at those within a hundred paces distance. I now regretted my absent gun-bearers, as I plainly saw that these village people would be worse than useless.

We determined to take a stroll along the base of the dam to reconnoitre the ground, as at present it seemed impossible to make an attack, and even were the elephants within the forest there appeared to be no possibility of following them up through such deep water and heavy ground with any chance of success. However, they were not in the forest, being safe, belly and shoulder deep in the tank.

We strolled through mud and water thigh deep for a few hundred paces, when we suddenly came upon the spot, where in ages past the old dam had been carried away. Here the natives had formed a mud embankment strengthened by sticks and wattels. Poor fellows! we were not surprised at their wishing the elephants destroyed; the repair of their fragile dam was now a daily occupation, for the elephants, as though out of pure mischief, had chosen this spot as their thoroughfare to and from the lake, and the dam was trodden down in all directions.

We found that the margin of the forest was everywhere flooded to a width of about 200 yards, after which it was tolerably dry. We therefore returned to our former post.

It struck me that the only way to secure a shot at the herd would be to employ a ruse, which I had once practised successfully some years ago. Accordingly we sent the greater part of the villagers for about half a mile along the edge of the lake, with orders to shout and make a grand hullaballoo on arriving at their station. It seemed most probable that upon being disturbed, the elephants would retreat to the forest by their usual thoroughfare; we accordingly stood on the alert, ready for a rush to any given point which the herd should attempt in their retreat.

Some time passed in expectation, when a sudden yell broke from the far point, as though twenty demons had cramp in the stomach. Gallant fellows are the Cingalese at making a noise, and a grand effect this had upon the elephants; up went tails and trunks, the whole herd closed together, and made a simultaneous rush for their old thoroughfare. Away we skipped through the water straight in shore through the forest, until we reached the dry ground, when, turning sharp to our right, we soon halted exactly opposite the point at which we knew the elephants would enter the forest. This was grand excitement; we had a great start of the herd, so that we had plenty of time to arrange gun-bearers, and take our positions for the *rencontre.*

In the mean time the roar of water caused by the rapid passage of so many large animals approached nearer and nearer. Palliser and I had taken splendid positions so as to command either side of the herd on their arrival, with our gun-bearers squatted around us behind our respective trees, while the non-sporting village followers, who now began to think the matter rather serious, and totally devoid of fun, scrambled up various large trees with ape-like activity.

A few minutes of glorious suspense, and the grand crash and roar of broken water approached close at hand; we distinguished the mighty phalanx headed by the largest elephants bearing down exactly upon us, and not a hundred yards distant. Here was luck! There was a grim and very murderous smile of satisfaction on either countenance as we quietly cocked the rifles and awaited the onset: it was our intention to let half the herd pass us before we opened upon them, as we should then be in the very centre of the mass, and be able to get good and rapid shooting.

On came the herd in gallant style, throwing the spray from the muddy water, and keeping a direct line for our concealed position. They were within twenty yards, and we were still undiscovered, when those rascally villagers, who had already taken to the trees, scrambled still higher in their fright at the close approach of the elephants, and by this movement they gave immediate alarm to the leaders of the herd.

Round went the colossal heads ; right about, was the word, and away dashed the whole herd back towards the tank. In the same instant we made a rush in among them, and I floored one of the big leaders by a shot behind the ear, and immediately after, as bad luck would have it, Palliser and I both took the same bird, and down went another to the joint shots. Palliser then got another shot and bagged one more, when the herd pushed straight out to the deep lake, with the exception of a few elephants, who turned to the right ; after which, Palliser hurried through the mud and water, while I put on all steam in chase of the main body of the herd. It is astonishing to what an amount a man can get up this said steam in such a pitch of excitement. However, it was of no use in this case, as I was soon hip deep in water, and there was an end to all pursuit in that direction.

It immediately struck me that the elephants would again retreat to some other part of the forest after having made a circuit in the tank ; I accordingly waded back at my best speed to *terra firma*, and then, striking off to my right, I ran along parallel to the water for about half a mile, fully expecting to meet the herd once more on their entrance to the jungle. It was now that I deplored the absence of my regular gun-bearers; the village people had no taste for this gigantic scale of amusement, and the men who carried my guns would not keep up; fortunately, Carrasi, the best gun-bearer, was there, and he had taken another loaded rifle, after handing me that which he had carried at the onset. I waited a few moments for the lagging men, and succeeded in getting them well together, just as I heard the rush of water, as the elephants were again entering the jungle, not far in advance of the spot upon which I stood.

This time they were sharp on the *qui vive*, and the bulls, being well to the front, were keeping a bright look-out. It was in vain that I endeavoured to conceal myself until the herd had got well into the forest; the gun-bearers behind me did not take the same precaution, and the leading elephants both saw and winded us, when at a hundred paces distant. This time, however, they were determined to push on for a piece of thicker jungle, which they knew lay in this direction, and upon seeing me running towards them, they did not turn back to the lake, but slightly altered their course in an oblique direction, still continuing to push on through the forest, while I was approaching at right angles with the herd.

Hallooing and screaming at them with all my might, to tease some of the old bulls into a charge, I ran at top speed through the fine open forest, and soon got among a whole crowd of half-grown elephants, at which I would not fire ; there were a lot of fine beasts pushing along in the front, and towards these I ran as hard as I could go. Unfortunately, the herd seeing me so near, and gaining upon them, took to the ruse of a beaten fleet and scattered in all directions ; but I kept a few big fellows in view, who were still pretty well together, and managed to overtake the rearmost and knock him over. Up went the tail and trunk of one of the leading bulls at the report of the shot, and trumpeting shrilly, he ran first to one side then to the other, with his ears cocked, and sharply turning his head. I knew this fellow had his monkey up, and that a little teasing would bring him round for a charge. I therefore redoubled my shouts and yells, and kept on in full chase, as the elephants were straining every nerve to reach a piece of thick jungle, within a couple of hundred paces.

I could not go any faster, and I saw that the herd, which was thirty or forty yards ahead of me, would gain the jungle before I could overtake them, as they were going at a slapping pace, and I was tolerably blown with a long run at full speed, part of which had been through deep mud and water. But I still

ATTACK ON THE HERD

teased the bull, who was now in such an excited state, that I felt convinced he would turn to charge.

The leading elephants rushed into the thick jungle closely followed by the others, and, to my astonishment, my excited friend, who had lagged to the rear, followed their example. But it was only for a few seconds, for, on entering the thick bushes, he wheeled sharp round and came rushing out in full charge. This was very plucky, but very foolish, as his retreat was secured when in the thick jungle, and yet he courted further battle. This he soon had enough of, as I bagged him in his onset with my remaining barrel by the forehead shot.

I now heard a tremendous roaring of elephants behind me, as though another section was coming in from the tank; this I hoped to meet. I therefore reloaded the empty rifles as quickly as possible, and ran towards the spot. The roaring still continued, and was apparently almost stationary, and what was my disappointment on arrival, to find, in place of the expected herd, a young elephant of about four feet high, who had missed the main body in the retreat, and was now roaring for his departed friends. These young things are excessively foolhardy and wilful, and he charged me the moment I arrived. As I laid the rifle upon the ground, instead of firing at him, the rascally gun-bearers, with the exception of Carrasi, threw down the rifles and ran up the trees like so many monkeys, just as I had jumped on one side and caught the young elephant by the tail. He was far too strong for me to hold, and, although I dug my heels into the ground and held on with all my might, he fairly ran away with me through the forest. Carrasi now came to my assistance, and likewise held on by his tail; but away we went like the tender to a steam-engine; wherever the elephant went, there we were dragged in company. Another man now came to the rescue; but his assistance was not of the slightest use, as the animal was so powerful and of such weight that he could have run away with half a dozen of us unless his legs were tied. Unfortunately, we had no rope, or I could have secured him immediately, and seeing that we had no power over him whatever, I was obliged to run back for one of the guns to shoot him. On my return, it was laughable to see the pace at which he was running away with the two men who were holding on to his tail like grim death, the elephant not having ceased roaring during the run. I accordingly settled him, and returned to have a little conversation with the rascals who were still perched in the trees. I was extremely annoyed, as these people, if they had possessed a grain of sense, might have tied their long comboys (cotton cloths about eight feet long) together, and we might have thus secured the elephant without difficulty, by tying his hind legs.

It was a great loss, as he was so large that he might have been domesticated and driven to Newera Ellia without the slightest trouble. All this was occasioned by the cowardice of these villanous Cingalese, and upon my lecturing one fellow on his conduct, he began to laugh. This was too much for any person's patience, and I began to look for a stick, which the fellow perceiving, he immediately started off through the forest like a deer. He could run faster than I could, being naked, and having the advantage of bare feet; but I knew I could run him down in the course of time, especially as, being in a fright, he would soon get blown. We had a most animated hunt through water, mud, roots of trees, open forest, and all kinds of ground; but I ran into him at last in heavy ground, and I dare say he recollects the day of the month.

In the mean time, Palliser had heard the roaring of the elephant, followed by the screaming of the coolies, and succeeded by a shot. Shortly after, he heard the prolonged yells of the hunted villager, while he was hastening towards my direction. This combination of sounds naturally led him to expect that some accident had occurred, especially as the cries indicated that somebody had come to grief. This caused him a very laborious run, and he arrived thoroughly blown, and with a natural desire to kick the recreant villager who had caused the uproar.

If the ground had been even tolerably dry, we should have killed a large number of elephants out of this herd; but, as it happened, in such deep mud and water, the elephants had it all their own way, and our joint bag could not produce more than seven tails; however, this was far more than I had expected when I first saw the herd in such a secure position.

On our return to the village, we found Palliser's horse terribly gored by a buffalo, and we were obliged to leave him behind for some weeks; fortunately there was an extra pony, which served him as a mount home, a distance of 150 miles.

* * * * * *

This has been a sad digression from our argument upon instinct and reason, a most unreasonable departure from the subject; but this is my great misfortune: so sure as I bring forward the name of an elephant, the pen lays hold of some old story, and runs madly away in a day's shooting. I now have to speak of the reasoning powers of the canine race, and I confess my weakness. I feel perfectly certain that the pen will serve me the same trick, and that it will be plunging through a day's hunting to prove the existence of reason in a hound, and the want of it in the writer. Thrash me, good critics, I deserve it; lay it on with an unsparing thong. I am humiliated, but still wilful; I know my fault, but still continue it.

Let us think;—what was the subject? Reason in dogs, to be sure. Well, every one who has a dog must admit that he has a strong share of reason: only observe him as he sits by your side and wistfully watches the endless transit of piece after piece, bit after bit, as the fork is conveying delicate morsels to your mouth. There is neither hope nor despair exhibited in his countenance,—he knows those pieces are not for him. There is an expression of impatience about the eye, as he scans your features, which seems to say, 'Greedy fellow, what, not one bit for me?' Only cut a slice from the exterior of the joint, a piece that he knows you will not eat, and watch the change and eagerness of his expression; he knows as well as you do that this is intended for him,—he has reasoned upon it.

This is the simple and every-day performance of a common house-dog. Observe the pointers in a field of close-cut stubble—two well broken, reasonable old dogs. The birds are wild, and have been flushed several times during the day, and the old dog has winded them now in this close-cut stubble, from which he knows the covey will rise at a long range. Watch his expression of intense, and yet careful excitement as he draws upon his game, step by step, crouching close to the ground, and occasionally moving his head slowly round to see if his master is close up. Look at the bitch at the other end of the field, backing him like a statue, while the old dog still creeps on. Not a step further will he move; his lower jaw trembles with excitement; the guns advance to a line with his shoulder; up they rise, whiz-z-z-z-z-z-z!—bang!—bang! See how the excitement of the dog is calmed as he falls to the down charge, and afterwards with what pleasure he follows up and stands to the dead birds. If this is not reason, there is no such thing in existence.

Again, look at the sheep-dog, what can be more beautiful than to watch the judgment displayed by these dogs in driving a large flock of sheep? Then turn to the Mont St. Bernard dog, and the Newfoundland, and countless instances could be produced as proofs of their wonderful share of reasoning power.

The different classes of hounds being kept in kennels do not exhibit this quality to the same amount as many others, as they are not sufficiently domesticated, and their intercourse with man is confined to the one particular branch of hunting; but in this pursuit they will afford many striking proofs that they, in like manner with their other brethren, are not devoid of the reasoning power.

Poor old 'Bluebeard;'—he had an almost human share of understanding, but being simply a hound, this was confined to elk hunting. He was like the fox-hunter of the last century, whose ideas did not extend beyond his sport; but in this he was perfect.

Bluebeard was a foxhound, bred at Newera Ellia in 1847 by F. J. Templer, Esq. He subsequently belonged to F. H. Palliser, Esq., who kindly added him to my kennel.

He was a wonderful hound on a cold scent, and so thoroughly was he versed in all the habits of an elk, that he knew exactly where to look for one. I am convinced that he knew the date of a track from its appearance, as I have constantly seen him shove his nose into the deep impression, to try for a scent when the track was some eight or ten hours old.

It was a curious thing to watch his cleverness at finding on a patina. In most of the plains in the neighbourhood of Newera Ellia, a small stream flows through the centre. To this the elk, who are out feeding in the night, are sure to repair at about four in the morning for their last drink, and I usually try along the banks a little after daylight for a find, where the scent is fresh, and the tracks are distinctly visible.

When every hound has been eagerly winding the scent upon the circuitous route which the elk has made in grazing, Bluebeard would never waste his time in attempting to follow the innumerable windings, but, taking a fresh cast, he would invariably strike off to the jungle and try along the edge, until he reached the spot at which the elk had entered. At these times he committed the only fault which he possessed (for an elk hound); he would immediately open upon the scent, and, by alarming the elk at too great a distance, would give him too long a start. Nevertheless, he made up for this by his wonderful correctness and knowledge of his game, and if the run was increased in length by his early note, we nevertheless ran into our game at last.

Some years ago he met with an accident, which partly deprived him of the use of one of his hind legs; this made the poor old fellow very slow; but it did not interfere with his finding and hunting, although the rest of the pack would shoot ahead, and the elk was frequently brought to bay and killed before old Bluebeard had finished his hunt; but he was never thrown out, and was sure to come up at last; and if the pack were at fault during the run, he was the hound to show them the right road on his arrival.

I once saw an interesting proof of his reasoning powers during a long and difficult hunt.

I was hunting for a few days at the Augora patinas, accompanied by Palliser. These are about five hundred feet lower than Newera Ellia, and are situated in the district of Dimboola. They are composed of undulating knolls of fine grass, with a large and deep river flowing through the centre. These patinas are surrounded by wooded hills of good open jungle.

We had found upon the patina at break of day, and the whole pack had gone off in full cry; but the whereabouts was very uncertain, and having long lost all sound of the hounds, we wandered here and there to no purpose. At length we separated, and took up our stations upon different knolls to watch the patina, and to listen.

The hill upon which I stood commanded an extensive view of the patina, while the broad river flowed at the base, after its exit from the jungle. I had been only a few minutes at my post, when I observed, at about 600 yards' distance, a strong ripple in the river like the letter V, and it immediately struck me that an elk had come down the river from the jungle, and was swimming down the stream. This was soon proved to be the case, as I saw the head of a doe elk in the acute angle of the ripple.

I had the greyhounds with me, 'Lucifer,' 'Lena,' 'Hecate,' and 'Bran,' and I ran down the hill with these dogs, hoping to get them a view of her as she landed on the patina. I had several bogs and hollows to cross, and I accordingly lost sight of the elk; but upon arriving at the spot where I imagined the elk would land, I saw her going off across the patina, a quarter of a mile away. The greyhounds saw her, and away they flew over the short grass, while the pack began to appear from the jungle, having come down to the halloo that I had given on first seeing the elk swimming down the river.

The elk seemed determined to give a beautiful course, for, instead of pushing straight for the jungle, she made a great circuit on the patina as though in the endeavour to make once more for the river. The long-legged ones were going at a tremendous pace, and, being fresh, they rapidly overhauled her; gradually the distance between them diminished, and at length they had a fair course down a gentle inclination which led towards the river. Here the greyhounds soon made an end of the hunt; their game was within a hundred yards, going at top speed; but it was all up with the elk; the pace was too good, and they ran into her and pulled her down just as the other hounds had come down upon my scent.

We were cutting up the elk, when we presently heard old Bluebeard's voice far away in the jungle, and, thinking that he might perhaps be running another elk, we ran to a hill which overlooked the river and kept a bright look-out. We soon discovered that he was true upon the same game, and we watched his plan of hunting, being anxious to see whether he could hunt up an elk that had kept to water for so long a time.

On his entrance to the patina by the river's bank he immediately took to water and swam across the stream; here he carefully hunted the edge for several hundred yards down the river, but, finding nothing, he returned to the jungle at the point from which the river flowed. Here he again took to water, and, swimming back to the bank from which he had at first started, he landed and made a vain cast down the hollow. He returned back after his fruitless search, and once more took to water. I began to despair of the possibility of his finding; but the true old hound was now swimming steadily down the stream, crossing and re-crossing from either bank, and still pursuing his course down the river. At length he neared the spot where I knew that the elk had landed, and we eagerly watched to see if he would pass the scent, as he was now several yards from the bank. He was nearly abreast of the spot, when he turned sharp in and landed in the exact place; his deep and joyous note rang across the patinas, and away went the gallant old hound in full cry upon the scent, while I could not help shouting 'Hurrah for old Bluebeard!' In a few minutes he was by the side of the dead elk, a specimen of a true hound, who certainly had exhibited a large share of 'reason.'

CHAPTER X.

Wild Fruits—Ingredients for a *Soupe maigre*—Orchidaceous Plants—Wild Nutmegs—Native Oils—Cinnamon—Primeval Forests—Valuable Woods—The Mahawelli River—Variety of Palms—Cocoa-nut Toddy—Arrack—Cocoa-nut Oil—Cocoa-nut Planting—The Talipot Palm—The Areca Palm—Betel Chewing—Sago Nuts—Variety of Bees—Waste of Bees'-wax—Edible Fungi—Narcotic Puff Ball—Intoxicating Drugs—Poisoned Cakes—The 'Sack Tree'—No Gum Trees of Value in Ceylon.

AMONG the inexperienced there is a prevalent idea connected with tropical forests and jungles, that they teem with wild fruits, which Nature is supposed to produce spontaneously. Nothing can be more erroneous than such an opinion; even edible berries are scantily supplied by the wild shrubs and trees, and these, in lieu of others of superior quality, are sometimes dignified by the name of fruit.

The Guava and the Katumbillé are certainly very numerous throughout the Ouva district; the latter being a dark red, rough-skinned kind of plum, the size of a greengage, but free from stone. It grows upon a thorny bush about fifteen feet high; but the fruit is too acid to please most palates; the extreme thirst produced by a day's shooting in a burning sun makes it refreshing when plucked from the tree; but it does not aspire to the honour of a place at the table, where it can only appear in the form of red currant jelly, for which it is an undeniable substitute.

Excellent blackberries and a very large and full-flavoured black raspberry grow at Newera Ellia; likewise the Cape gooseberry, which is of the genus 'Solanum.' The latter is a round yellow berry, the size of a cherry; this is enclosed in a loose bladder, which forms an outer covering. The flavour is highly aromatic, but, like most Ceylon wild fruits, it is too acid.

The sweetest and best of the jungle productions is the 'Morra.' This is a berry about the size of a small nutmeg, which grows in clusters upon a large tree of rich dark foliage. The exterior of the berry is brown and slightly rough; the skin, or rather the case, is brittle, and of the consistence of an egg-shell; this, when broken and peeled off, exposes a semi-transparent pulp, like a skinned grape in appearance and in flavour. It is extremely juicy; but, unfortunately, a large black stone occupies the centre and at least one-half of the bulk of the entire fruit.

The Jambo apple is a beautiful fruit in appearance, being the fac-simile of a snow-white pear formed of wax, with a pink blush upon one side. Its exterior beauty is all that it can boast of, as the fruit itself is vapid and tasteless. In fact, all wild fruits are for the most part great exaggerations. I have seen in a work on Ceylon the miserable little acid berry of the rattan, which is no larger than a currant, described as a fruit: hawthorn berries might with equal justice be classed among the fruits of Great Britain.

I will not attempt to describe these paltry productions in detail; there is necessarily a great variety throughout the island; but their insignificance does not entitle them to a description, which would raise them far above their real merit.

It is nevertheless most useful to a sportsman in Ceylon to possess a sufficient stock of botanical information for his personal convenience. A man may be lost in the jungles, or hard up for provisions in some out-of-the-way place, where, if he has only a saucepan, he can generally procure something eatable in the way of herbs. It is not to be supposed, however, that he would succeed in making a good dinner; the reader may at any time procure something similar in England by restricting himself to nettle-tops—an economical, but not a fattening, vegetable. Anything, however simple, is better than an empty stomach, and when the latter is positively empty, it is wonderful how the appetite welcomes the most miserable fare.

At Newera Ellia the jungles would always produce a supply for a *soupe maigre.* There is an esculent nillho which grows in the forest in the bottoms of the swampy ravines. This is a most succulent plant, which grows to the height or length of about seven feet, as its great weight keeps it close to the ground. It is so brittle that it snaps like a cucumber when struck by a stick, and it bears a delicate dark blue blossom. When stewed, it is as tender as the vegetable marrow; but its flavour approaches more closely to that of the cucumber. Wild ginger also abounds in the forests. This is a coarse variety of the 'Amomum zingiber.' The leaves, which spring from the ground, attain a height of seven or eight feet; a large crimson fleshy blossom also springs from the ground in the centre of the surrounding leaf-stems. The root is coarse, large, but wanting in fine flavour, although the young tubers are exceedingly tender and delicate. This is the favourite food of elephants on the Ceylon mountains; but it is a curious fact that they invariably reject the leaves which anyone would suppose would be their choicest morsel, as they are both succulent and plentiful. The elephants simply use them as a handle for tearing up the roots, which they bite off and devour, throwing the leaves on one side.

The wild parsnip is also indigenous to the plains on the mountains. As usual with most wild plants of this class, they have little or no root, but run to leaf. The seeds are very highly flavoured, and are gathered by the natives for their curries.

There is likewise a beautiful orchidaceous plant,

which is very common throughout the patinas on the mountains, and which produces the very finest quality of arrowroot. So much is this valued in the Nepaul country in India, that I have been assured by a person well acquainted with that locality that this quality of arrowroot is usually sold for its weight in rupees. In vain have I explained this to the Cingalese ; they will not attempt its preparation, because their fathers did not eat it ; and yet these same men will walk forty miles to cut a bundle of sticks of the Galla Gaha tree for driving buffaloes!—their fathers did this, and therefore they do it. Thus this beautiful plant is only appreciated by those whose instinct leads them to its discovery. The wild hogs plough up the patinas and revel in this delicate food. The plant itself is almost lost in the rank herbage of the patinas ; but its beautiful pink hyacinth-shaped blossom attracts immediate attention. Few plants combine beauty of appearance, scent, and utility ; but this is the perfection of each quality—nothing can surpass the delicacy and richness of its perfume. It has two small bulbs about an inch below the surface of the earth, and these when broken, exhibit a highly granulated texture, semi-transparent like half-boiled sago. From these bulbs the arrowroot is produced by pounding them in water and drying the precipitated farina in the sun.

There are several beautiful varieties of orchidaceous plants upon the mountains, among others several species of the Dendrobium. Its rich yellow flowers hang in clusters from a withered tree, the only sign of life upon a giant trunk decayed, like a wreath upon a grave. The scent of this flower is well known as most delicious; one plant will perfume a large room.

There is one variety of this tribe in the neighbourhood of Newera Ellia, which is certainly unknown in English collections. It blossoms in April; the flowers are a bright lilac, and I could lay my hand upon it at any time, as I have never seen it but in one spot, where it flourishes in profusion. This is about fourteen miles from Newera Ellia; and I have never yet collected a specimen, as I have invariably been out hunting whenever I have met with it.

The black pepper is also indigenous throughout Ceylon. At Newera Ellia the leaves of this vine are highly pungent, although at this elevation it does not produce fruit. A very short distance towards a lower elevation effects a marked change, as within seven miles it fruits in great perfection.

At a similar altitude, the wild nutmeg is very common throughout the forests. This fruit is a perfect anomaly. The tree is entirely different to that of the cultivated species. The latter is small, seldom exceeding the size of an apple-tree, and bearing a light green myrtle-shaped leaf, which is not larger than that of a peach. The wild species, on the contrary, is a large forest tree, with leaves equal in size to those of the horse chestnut; nevertheless, it produces a perfect nutmeg. There is the outer rind of fleshy texture, like an unripe peach ; enclosed within is the nut-like shell, enveloped in the crimson network of mace, and within the shell is the nutmeg itself. All this is perfect enough, but, alas, the grand desideratum is wanting—it has no flavour or aroma whatever.

It is a gross imposition on the part of Nature ; a most stingy trick upon the public, and a regular do. The mace has no taste whatever, and the nutmeg has simply a highly acrid and pungent taste, without any spicy flavour, but merely abounding in a rank and disagreeable oil. The latter is so plentiful, that I am astonished it has not been experimented upon, especially by the natives, who are great adepts at expressing oils from many substances.

Those most common in Ceylon are the cocoa-nut and gingerly oils. The former is one of the grand staple commodities of the island ; the latter is the produce of a small grain, grown exclusively by the natives.

But, in addition to these, there are various other oils manufactured by the Cingalese. These are the Cinnamon, Castor, Margosse, Mee, Kenar, Meeheeria ; and both clove and lemon-grass oil are prepared by Europeans.

The first, which is the cinnamon oil, is more properly a kind of vegetable wax, being of the consistence of stearine. This is prepared from the berries of the cinnamon shrub, which are boiled in water until the fatty substance, or so-called oil, floats upon the surface; this is skimmed off, and, when a sufficient quantity is collected, it is boiled down until all watery particles are evaporated, and the melted fat is turned out into a shallow vessel to cool. It has a pleasant, though, perhaps, a rather faint aromatic smell, and is very delicious as an adjunct in the culinary art. In addition to this, it possesses gentle aperient properties, which render it particularly wholesome.

Castor oil is also obtained by the natives by boiling, and it is accordingly excessively rank after long keeping. The castor-oil plant is a perfect weed throughout Ceylon, being one of the few useful shrubs that will flourish in such poor soil without cultivation.

Margosse oil is extracted from the fruit of a tree of that name. It has an extremely fetid and disagreeable smell, which will effectually prevent the contact of flies or any other insect. On this account it is valuable as an application to open wounds, in addition to which it possesses powerful healing properties.

Mee oil is obtained from the fruit of the Mee tree. This fruit is about the size of an apricot, and is extremely rich in its produce; but the oil is of a coarse description, and is simply used by the natives for their rude lamps. Kenar oil and Meeheeria oil are equally coarse, and are quite unfit for any but native purposes.

Lemon-grass oil, which is known in commerce as citronella oil, is a delightful extract from the rank lemon grass, which covers most of the hill sides in the more open districts of Ceylon. An infusion of the grass is subsequently distilled; the oil is then discovered on the surface. This is remarkably pure, with a most pungent aroma. If rubbed upon the skin, it will prevent the attacks of insects, while its perfume remains; but the oil is so volatile, that the scent quickly evaporates, and the spell is broken.

Clove oil is extracted from the leaves of the cinnamon tree, and not from cloves, as its name would imply. The process is very similar to that employed in the manufacture of citronella oil.

Cinnamon is indigenous throughout the jungles of Ceylon. Even at the high elevation of Newera Ellia, it is one of the most common woods, and it grows to the dimensions of a forest tree, the trunk being usually about three feet in circumference. At Newera Ellia it loses much of its fine flavour, although it is still highly aromatic.

This tree flourishes in a white quartz sandy soil, and in its cultivated state it is never allowed to exceed the dimensions of a bush, being pruned down close to the ground every year. This system of close cutting induces the growth of a large number of shoots, in the same manner that withies are produced in England.

Every twelve months these shoots attain the length of six or seven feet, and the thickness of a man's finger. In the interim, the only cultivation required is repeated cleaning. The whole plantation is cut down at the proper period, and the sticks are then stripped of their bark by the peelers. These men are called 'Chalias,' and their labour is confined to this particular branch. The season being over, they pass the remaining portion of the year in idleness, their earnings during one crop being sufficient to supply their trifling wants until the ensuing harvest.

Their practice in this employment naturally renders them particularly expert, and in far less time than is occupied in the description, they run a sharp knife longitudinally along a stick, and at once divest it of the bark. On the following day, the strips of bark are scraped, so as entirely to remove the outer cuticle. One strip is then laid within the other, which upon becoming dry, contract, and form a series of enclosed pipes. It is subsequently packed in bales, and carefully sewed up in double sacks for exportation.

The essential oil of cinnamon is usually made

from the refuse of the crop; but the quantity produced, in proportion to the weight of cinnamon, is exceedingly small, being about five ounces of oil to half a hundredweight of the spice.

Although the cinnamon appears to require no more than a common quartz sand for its production, it is always cultivated with the greatest success, where the subsoil is light, dry, and of a loamy quality.

The appearance of the surface soil is frequently very deceitful. It is not uncommon to see a forest of magnificent trees growing in soil of apparently pure sand, which will not even produce the underwood with which Ceylon forests are generally choked. In such an instance the appearance of the trees is unusually grand, as their whole length and dimensions are exposed to view, and their uniting crowns throw a sombre shade over the barren ground beneath. It is not to be supposed that these mighty specimens of vegetation are supported by the poor sandy soil upon the surface; their tap roots strike down into some richer stratum, from which their nourishment is derived.

These forests are not common in Ceylon; their rarity accordingly enhances their beauty. The largest English oak would be a mere pigmy among the giants of these wilds, whose stature is so wonderful, that the eye never becomes tired of admiration. Often have I halted on my journey to ride around and admire the prodigious height and girth of these trees. Their beautiful proportions render them the more striking; there are no gnarled and knotty stems, such as we are accustomed to admire in the ancient oaks and beeches of England, but every trunk rises like a mast from the earth perfectly free from branches for ninety or a hundred feet, straight as an arrow, each tree forming a dark pillar to support its share of the rich canopy above, which constitutes a roof perfectly impervious to the sun. It is difficult to guess the actual height of these forest trees; but I have frequently noticed that it is impossible to shoot a bird on the higher branches with No. 5 shot.

It is much to be regretted that the want of the means of transport renders the timber of these forests perfectly valueless. From age to age these magnificent trees remain in their undisturbed solitudes, gradually increasing in their apparently endless growth, and towering above the dark vistas of everlasting silence. No one can imagine the utter stillness which pervades these gloomy shades. There is a mysterious effect produced by the total absence of animal life. In the depths of these forests I have stood and listened for some sound until my ears tingled with overstrained attention; not a chirp of a bird, neither the hum of an insect, but the mouth of Nature is sealed. Not a breath of air has rustled a leaf, nor even a falling fruit has broken the spell of silence. The undying verdure, the freshness of each tree, even in its mysterious age, create an idea of eternal vegetation, and the silvery, yet dim light adds to the charm of the fairy-like solitude.

I had ridden for fifteen or twenty miles through one of these forests without hearing a sound, except that of my horse's hoof occasionally striking against a root. Neither beast nor bird is to be seen, except upon the verge. The former has no food upon such barren ground; and the latter can find no berries, as the earth is sunless and free from vegetation. Not even monkeys are to be seen, although the trees must produce fruit and seed. Every thing appears to have deserted the country, and to have yielded it as the sole territory of Nature on a stupendous scale. The creepers lie serpent-like along the ground to the thickness of a man's waist, and, rearing their twisted forms on high, they climb the loftiest trees, hanging in festoons from stem to stem like the cables of a line-of-battle-ship, and extending from tree to tree for many hundred yards; now falling to the earth and striking a fresh root, then, with increased energy, remounting the largest trunks, and forming a labyrinth of twisted ropes among the ceiling of the forest. From these creepers hang the sabre beans. Every thing seems on a supernatural scale; the bean-pod four feet or more in length, by three inches in breadth; the beans two inches in diameter.

Here may be seen the most valuable woods of Ceylon. The ebony growing in great perfection and large quantity. This tree is at once distinguished from the surrounding stems by its smaller diameter and its sooty trunk. The bark is crisp, jet black, and has the appearance of being charred. Beneath the bark the wood is perfectly white until the heart is reached, which is the fine black ebony of commerce. Here also, equally immoveable, the Calamander is growing, neglected and unknown. This is the most esteemed of all Ceylon woods, and it is so rare that it realises a fancy price. It is something similar to the finest walnut; the colour being a rich hazel brown, mottled and striped with irregular black marks. It is superior to walnut in the extreme closeness of the grain and the richness of its colour.

There are upwards of eighty different woods produced in Ceylon, which are made use of for various purposes; but of these many are very inferior. Those most appreciated are,

Calamander, Ebony, Satinwood } chiefly used for furniture and cabinet work.

Suria (the tulip-tree).

Tamarind.

Jackwood.

Halmileel.

Cocoa-nut.

Palmyra.

The Suria is an elegant tree, bearing a beautiful yellow blossom something similar to a tulip, from which it derives its name. The wood is of an extremely close texture, and of a reddish brown colour. It is exceedingly tough, and it is chiefly used for making the spokes of wheels.

The Tamarind is a fine dark red wood, mottled with black marks; but is not in general use, as the tree is too valuable to be felled for the sake of its timber. This is one of the handsomest trees of the tropics, growing to a very large size, the branches widely spreading, something like the cedars of Lebanon.

Jackwood is a coarse imitation of mahogany, and is used for a variety of purposes, especially for making cheap furniture. The latter is not only economical, but exceedingly durable, and is manufactured at so low a rate, that a moderate-sized house might be entirely furnished with it for 150*l*.

The fruit of the jack grows from the trunk and branches of the tree, and when ripe it weighs about twenty pounds. The rind is rough, and when cut it exposes a yellow pulpy mass. This is formed of an infinite number of separate divisions of fleshy matter, which severally enclose an oval nut. The latter are very good when roasted, having a close resemblance to chestnuts. The pulp, which is the real fruit, is not usually eaten by Europeans, on account of its peculiar odour. This perfume is rather difficult to describe, but when a rainy day in London crams a waiting-room with well-soaked and steaming multitudes, the atmosphere somewhat approaches the smell of the jack-fruit.

The Halmileel is one of the most durable and useful woods in Ceylon, and is almost the only kind that is thoroughly adapted for making staves for casks. Of late years, the great increase of the oil-trade has brought this wood into general request, consequent upon the increased demand for barrels. So extensive and general is the present demand for this wood, that the natives are continually occupied in conveying it from certain districts which a few years ago were utterly neglected. Unfortunately the want of roads and the means of transport confine their operations to the banks of rivers, down which the logs are floated at the proper season.

I recollect some eight years ago crossing the Mahawelli river upon a raft which my coolies had hastily constructed, and reaching a miserable village near Monampitya, in the extreme north of the Veddah country. The river is here about four hundred paces wide, and in the rainy season a fine volume of water rolls along in a rapid stream towards Trincomalie, at which place it meets the sea. I was struck at the time with the magnificent timber in the forests on its banks, and no less surprised that with the natural facilities of transport it should be neglected. Two years ago I crossed at this same spot, and I remarked the wonderful change which a steady demand had effected in this wild country. Extensive piles of halmileel logs were collected along the banks of the river, while the forests were strewed with felled trees, in preparation for floating down the stream. A regular demand usually ensures a corresponding supply, which could not be better exemplified than in this case.

Among fancy woods, the Bread-fruit tree should not be omitted. This is something similar to the jack, but, like the tamarind, the value of the produce saves the tree from destruction.

This tree does not attain a very large size; but its growth is exceedingly regular, and the foliage peculiarly rich and plentiful. The fruit is something similar in appearance to a small unripe jack-fruit, with an equally rough exterior. In the opinion of most who have tasted it, its virtues have been grossly exaggerated. To my taste it is perfectly uneatable, unless fried in thin slices with butter; it is even then a bad imitation of fried potatoes. The bark of this tree produces a strong fibre, and a kind of very adhesive pitch is also produced by decoction.

The Cocoa-nut and Palmyra woods at once introduce us to the palms of Ceylon, the most useful and elegant class in vegetation. For upwards of 120 miles along the western and southern coasts of Ceylon one continuous line of cocoa-nut groves wave their green leaves to the sea breeze, without a single break, except where some broad, clear river cleaves the line of verdure as it meets the sea.

Ceylon is rich in palms, including the following varieties :—

The Cocoa-nut.
The Palmyra.
The Kittool.
The Areca.
The Date.
The Sago.
The Talipot.

The wonderful productions of this tribe can only be appreciated by those who thoroughly understand the habits and necessities of the natives ; and upon examination it will be seen that Nature has opened wide her bountiful hand, and in the midst of a barren soil she has still remembered and supplied the wants of the inhabitants.

As the stream issued from the rock in the wilderness, so the cocoa-nut tree yields a pure draught from a dry and barren land ; a cup of water to the temperate and thirsty traveller ; cream from the pressed kernel ; refreshing and sparkling toddy to the early riser ; arrack to the hardened spirit-drinker; and a cup of oil, by the light of which I now extol its merits,—five separate and distinct liquids from the same tree!

A green or unripe cocoa-nut contains about a pint of sweetish water. In the hottest weather this is deliciously cool, in comparison to the heat of the atmosphere.

The ripe nut, when scraped into a pulp by a little serrated semi-circular iron instrument, is squeezed in a cloth by the hand, and about a quarter of a pint of delicious, thick cream, highly flavoured by cocoa-nut, is then expressed. This forms the chief ingredient in a Cingalese curry, from which it entirely derives its richness and fine flavour.

The toddy is the sap, which would nourish and fructify the blossom and young nuts, were it allowed to accomplish its duties. The toddy-drawer binds into one rod the numerous shoots, which are garnished with embryo nuts, and he then cuts off the ends, leaving an abrupt and brush-like termination. Beneath this he secures an earthen chatty, which will hold about a gallon. This remains undisturbed for twenty-four hours, until sunrise on the following morning; the toddy-drawer then reascends the tree, and lowers the chatty by a line to an assistant below, who empties the contents into a larger vessel, and the chatty is replaced under the productive branch, which continues to yield for about a month.

When first drawn, the toddy has the appearance

of thin milk-and-water, with a combined flavour of milk and soda-water, with a tinge of cocoa-nut. It is then very pleasant and refreshing, but in a few hours after sunrise a great change takes place, and the rapidity of the transition from the vinous to the acetous fermentation is so great that by midday it resembles a poor and rather acid cider. It now possesses intoxicating properties, and the natives accordingly indulge in it to some extent; but from its flavour and decided acidity, I should have thought the stomach would be affected some time before the head.

From this fermented toddy the arrack is procured by simple distillation.

This spirit to my taste is more palatable than most distilled liquors, having a very decided and peculiar flavour. It is a little fiery when new, but as water soon quenches fire, it is not spared by the native retailers, whose arrack would be of a most innocent character were it not for their infamous addition of stupifying drugs and hot peppers.

The toddy contains a large proportion of saccharine, without which the vinous fermentation could not take place. This is procured by evaporation in boiling, on the same principle that sugar is produced from cane-juice. The syrup is then poured into small saucers to cool, and it shortly assumes the consistence of hardened sugar. This is known in Ceylon as 'jaggery,' and is manufactured exclusively by the natives.

Cocoa-nut oil is now one of the greatest exports of Ceylon, and within the last few years the trade has increased to an unprecedented extent. In the two years of 1849 and 1850, the exports of cocoa-nut oil did not exceed 443,600 gallons, while in the year 1853, they had increased to 1,033,900 gallons, the trade being more than quadrupled in three years.

The manufacture of the oil is most simple. The kernel is taken from the nut, and, being divided, it is exposed to the sun, until all the watery particles are evaporated. The kernel thus dried is known as 'Copperah.' This is then pressed in a mill, and the oil flows into a reservoir.

This oil, although clear and limpid in the tropics, hardens to the consistence of lard at any temperature below 72° Fahr. Thus it requires a second preparation on its arrival in England. There it is spread upon mats (formed of coir) to the thickness of an inch, and then covered by a similar protection. These fat sandwiches are two feet square, and being piled one upon the other to a height of about six feet in an hydraulic press, are subjected to a pressure of some hundred tons. This disengages the pure oleaginous parts from the more insoluble portions, and the fat residue, being increased in hardness by its extra density, is mixed with stearine, and by a variety of preparations is converted into candles. The pure oil thus expressed, is that known in the shops as cocoa-nut oil.

The cultivation of the cocoa-nut tree is now carried to a great extent both by natives and Europeans; by the former it is grown for a variety of purposes, but by the latter its profits are confined to oil, coir, and poonac. The latter is the refuse of the nut after the oil has been expressed, and corresponds in its uses to the linseed oil cake of England, being chiefly employed for fattening cattle, pigs, and poultry.

The preparation of coir is a dirty and offensive occupation. The husk of the cocoa-nut is thrown into tanks of water, until the woody or pithy matter is loosened by fermentation from the coir fibre. The stench of putrid vegetable matter arising from these heaps must be highly deleterious. Subsequently the husks are beaten, and the fibre is separated and dried. Coir rope is useful on account of its durability and power of resisting decay during long immersion. In the year 1853, 2,380 tons of coir were exported from Ceylon.

The great drawback to the commencement of a cocoa-nut plantation is the total uncertainty in the price of oil during the interval of eleven years which must elapse before the estate comes into bearing. In this era of invention, when improvements in every branch of science follow each other with such rapid strides, it is a dangerous speculation to make any outlay that will remain so long invested without producing a return. Who can be so presumptuous as to predict the changes of future years? Oil may have ceased to be the common medium of light; our rooms may be illuminated by electricity, or from fifty other sources, which now are never dreamed of. In the mean time, the annual outlay during eleven years is an additional incubus upon the prime cost of the plantation, which at the expiration of this term may be reduced to one-tenth of its present value.

The cocoa-nut tree requires a sandy and well-drained soil; and although it flourishes where no other tree will grow, it welcomes a soil of a richer quality, and produces fruit in proportion. Eighty nuts per annum are about the average income from a healthy tree in full bearing; but this, of course, depends much upon the locality. This palm delights in the sea-breeze, and never attains the same perfection inland that it does in the vicinity of the coast. There are several varieties, and that which is considered superior is the yellow species, called the 'King Cocoa-nut.' I have seen this on the Maldive Islands in great perfection. There it is the prevailing description.

At the Seychelles there is a variety peculiar to those islands, differing entirely in appearance from the common cocoa-nut. It is fully twice the size, and is shaped like a kidney that is laid open. This is called by the French the '*Coco de mer*,' from the large numbers that are found floating in the sea in the neighbourhood of the islands.

The wood of the cocoa-nut tree is strong and durable; it is a dark brown, traversed by longitudinal black lines.

There are three varieties of toddy-producing palms in Ceylon; these are the cocoa-nut, the kittool, and the palmyra. The latter produces the finest quality of jaggery. This cannot be easily distinguished from crumbled sugar-candy, which it exactly resembles in flavour. The wood of the palmyra is something similar to the cocoa-nut, but it is of a superior quality, and is much used for rafters, being durable and of immense strength.

The kittool is a very sombre and peculiar palm. Its crest very much resembles the drooping plume upon a hearse, and the foliage is a dark green, with a tinge of grey. The wood of this palm is almost black, being apparently a mass of longitudinal strips, or coarse lines of whalebone running close together from the top to the root of the tree. This is the toughest and most pliable of all the palm woods, and is principally used by the natives in making 'pingos:' these are flat bows about eight feet in length, and are used by the Cingalese for carrying loads upon the shoulder. The weight is slung at either end of the pingo, and the elasticity of the woodaccommodates itself to the spring of each step, thereby reducing the dead weight of the load. In this manner a stout Cingalese will carry and travel with eighty pounds, if working on his own account, or with fifty if hired for a journey. A Cingalese will carry a much heavier weight than an ordinary Malabar, as he is a totally different man in form and strength. In fact, the Cingalese are generally a compactly built and well-limbed race, while the Malabar is a man averaging full a stone lighter weight.

The most extraordinary in the list of palms is the Talipot. The crest of this beautiful tree is adorned by a crown of nearly circular fan-shaped leaves, of so tough and durable a texture, that they are sewn together by the natives for erecting portable tents or huts. The circumference of each leaf at the extreme edge is from twenty to thirty feet, and even this latter size is said to be frequently exceeded.

Every Cingalese throughout the Kandian district is provided with a section of one of these leaves which forms a kind of fan about six feet in length. This is carried in the hand, and is only spread in case of rain, when it forms an impervious roofing of about three feet in width at the broad extremity. Four or five of these sections will form a circular roof for a small hut which resembles a large umbrella, or Brobdingnag mushroom.

There is a great peculiarity in the talipot palm.

It blossoms only once in a long period of years, and after this it dies. No flower can equal the elegance and extraordinary dimensions of this blossom; its size is proportionate to its leaves, and it usurps the place of the faded crest of green, forming a magnificent crown or plume of snow-white ostrich feathers, which stand upon the summit of the tall stem, as though they were the natural head of the palm.

There is an interesting phenomenon at the period of flowering. The great plume already described, prior to its appearing in bloom, is packed in a large case or bud, about four feet long. In this case, the blossom comes to maturity, at which time the tightened cuticle of the bud can no longer sustain the pressure of the expanding flower. It suddenly bursts with a loud report, and the beautiful plume, freed from its imprisonment, ascends at this signal and rapidly unfolds its feathers, towering above the drooping leaves which are hastening to decay.

The Areca is a palm of great elegance; it rises to a height of about eighty feet, and a rich feathery crest adorns the summit. This is the most delicate stem of all the palm tribe; that of a tree of eighty feet in length would not exceed five inches in diameter. Nevertheless, I have never seen an areca palm overturned by a storm; they bow gracefully to the wind, and the extreme elasticity of the wood secures them from destruction.

This tree produces the commonly called 'betel nut,' but more properly, the areca nut. They grow in clusters beneath the crest of the palm, in a similar manner to the cocoa-nut, but the tree is more prolific, as it produces about 200 nuts per annum. The latter are very similar to large nutmegs both in size and appearance, and, like the cocoa-nut, they are enclosed in an outer husk of a fibrous texture.

The consumption may be imagined, when it is explained that every native is perpetually chewing a mixture of this nut and betel leaf. Every man carries a betel bag, which contains the following list of treasures: A quantity of areca nuts, a parcel of betel leaves, a roll of tobacco, a few pieces of ginger, an instrument similar to pruning scissors, and a brass or silver case (according to the wealth of the individual), full of chunam paste,—viz., a fine lime produced from burnt coral, slacked. This case very much resembles an old-fashioned warming-pan breed of watch and chateleine, as numerous little spoons for scooping out the chunam are attached to it by chains.

The betel is a species of pepper, the leaf of which very much resembles that of the black pepper, but is highly aromatic and pungent. It is cultivated to a very large extent by the natives, and may be seen climbing round poles and trees in every garden.

It has been said by some authors that the betel has powerful narcotic properties; but, on the contrary, its stimulating qualities have a directly opposite effect. Those who have attributed this supposed property to the betel leaf must have indulged in a regular native 'chew' as an experiment, and have nevertheless been ignorant of the mixture.

We will make up a native 'chew' after the most approved fashion, and the reader shall judge for himself in which ingredient the narcotic principle is displayed.

Take a betel leaf, and upon this spread a piece of chunam,[1] as large as a pea; then with the pruning scissors cut three very thin slices of areca nut, and lay them in the leaf; next, add a small piece of ginger; and, lastly, a good-sized piece of *tobacco.* Fold up this mixture in another betel leaf in a compact little parcel, and it is fit for promoting several hours' enjoyment in chewing, and spitting a disgusting blood-red dye in every direction. The latter is produced by the areca nut. It is the tobacco which possesses the narcotic principle; if this is omitted, the remaining ingredients are simple stimulants.

The teeth of all natives are highly discoloured by the perpetual indulgence in this disgusting habit: nor is this the only effect produced; cancer in the cheek is a common complaint among them, supposed to be produced by the caustic lime which is so continually in the mouth.

[1] Lime made from burnt coral.

The exports of areca nuts from Ceylon will give some idea of the supply of palms. In 1853 no less than 3,000 tons were shipped from this colony, valued at about 45,000*l.* The greater portion is consumed in India.

Two varieties of palms remain to be described,—the Date, and the Sago.

The former is a miserable species, which does not exceed the height of three to five feet, and the fruit is perfectly worthless.

The latter is indigenous throughout the jungles in Ceylon, but it is neither cultivated, nor is the sago prepared from it.

The height of this palm does not exceed fifteen or twenty feet, and even this is above the general average. It grows in the greatest profusion in the Veddah country. The stem is rough, and a continuation of rings divides it into irregular sections. The leaves are a rich dark green, and very light and feathery, beneath which, the nuts grow in clusters similar to those of the areca palm.

The only use that the natives make of the produce of this tree is the preparation of flour from the nuts. Even this is not very general, which is much to be wondered at, as the farina is far superior in flavour to that produced from most grains.

The natives ascribe intoxicating properties to the cakes made from this flour ; but I have certainly eaten a fair allowance at one time, and I cannot say that I had the least sensation of elevation.

The nut, which is something similar to the areca in size, is nearly white when divested of its outer husk; this is soaked for about twenty-four hours in water. A slight fermentation takes place, and the gas generated, splits the nut open at a closed joint like an acorn. This fermentation may, perhaps, take some exhilarating effect upon the natives' weak heads.

The nuts, partially softened by this immersion, are dried in the sun, and subsequently pounded into flour in a wooden mortar. This flour is sifted, and the coarser parts being separated, are again pounded, until a beautiful snow-white farina is produced. This is made into a dough by a proper admixture with water, and being formed into small cakes, they are baked for about a quarter of an hour in a chatty. The fermentation, which has already taken place in the nut, has impregnated the flour with a leaven; this, without any further addition, expands the dough when in the oven, and the cake produced is very similar to a crumpet, both in appearance and flavour.

The village in which I first tasted this preparation of the sago nut was a tolerable sample of such places, on the borders of the Veddah country. The population consisted of one old man, and a corresponding old woman, and one fine stout young man, and five young women. A host of little children, who were so similar in height that they must have been one litter, and three or four most miserable dogs and cats, were additional tenants of the village.

These people lived upon sago cakes, pumpkins, wild fruits, and berries, river fish, and wild honey. The latter is very plentiful throughout Ceylon, and the natives are very expert in finding out the nests, by watching the bees in their flight, and following them up. A bee-hunter must be a most keen-sighted fellow, although there is not so much difficulty in the pursuit as may at first appear. No one can mistake the flight of a bee *en route* home, if he has once observed him. He is no longer wandering from flower to flower, in an uncertain course, but he rushes through the air in a straight line for the nest. If the bee-hunter sees one bee thus speeding homewards, he watches the vacant spot in the air, until assured of the direction by the successive appearance of these insects, one following the other nearly every second in their hurried race to the comb. Keeping his eye upon the passing bees, he follows them, until he reaches the tree in which the nest is found.

There are five varieties of bees in Ceylon; these are all honey-makers, except the carpenter bee. This species is entirely unlike a bee in all its habits. It is a bright tinsel-green colour, and the size of a large walnut, but shaped like the humble bees of England. The mouth is armed with a very powerful pair of mandibles, and the tail with a sting even larger and more venomous than that of the hornet. These carpenter bees are exceedingly destructive, as they bore holes in beams and posts, in which they lay their eggs, the larvæ of which, when hatched, feed upon the timber.

The honey bees are of four very distinct varieties, each of which forms its nest on a different principle. The largest and most extensive honey-maker is the 'Bambera.' This is nearly as large as a hornet, and it forms its nest upon the bough of a tree, from which the comb hangs like a Cheshire cheese, being about the same thickness, but five or six inches greater in diameter. The honey of this bee is not so much esteemed as that from the smaller varieties, as the flavour partakes too strongly of the particular flower which the bee has frequented ; thus in different seasons the honey varies in flavour, and is sometimes so highly aperient that it must be used with much caution. This property is, of course, derived from the flower which the bee prefers at that particular season. The wax of the comb is the purest and whitest of any kind produced in Ceylon. So partial are these bees to particular blossoms, that they migrate from place to place at different periods, in quest of flowers which are then in bloom.

This is a very wonderful and inexplicable arrangement of Nature, when it is considered that some flowers, which particularly attract these migrations, only blossom once in '*seven years*.' This is the case at Newera Ellia, where the nillho induces such a general rush of this particular bee to the district, that the jungles are swarming with them in every direction, although during the six preceding years hardly a bee of the kind is to be met with.

There are many varieties of the nillho. These vary from a tender dwarf plant to the tall and heavy stem of the common nillho, which is nearly as thick as a man's arm, and about twenty feet high.

The next honey-maker is very similar in size and appearance to our hive-bee in England. This variety forms its nest in hollow trees, and in holes in rocks. Another bee, similar in appearance, but not more than half the size, suspends a most delicate comb to the twigs of a tree. This nest is no larger than an orange, but the honey of the two latter varieties is of the finest quality, and quite equal in flavour to the famed 'Miel vert' of the Isle de Bourbon, although it has not the delicate green tint which is so much esteemed in the latter.

The last of the Ceylon bees is the most tiny, although an equally industrious workman. He is a little smaller than our common house-fly, and he builds his diminutive nest in the hollow of a tree, where the entrance to his mansion is a hole no larger than would be made by a lady's stiletto.

It would be a natural supposition, that so delicate an insect would produce a honey of corresponding purity. but instead of the expected treasure, we find a thick, black, and rather pungent, but highly aromatic, molasses. The natives, having naturally coarse tastes and strong stomachs, admire this honey beyond any other. Many persons are surprised at the trifling exports of wax from Ceylon. In 1853, these amounted to no more than *one ton.*

Cingalese are curious people, and do not trouble themselves about exports; they waste or consume all the bees'-wax. While we are contented with the honey, and carefully reject the comb, the native (in some districts) crams his mouth with a large section, and giving it one or two bites, he bolts the luscious morsel and begins another. In this manner immense quantities of this valuable article are annually wasted. Some few of the natives in the poorest villages save a small quantity, to exchange with the travelling Moormen for cotton cloths, &c., and in this manner the trifling amount exported is collected.

During the honey year at Newera Ellia, I gave a native permission to hunt bees in my forests, on condition that he should bring me the wax. Of course he stole the greater portion, but, nevertheless, in a few weeks, he brought me seventy-two pounds' weight of well-cleaned and perfectly white wax, which he had made up into balls, about the size of an eighteen-pound shot. Thus in so short a time, one man had collected about the thirtieth part of the annual export from Ceylon ; or, allowing that he stole at least one half, this would amount to the fifteenth.

It would be a vain attempt to restrain these people from their fixed habit; they would as soon think of refraining from betel-chewing as giving up a favourite food. Neither will they be easily persuaded to indulge in a food of a new description. I once showed them the common British mushroom, which they declared was a poisonous kind.[1] To prove the contrary, I had them several times at table, and found them precisely similar in appearance and flavour to the well-known 'Agaricus campestris;' but, notwithstanding this actual proof, the natives would not be convinced, and, although accustomed to eat a variety of this tribe, they positively declined this experiment. There is an edible species which they prefer, which, from its appearance, an Englishman would shun : this is perfectly white, both above and below, and the upper cuticle cannot be peeled off. I have tasted this, but it is very inferior in flavour to the common mushroom.

Experiments in these varieties of fungi are highly dangerous, as many of the most poisonous so closely resemble the edible species that they can with difficulty be distinguished. There is one kind of fungus

[1] English people are quite as obstinate in neglecting esculent fungi, which are accordingly wasted.

that I have met with in the forests which, from its offensive odour and disgusting appearance, should be something superlatively bad. It grows about four inches high; the top is round, with a fleshy and inflamed appearance; the stalk is out of all proportion in its thickness, being about two inches in diameter and of a livid white colour; this, when broken, is full of a transparent gelatinous fluid, which smells like an egg in the last stage of rottenness.

This fungus looks like an unhealthy excrescence on the face of Nature, who, as though ashamed of the disgusting blemish, has thrown a veil over the defect. The most exquisite fabric that can be imagined—a scarlet veil, like a silken net—falls over this ugly fungus, and, spreading like a tent at its base, it is there attached to the ground.

The meshes of this net are about as fine as those of a very delicate silk purse, and the gaudiness of the colour and the size of the fungus make it a very prominent object among the surrounding vegetation. In fact, it is a diminutive, though perfect circular tent of net-work, the stem of the fungus forming the pole in the centre.

I shall never forget my first introduction to this specimen. It was growing in an open forest, free from any underwood, and it seemed like a fairy bivouac beneath the mighty trees which overshadowed it. Hardly believing my own eyes at so strange and exquisite a structure, I jumped off my horse and hastened to secure it. But the net-work once raised was like the uncovering of the veiled prophet of Khorassan, and the stem, crushing in my fingers, revealed all the disgusting properties of the plant, and proved the impossibility of removing it entire. The elegance of its exterior only served to conceal its character.

There are two varieties of narcotic fungi whose properties are so mild that they are edible in small quantities. One is a bright crimson on the surface. This is the most powerful, and is seldom used. The other is a white solid puff-ball, with a rough outer skin or rind.

I have eaten the latter on two occasions, having been assured by the natives that they were harmless. The flavour somewhat resembles a truffle, but I could not account for the extreme drowsiness that I felt soon after eating. This wore off in the course of two or three hours. On the following day I felt the same effect, but to a still greater degree, as, having convinced myself that they were really eatable, I had taken a larger quantity. Knowing that the narcotic principle is the common property of a great variety of fungi, it immediately struck me that the puff-balls were the cause. On questioning the natives, it appeared that it was this principle that they admired, as it produced a species of mild intoxication.

All people, of whatever class or clime, indulge in some narcotic drug or drink. Those of the Cingalese are arrack, tobacco, fungi, and the Indian hemp. The use of the latter is, however, not so general among the Cingalese as the Malabars. This drug has a different effect from opium, as it does not injure the constitution, but simply exhilarates, and afterwards causes a temporary lethargy.

In appearance it very nearly resembles the common hemp. The leaves and blossom are dried, and are either smoked like tobacco, or formed into a paste with various substances and chewed.

When the plant approaches maturity, a gummy substance exudes from the leaves; this is gathered by men clothed in dry raw hides, who, by walking through the plantation, become covered with this gum or glue. This is scraped off and carefully preserved, being the very essence of the plant, and exceedingly powerful in its effects.

The sensation produced by the properties of this shrub is a wild dreamy kind of happiness; the ideas are stimulated to a high degree, and all that are most pleasurable are exaggerated, till the senses at length sink into a vague and delightful Elysium.

The reaction after this unnatural excitement is a temporary depression, but the sufferer is set all right again by some trifling stimulant, such as a glass of wine or spirits.

It is supposed, and confidently asserted, by some that the Indian hemp is the foundation of the Egyptian 'hashisch,' the effects of which are precisely similar.[1]

However harmless the apparent effect of a narcotic drug, common sense must at once perceive that a repeated intoxication, no matter how it is produced, must be ultimately hurtful to the system. The brain, accustomed to constant stimulants, at length loses its natural power, and requires these artificial assistants to enable it to perform its ordinary functions, in the same manner that the stomach, from similar treatment, would at length cease to act. This being continued, the brain becomes semi-torpid, until wakened up by a powerful stimulant; and the nervous system is at length worn out by a succession of exciting causes and reactions. Thus a hard drinker appears dull and heavy until under the influence of his secret destroyer, when he brightens up and, perhaps, shines in conversation; but every reaction requires a stronger amount of stimulant to lessen its effect, until mind and body at length became involved in the common ruin.

The seed of the lotus is a narcotic of a mild description, and it is carefully gathered when ripe, and eaten by the natives.

The lotus is seen in two varieties in Ceylon,—

[1] This is correct.

the pink and the white. The former is the most beautiful; and they are both very common in all tanks and sluggish streams. The leaves are larger than those of the water-lily, to which they bear a great resemblance, and the blossoms are full double the size. When the latter fade, the petals fall, and the base of the flower and seed-pod remains in the shape of a circular piece of honeycomb, full of cells sufficiently large to contain a hazel-nut. This is about the size of the seed; but the shape is more like an acorn without its cup. The flavour is pleasant, being something like a filbert, but richer and more oily.

Stramonium (*Datura stramonium*), which is a powerful narcotic, is a perfect weed throughout the island; but it is not used by the natives otherwise than medicinally, and the mass of the people are ignorant of its qualities, which are only known to the Cingalese doctors. I recollect some years ago, in Mauritius, where this plant is equally common, its properties were not only fully understood, but made use of by some of the Chinese emigrants. These fellows made cakes of manioc, and poisoned them with stramonium. Hot manioc cakes are the common every-day accompaniment to a French planter's breakfast at Mauritius, and through the medium of these, the Chinese robbed several houses. Their plan was simple enough.

A man with cakes to sell, appeared at the house at an early hour, and these being purchased, he retired until about two hours after breakfast was concluded. By this time the whole family were insensible, and the thieves robbed the house at their leisure. None of these cases terminated fatally; but, from the instant that I heard of it, I made every cake-seller who appeared at the door devour one of his own cakes before I became a purchaser. These men, however, were *bonâ fide* cake-merchants, and I did not meet with an exception.

There are a great variety of valuable medicinal plants in the jungles of Ceylon, many of which are unknown to any but the native doctors. Those most commonly known to us, and which may be seen growing wild by the road-side, are the nux vomica, ipecacuanha, gamboge, sarsaparilla, cassia fistula, cardamoms, &c.

The ipecacuanha is a pretty delicate plant, which bears a bright orange-coloured cluster of flowers.

The cassia fistula is a very beautiful tree, growing to the size of an ash, which it somewhat resembles in foliage. The blossom is very beautiful, being a pendant of golden flowers similar to the laburnum, but about two and a half feet long, and the individual flowers on the bunch are large in proportion. When the tree is in full flower it is very superb, and equally as singular when its beauty has faded and the seedpods are formed. These grow to a length of from two to three feet; when ripe they are perfectly black, round, and about three-quarters of an inch in diameter. The tree has the appearance of bearing a prolific crop of ebony rulers, each hanging from the bough by a short string.

There is another species of cassia fistula, the foliage of which assimilates to the mimosa. This bears a thicker, but much shorter, pod, of about a foot in length. The properties of both are the same, being laxative. Each seed within the pod is surrounded by a sweet, black, and honey-like substance, which contains the property alluded to.

The gamboge-tree is commonly known in Ceylon as the 'Ghorka.' This grows to the common size of an apple-tree, and bears a corrugated and intensely acid fruit. This is dried by the natives, and used in curries. The gamboge is the juice of the tree obtained by incisions in the bark. This tree grows in great numbers in the neighbourhood of Colombo, especially among the cinnamon gardens. Here, also, the cashew-tree grows to great perfection. The bark of the latter is very rich in tannin, and is used by the natives in the preparation of hides. The fruit is like an apple in appearance, and small, but is highly astringent. The well-known cashew nut grows like an excrescence from the end of the apple.

Many are the varieties and uses of vegetable productions in Ceylon, but of these none are more singular and interesting than the 'Sack Tree,' the Rita Gaha of the Cingalese. From the bark of this tree an infinite number of excellent sacks are procured, with very little trouble or preparation. The tree being felled, the branches are cut into logs of the length required, and sometimes are soaked in water; but this is not always necessary. The bark is then well beaten with a wooden mallet, until it is loosened from the wood; it is then stripped as a stocking is drawn off the leg. It is subsequently bleached, and one end being sewn up, completes a perfect sack, of a thick fibrous texture, somewhat similar to felt.

These sacks are in general use among the natives, and are preferred by them to any other, as their durability is such, that they sometimes descend from father to son. By constant use they stretch and increase their original size nearly one half. The texture necessarily becomes thinner, but the strength does not appear to be materially decreased.

There are many fibrous barks in Ceylon, some of which are so strong, that thin strips require a great amount of strength to break them; but none of these have yet been reduced to a marketable fibre. Several barks are more or less aromatic; others would be valuable to the tanners; some are highly esteemed by the natives as valuable astringents; but hitherto none have received much notice from Europeans. This may be caused by the general want of success of all experiments with indigenous produce. Although the jungles of Ceylon produce a long list of articles of much interest, their value chiefly lies in their curiosity; they are useful to the native, but comparatively of little worth to the European. In fact, few things will actually pay for the trouble and expense of collecting and transporting. Throughout the vast forests and jungles of Ceylon, although the varieties of trees are endless, there is not one valuable gum known to exist. There are a great variety of coarse unmarketable productions, about equal to the gum of the cherry-tree, &c.; but there is no such thing as a high-priced gum in the island.

The export of dammer is a mere trifle; four tons in 1852, twelve tons in 1853. This is a coarse and comparatively valueless commodity. No other tree but the doom produces any gum worth collecting; this species of rosin exudes in large quantities from an incision in the bark, but the small amount exported shows its insignificance. It is a fair sample of Ceylon productions; nothing that is uncultivated is of much pecuniary value.

CHAPTER XI.

Indigenous Productions—The Botanical Gardens—Suggested Experiments—Lack of Encouragement to Gold-diggers—The Prospects of Gold-digging—We want 'Nuggets'—Who is to Blame?—Governor's Salary—Fallacies of a Five Years' Reign—Neglected Education of the People—Responsibilities of Conquest—Progress of Christianity.

THE foregoing chapter may appear to decry *in toto* the indigenous productions of Ceylon, as it is asserted that they are valueless in their natural state. Nevertheless, I do not imply that they must necessarily remain useless. Where nature simply creates a genus, cultivation extends the species; and from an insignificant parent stock we propagate our finest varieties of both animals and vegetables. Witness the wild kale, parsnip, carrot, crab-apple, sloe, &c., all utterly worthless, but nevertheless the first parents of their now choice descendants.

It is therefore impossible to say what might not be done in the improvement of indigenous productions, were the attention of science bestowed upon them. But all this entails expense, and upon whom is this to fall? Out of a hundred experiments, ninety-nine might fail. In Ceylon we have no wealthy experimentalists, no agricultural exhibitions, no model farms; but every man who settles in a colony has left the mother-country to better himself, therefore no private enterprise is capable of such speculation. It clearly rests upon the government to develop the resources of the country, to prove the value of the soil, which is delivered to the purchaser at so much per acre, good or bad. But no; it is not in the nature of our government to move from an established routine As the squirrel revolves his cage, so governor after governor rolls his dull course along, pockets his salary, and leaves the poor colony as he found it.[1]

The government may direct the attention of the public, in reply, to their own establishment—to the Botanical Gardens. Have we not Botanical Gardens? We have, indeed, and much good they should do, if conducted upon the principle of developing local resources; but this would entail expense, and, like *everything* in the hands of government, it dies in its birth for want of consistent management.

With an able man as superintendent, at a good salary, the beautiful gardens at Peredenia are rendered next to useless, for want of a fund at his disposal. Instead of being conducted as an experimental farm,

[1] This was the wretched state of affairs in 1853, but the healthy change since that time is due to the character and ability of the subsequent governors.

they are little more than ordinary pleasure-grounds, filled with the beautiful foliage of the tropics, and kept in perfect order. What benefit have they been to the colony? Have the soils of various districts been tested?—have new fibres been manufactured from the countless indigenous fibrous plants?—have new oils been extracted?—have medicinal drugs been produced?—have dyes been extracted?—have improvements been suggested in the cultivation of any of the staple articles of Ceylon export? In fact, has ANYTHING ever been done by government for the interest of the private settler?

This is not the fault of the manager of the gardens; he has the will, but no funds. My idea of the object of a botanical garden is, that agricultural theories should be reduced to facts, upon which private enterprise may speculate, and by such success the government should ultimately benefit.[1]

It is well known to the commonest schoolboy, that soil which may be favourable to one plant is not adapted to another; therefore, where there is a diversity of soils, it stands to reason that there should be a corresponding variety of crops to suit those soils, so as to make the whole surface of the land yield its proportion.

[1] Since this was written the Ceylon government has established gardens for experiments, and the cinchona plant has been successfully introduced.

In Ceylon, where the chief article of production is coffee, land (upon an estate) which is not suitable to this cultivation is usually considered waste. Thus the government and the private proprietor are alike losers, in possessing an amount of unprofitable soil.

Now surely it is the common sense object in the establishment of a botanical garden, to discover for each description of soil a remunerating crop, so that an estate should be cultivated to its uttermost, and the word 'waste' be unknown upon the property.

Under the present system of management this is impossible; the sum allowed per annum is but just sufficient to keep the gardens in proper condition, and the abilities of the botanist in charge are sacrificed. Many a valuable plant now lies screened in the shades of remote jungles, which the enterprising botanist would bring to light, were he enabled by government to make periodical journeys through the interior. These journeys should form a part of his duties; his botanical specimens should be his game, and they should be pursued with the ardour of the chase itself, and subsequently transferred to the gardens, and their real merits discovered by experiments.

But what can be expected from an apathetic system of government? Dyes, fibres, gums may abound in the forests, metals and even gold may be concealed beneath our feet; but the governor does not consider it a part of his duty to prosecute the search, or even to render facilities to those of a more industrious temperament. What can better exemplify the case than the recent discovery of gold at Newera Ellia?

Here was the plain fact, that gold was found in small specks, not in one spot, but *everywhere* throughout the swamps for miles in the vicinity. At a depth of two or three feet from the surface, this proof was adduced of its presence; but the governor positively refused to assist the discoverers, ('diggers,' who were poor sailors visiting Ceylon), although they merely asked for subsistence until they should be able to reach a greater depth. This may appear too absurd to be correct, but it is nevertheless true.

At the time that I commenced these sketches of Ceylon, the gold was just discovered, and I touched but lightly upon it, in the expectation that a few months of labour, aided by government support, would have established its presence in remunerating quantities. The swampy nature of the soil rendered the digging impossible, without the aid of powerful pumps to reduce the water; which filled the shaft so rapidly, that no greater depth could be obtained than 18 feet.

The diggers were absolutely penniless, and but for assistance received from private parties they must have starved. The rainy season was at its height, and torrents fell night and day with little intermission. Still these poor fellows worked early and late, wet and dry, ever sanguine of success, and they at length petitioned the government to give them the means of subsistence for a few months—'subsistence' for two men, and the assistance of a few coolies. This was refused, and the reply stated that the government intended to leave the search for gold to 'private enterprise.' No reward was offered for its discovery as in other colonies, but the governor would leave it to 'private enterprise.' A promising enterprise truly, when every landholder in Ceylon, on referring to his title-deeds, observes the *reservation of all precious metals to the crown.* This is a fair sample of the narrow-minded, selfish policy of a government which, in endeavouring to save a little, loses all; a miserable tampering with the public, in attempting to make a cat's paw of private enterprise.

How has this ended? The diggers left the island in disgust. If the gold is there in quantity, there it remains to the present time, unsought for. The subject of gold is so generally interesting, and in this case of such importance to the colony, that, believing as I do that it does exist in large quantities, I must claim the reader's patience in going into this subject rather fully.

Let us take the matter as it stands.

I mentioned at an early part of these pages, that gold was first discovered in Ceylon by the diggers in the bed of a stream near Kandy; that they subsequently came to Newera Ellia, and there discovered gold likewise.

It must be remembered that the main features of the country at Newera Ellia and the vicinity are broad flats or swampy plains, surrounded by hills and mountains: the former covered with rank grass and intersected by small streams, the latter covered with dense forest. The soil abounds with rocks of gneiss and quartz; some of the latter rose-colour, some pure white. The gold has hitherto been found in the plains only. These plains extend over some thirty miles of country, divided into numerous patches by intervening jungles.

The surface soil is of a peaty nature, perfectly black, soapy when wet, and as light as soot when dry; worthless for cultivation. This top soil is about eighteen inches thick, and appears to have been the remains of vegetable matter washed down from the surrounding hills and forests.

This swampy black soil rests upon a thin stratum of brownish clay, not more than a few inches thick, which, forming a second layer, rests in its turn upon a snow-white rounded quartz gravel intermixed with white pipeclay.

This contains gold, every shovelful of earth producing, when washed, one or more specks of the precious metal.

The stratum of rounded quartz is about two feet thick, and is succeeded by pipeclay, intermixed with quartz gravel, to a depth of eighteen feet. Here another stratum of quartz gravel is met with perfectly water-worn, and rounded to the size of a twelve-pound shot.

In this stratum the gold was of increased size, and some pieces were discovered as large as small grains of rice; but no greater depth was attained, viz., eighteen feet from the surface.

No other holes were sunk below ten feet, on account of the influx of water, but similar shafts were made in various places, and all with equal success.

From the commencement of the first stratum of quartz throughout to the greatest depth attained, gold was present.

Upon washing away the clay and gravel, a great number of gems of small value remained (chiefly sapphire, ruby, jacinth, and green tourmaline). These being picked out, there remained a jet black fine sand, resembling gunpowder. This was of great specific gravity, and when carefully washed, discovered the gold, some in grains, some in mere specks, and some like fine golden flour.

At this interesting stage the search has been given up; although the cheering sight of gold can be obtained in nearly every pan of earth, at such trifling depths, and literally in every direction, the prospect is abandoned. The government leave it to private enterprise; but the enterprising public have no faith in the government.

Without being over sanguine, or, on the other side, closing our ears with asinine stubbornness, let us take an impartial view of the facts determined, and draw rational conclusions.

It appears that from a depth of two and a half feet from the surface to the greatest depth as yet attained, (eighteen feet), gold exists throughout.

It also appears that this is not only the case in one particular spot, but all over this part of the country, and that this fact is undeniable; and, nevertheless, the government did not believe in the *existence* of gold in Ceylon until these diggers discovered it; and when discovered, they gave the diggers neither reward nor encouragement, but they actually met the discovery by a published *prohibition* against the search; they then latterly withdrew the prohibition, and left it to private enterprise, but neglected the unfortunate diggers. In this manner is the colony mismanaged, in this manner is all public spirit damped, all private enterprise checked, and all men who have anything to venture disgusted.

The liberality of a government must be boundless where the actual subsistence for a few months is refused to the discoverers of gold in a country where, hitherto, its presence had been denied!

It would be speculative to anticipate the vast changes that an extended discovery would effect in such a colony as Ceylon. We have before us the two pictures of California and Australia, which have been changed as though by the magician's wand within the last few years. It becomes us now simply to consider the probability of the gold being in such quantities in Ceylon as to effect such changes. We have at present these simple data,—that in a soft swampy soil gold has been found close to the surface in small specks, gradually increasing in size and quantity as a greater depth has been attained.

From the fact that gold will naturally lie deep, from its specific gravity, it is astonishing that any vestige of such a metal should be discovered in such spongy soil so close to the surface. Still more astonishing that it should be so generally disseminated throughout the locality. This would naturally be accepted as a proof that the earth is rich in gold. But the question will then arise—Where is the gold? The quantities found are a mere nothing, it is only dust: we want 'nuggets.'

The latter is positively the expression that I myself frequently heard in Ceylon,—'We want nuggets.'

Who does not want nuggets? But people speak of 'nuggets' as they would of pebbles, forgetting that the very principle which keeps the light dust at the surface, has forced the heavier gold to a greater depth, and that, far from complaining of the lack of nuggets when digging has hardly commenced, they should gaze with wonder at the bare existence of the gold in its present form and situation.

The diggings at Ballarat are from 100 to 160 feet deep in hard ground, and yet people in Ceylon expect to find heavy gold in mere mud, close to the surface. The idea is preposterous, and I conceive it only reasonable to infer from the present appearances, that gold does exist in large quantities in Ceylon. But as it is reasonable to suppose such to be the case, so it is unreasonable to suppose that private individuals will invest capital in so uncertain a speculation as mining, without facilities from the Government, and in the very face of the clause in their own title-deeds 'that all precious metals belong to the crown.'

This is the anomalous position of the gold in Ceylon under the governorship of Sir G. Anderson.

Nevertheless it becomes a question whether we should blame the man or the system ; but the question arises in this case, as with everything else in which Government is concerned, 'Where is the fault?' 'echo answers "Where?"' But the public are not satisfied with echoes, and in this matter of fact age people look to those who fill ostensible posts and draw *bonâ fide* salaries ; and if these men hold the appointments, no matter under what system, they become the deserved objects of either praise or censure.

Thus it may appear too much to say that Sir G.

Anderson is liable for the mismanagement of the colony *in toto*—for the total neglect of the public roads. It may appear too much to say, when you came to the colony you found the roads in good order: they are now impassable; communication is actually cut off from places of importance. This is your fault, these are the fruits of your imbecility; your answer to our petitions for repairs was, 'There is no money;' and yet at the close of the year you proclaimed and boasted of a saving of 27,000*l.* in the treasury! This seems a fearful contradiction; and the whole public received it as such. The governor may complain that the public expect too much; the public may complain that the governor does too little.

Upon these satisfactory terms, governors and their dependants bow each other out, the colony being a kind of opera stall, a reserved seat for the governor during the performance of five acts (as we will term his five years of office); and the fifth act, as usual in tragedies, exposes the whole plot of the preceding four, and winds up with the customary disasters.

Now the question is, how long this age of misrule will last.

Every one complains, and still every one endures. Each man has a grievance, but no man has a remedy. Still the absurdity of our colonial appointments is such, that if steps were purposely taken to ensure the destruction of the colonies, they could not have been more certain.

We will commence with a new governor dealt out to a colony. We will simply call him a governor, not troubling ourselves with his qualifications, as of course they have not been considered at the Colonial Office. He may be an upright, clear-headed, indefatigable man, in the prime of life; or he may be old, crotchety, pigheaded, and mentally and physically incapable. He may be either; it does not much matter, as he can only remain for five years, at which time his term expires.

We will suppose that the crotchety old gentleman arrives first. The public will be in a delightful perplexity as to what the new governor will do; whether he will carry out the views of his predecessor, or whether he will upset everything that has been done in the past five years,—all is uncertainty. The only thing known positively is, that, good or bad, he will pocket seven thousand a year!

His term of government will be chequered by many disappointments to the public, and, if he has any feeling at all, by many heartburnings to himself. Physically incapable of much exertion, he will be unable to travel over so wild a country as Ceylon. A good governor in a little island may be a very bad governor in a large island, as a good cab-driver might make a bad four-in-hand man thus our old governor would have no practical knowledge of the country, but would depend upon prejudiced accounts for his information. Thus he would never arrive at any correct conclusion ; he would receive all testimony with doubt, considering that each had some personal motive in offering advice, and one tongue would thus nullify the other until he would at length come to the conclusion of David in his haste, 'that all men are liars.' Incredulity would enable him to pass the rest of his term without any active blunders, and he might vary the passive monotony of his existence by a system of contradiction to all advice gratis. A little careful pruning of expenses during the last two years of his term might give a semblance of increase of revenue over expenditure, to gain a smile from the Colonial Office. On his return, the colony would be left with neglected roads, consequent upon the withdrawal of the necessary funds.

This incubus at length removed from the colony, might be succeeded by a governor of the first class.

He arrives ; finds everything radically wrong ; the great arteries of the country (the roads) in disorder ; a large outlay required to repair them. Thus his first necessary act begins by an *outlay* at a time when all outlay is considered equivalent to crime. This gains him a frown from the Colonial Office. Conscious of right, however, he steers his own course ; he travels over the whole country, views its features personally, judges of its requirements and resources, gathers advice from capable persons, forms his own opinion, and acts accordingly.

We will allow two years of indefatigable research to have passed over our model governor; by that time, and not before, he may have become thoroughly conversant with the colony in all its bearings. He has comprehended the vast natural capabilities, he has formed his plans methodically for the improvement of the country; not by any rash and speculative outlay, but, step by step, he hopes to secure the advancement of his schemes.

This is a work of time; he has much to do. The country is in an uncivilized state; he sees the vestiges of past grandeur around him, and his views embrace a wide field for the renewal of former prosperity. Tanks must be repaired, canals re-opened, emigration of Chinese and Malabars encouraged, forests and jungles cleared, barren land brought into fertility. The work of years is before him, but the expiration of his term draws near. Time is precious; but nevertheless he must refer his schemes to the Colonial Office. What do they know of Ceylon?—to them his plans seem visionary; at all events, they will require an *outlay*. A correspondence ensues,—that hateful correspondence,—this insures delay. Time flies, the expiration of his term draws near. Even his sanguine temperament has ceased to hope, his plans are not yet commenced, to work out which would require years; he never could see them realized, and his successor might neglect them, and lay the onus of the failure upon him, the originator, or claim the merit of their success.

So much for a five years' term of governorship, the absurdity of which is superlative. It is so entirely contrary to the system of management in private affairs, that it is difficult to imagine the cause that could have given rise to such a regulation. In matters great or small, the *capability* of the manager is the first consideration; and if this be proved, the value of the man is enhanced accordingly; no employer would lose him.

But in colonial governments the system is directly opposite, for no sooner does the governor become competent, than he is withdrawn, and transferred to another sphere. Thus every colony is like a farm held on a short lease, which effectually debars it from improvement, as the same feeling which actuates the individual in neglecting the future, because he will not personally enjoy the fruits of his labour, must in some degree fetter the enterprise of a five years' governor. He is little better than the Lord Mayor, who flutters proudly for a year, and then drops his borrowed feathers in his moulting season.

Why should not governors serve an apprenticeship as *colonial secretaries* to the colonies they are destined for, if five years is still to be the limited term of their office? This would insure a knowledge of the colony at a secretary's salary, and render them fit for both the office and salary of governor when called upon; whereas, by the present system, they at once receive a governor's salary before they understand their duties.

In casually regarding the present picture of Ceylon, it is hard to say which point has been most neglected; but a short residence in the island will afford a fair sample of government inactivity in the want of education among the people.

Upon this subject more might be said than lies in my province to dwell upon; nevertheless, after fifty years' possession of the Kandian districts, this want is so glaring that I cannot withhold a few remarks upon the subject, as I consider the ignorant state of the native population a complete check to the advancement of the colony.

In commencing this subject, I must assume that the conquerors of territory are responsible for the moral welfare of the inhabitants; therefore our responsibility increases with our conquests. A mighty onus thus rests upon Great Britain, which few consider when they glory in the boast that 'the sun never sets upon her dominions.'

This thought leads us to a comparison of power between ourselves and other countries, and we trace the small spot upon the world's map which marks our little island, and in every sphere we gaze with wonder at our vast possessions. This is a picture of the present. What will the future be in these days of advancement? It were vain to hazard a conjecture; but we can look back upon the past, and build upon this foundation our future hopes.

When the pomps and luxuries of eastern cities spread throughout Ceylon, and millions of inhabitants fed on her fertility; when the hands of her artists chiselled the figures of her gods from the rude rock; when her vessels, laden with ivory and spices, traded with the West, what were we? A forest-covered country, peopled by a fierce race of savages clad in skins, bowing before Druidical idolatry, paddling along our shores in frames of wicker-work and hide.

The ancient deities of Ceylon are in the same spots, unchanged; the stones of the Druids stand unmoved in Britain; but what has become of the nations? Those of the East have faded away, and their strength has perished. Their ships are crumbled; the rude canoe glides over their waves; the spices grow wild in their jungles; and, unshorn and unclad, the inhabitants wander on the face of the land.

Is it '*chance*' that has worked this change? Where is the forest-covered country and its savage race, its skin-clad warriors and their frail coracles.

There, where the forest stood, from north to south

and from east to west, spreads a wide field of rich fertility. There, on those rivers where the basket-boats once sailed, rise the taunt spars of England's navy. Where the rude hamlet rested on its banks in rural solitude, the never weary din of commerce rolls through the city of the world. The locomotive rushes like a thunder-roll upon the rail; the steamer ploughs against the adverse wind; and, rapid as lightning, the telegraph cripples time. The once savage land is the nucleus of art and civilization. The nation that from time to time was oppressed, invaded, conquered, but never subjected, still pressed against the weight of adversity, and as age after age rolled on, and mightier woes and civil strife gathered upon her, still the germ of her destiny, as it expanded, threw off her load, until she at length became a nation envied and feared.

It was then that the powers of the world were armed against her, and all Europe joined to tear the laurels from her crown, and fleets and armies thronged from all points against the devoted land; and her old enemy, the Gaul, hovered like his own eagle over the expected prey.

The thunder of the cannon shook the world, and blood tinged the waves around the land, and war and tumult shrieked like a tempest over the fair face of Nature; the din of battle smothered all sounds of peace, and years passed on, and thicker grew the gloom. It was then the innate might of the old Briton roused itself to action, and strained those giant nerves which brought us victory. The struggle was past, and as the smoke of battle cleared from the surface of the world, the flag of England waved in triumph on the ocean; her fleets sat swanlike on the waves, her standard floated on the strongholds of the universe, and far and wide stretched the vast boundaries of her conquests.

Again I ask, is this the effect of 'chance?' or is it the mighty will of Omnipotence, which, choosing His instruments from the humbler ranks, has snatched England from her lowly state, and has exalted her to be the apostle of Christianity throughout the world?

Here lies her responsibility. The conquered nations are in her hands, they have been subject to her for half a century; but they know neither her language nor her religion.

How many millions of human beings of all creeds and colours does she control? Are they or their descendants to embrace our faith?—that is, are we the divine instrument for accomplishing the vast change that we expect by the universal acknowledgment of Christianity, or are we—I pause before the suggestion—are we but another of those examples of human insignificance, that as from dust we rose, so to dust we shall return?—shall we be but another in the long list of nations whose ruins rest upon the solitudes of nature, like warnings to the proud cities which triumph in their present strength? Shall the traveller in future ages place his foot upon the barren sod, and exclaim, 'Here stood their great city!'

The inhabitants of Nineveh would have scoffed at such a supposition. And yet they fell; and yet the desert sand shrouded their cities as the autumn leaves fall on the faded flowers of summer.

To a fatalist it can matter but little whether a nation fulfils its duty, or whether, by neglecting it, punishment should be drawn down upon its head. According to his theory, neither good nor evil acts would alter a predestined course of events. There are fatalist governments which, absorbed in the fancied prosperity of the present, legislate for temporal advantages only.

Thus we see the most inconsistent and anomalous conditions imposed in treaties with conquered powers; we see, for instance, in Ceylon a protection granted to the Buddhist religion while flocks of missionaries are sent out to convert the heathen. We even stretch the point so far as to place a British sentinel on guard at the Buddhist temple in Kandy, as though in mockery of our Protestant church a hundred paces distant.

At the same time that we acknowledge and protect the Buddhist religion, we pray that Christianity shall spread through the whole world, and we appoint bishops to our colonies. To our disgrace we neglect the education of the inhabitants, who, by conquest, have become our subjects.

When I say we neglect the education, I do not mean to infer that there are no government schools, but that the education of the people, instead of being one of the most important objects of the government, is considered of so little moment that it is tantamount to neglected.

There are various opinions as to the amount of learning which constitutes education, and at some of the government schools the native children are crammed with useless nonsense which, by raising them above their natural position, totally unfits them for their proper sphere. This is what the government calls education; and the same time and expense thus employed in teaching a few, would educate triple the number in plain English. It is too absurd to hear the arguments in favour of mathematics, geography, &c. &c., for the native children, when a large proportion of our own population in Great Britain can neither read nor write.

The great desideratum in native education is a thorough knowledge of the English tongue, which naturally is the first stone for any superstructure of more extended learning. This brings them within the reach of the missionary, not only in conversation, but it enables them to benefit by books, which are otherwise useless. It lessens the distance between the white man and the black, and an acquaintance with the English language engenders a taste for English habits. The first dawn of civilization commences with a knowledge of our language. The native immediately adopts some English customs and ideas, and drops a corresponding number of his own. In fact he is a soil fit to work upon, instead of being a barren rock as hitherto, firm in his own ignorance and prejudices.

In the education of the rising native generation lies the hope of ultimate conversion. You may as well try to turn pitch into snow as to eradicate the dark stain of heathenism from the present race. Nothing can be done with them; they must be abandoned, like the barren fig-tree, and the more attention bestowed upon the young shoots.

But unfortunately this is a popular error, and, like all such, one full of prejudice. Abandon the present race!! Methinks I hear the cry from Exeter Hall. But the good people at home have no idea to what an extent they are at present, and always have been, abandoned. Where the children who can be educated with success are neglected at the present day, it may be imagined that the parents have been but little cared for; thus, in advocating their abandonment, it is simply proposing an extra amount of attention to be bestowed upon the next generation.

There are many large districts of Ceylon where no schools of any kind are established. In the Ouva country, which is one of the most populous, I have had applications from the natives, begging me to interest myself in obtaining some arrangement of the kind. Throngs of natives applied, describing the forlorn condition of their district, all being not only anxious to send their children to some place where they could learn free of expense, but offering to pay a weekly stipend in return. 'They are growing up as ignorant as our young buffaloes,' was a remark made by one of the headmen of the villages, and this within twelve miles of Newera Ellia.

Now, leaving out the question of policy in endeavouring to make English the common tongue of a conquered colony, it must be admitted that, simply as a question of duty, it is incumbent upon the government to do all in their power for the moral advancement of the native population. It is known that the knowledge of our language is the first step necessary to this advancement, and nevertheless it is left undone; the population is therefore neglected.

I have already adverted to the useless system in the government schools of forcing a superabundant amount of knowledge into the children's brains, and thereby raising them above their position. A contrasting example of good common sense education has recently been given by the Rev. Mr. Thurston (who is indefatigable in his profession) in the formation of an industrial school at Colombo.

This is precisely the kind of education which is required; and it has already been attended with results most beneficial on its limited scale.

This school is conducted on the principle that the time of every boy shall not only be of service to himself, but shall likewise tend to the support of the establishment. The children are accordingly instructed in such pursuits as shall be the means of earning a livelihood in future years; some are taught a trade, others are employed in the cultivation of gardens, and subsequently in the preparation of a variety of produce. Among others, the preparation of tapioca from the root of the manioc has recently been attended with great success. In fact they are engaged during their leisure hours in a variety of experiments, all of which tend to an industrial turn of mind, benefiting not only the lad and the school, but also the government, by preparing for the future men who will be serviceable and industrious in their station.

Here is a lesson for the government which, if carried out on an extensive scale, would work a greater change in the colony within the next twenty years than all the preaching of the last fifty.

Throughout Ceylon in every district there should be established one school upon this principle for every hundred boys, and a small tract of land granted to each. One should be attached to the Botanical Gardens at Peredenia, and instruction should be given to enable every school to form its own experiments in agriculture. By this means, in the course of a few years we should secure an educated and useful population, in lieu of the present indolent and degraded race;—an improved system of cultivation, new products, a variety of trades, and in fact a test of the capabilities of the country would be ensured, without risk to the government and to the ultimate prosperity of the colony. Heathenism could not exist in such a state of affairs; it would die out. Minds exalted by education upon such a system would look with ridicule upon the vestiges of former idolatry, and the rocky idols would remain without a worshipper, while a new generation flocked to the Christian altar.

This is no visionary prospect. It has been satis factorily proved that the road to conversion to Christianity is through knowledge, and this once attained, heathenism shrinks into the background. This knowledge can only be gained by the young when such schools are established as I have described.

Our missionaries should, therefore, devote their attention to this object, and cease to war against the impossibility of adult conversion. If one third of the enormous sums hitherto expended with little or no results upon missionary labour had been employed in the establishments as proposed, our colonies would now possess a Christian population. But are our missionaries capable? Here commences another question, which again involves others in their turn, all of which, when answered, thoroughly explain the stationary if not retrograde position of the Protestant Church among the heathen.

What is the reader's conceived opinion of the duties and labours of a missionary in a heathen land? Does he or does he not imagine, as he pays his subscription towards this object, that the devoted missionary quits his native shores like one of the apostles of old, to fight the good fight?—that he leaves all to follow 'Him'?—and that he wanders forth in his zeal to propagate the gospel, penetrating into remote parts, preaching to the natives, attending on the sick, living a life of hardship and self-denial?

It is a considerable drawback to this belief in missionary labour, when it is known that the missionaries are not educated for the particular colonies to which they are sent; upon arrival, they are totally ignorant of the language of the natives;—accordingly they are perfectly useless for the purpose of 'propagating the gospel among the heathen.' Their mission should be that of instructing the young, and for this purpose they should first be instructed themselves.

I do not wish to throw a shade upon the efforts of missionary labour; I have no doubt that they use great exertions privately, which the public on the spot do not observe; but taking this for granted as the case, the total want of success in the result becomes the more deplorable.

I have also no doubt that the missionaries penetrate into the most remote parts of Ceylon, and preach the gospel. For many years I have traversed the wildernesses of Ceylon at all hours and at all seasons. I have met many strange things during my forest journeys, but I never recollect a missionary. The Bishop of Colombo is the only man I know who travels *out of the high road* for this purpose; and he, both in this and many other respects, offers an example which few appear to follow.

Nevertheless, although Protestant missionaries are so rare in the jungles of the interior, and, if ever there, no vestige ever remains of such a visit, still, in spots where it might be least expected, may be seen the humble mud hut, surmounted by a cross, the certain trace of some persevering priest of the Roman faith. These men display an untiring zeal, and no point is too remote for their good offices. Probably they are not so comfortable in their quarters in the towns as the Protestant missionaries, and thus they have less hesitation in leaving home.

The few converts that have been made are chiefly

Roman Catholics, as, among the confusion arising from our multitudinous sects and schisms, the native is naturally bewildered. What with High Church, Low Church, Baptists, Wesleyans, Presbyterians, &c. &c. &c., the ignorant native is perfectly aghast at the variety of choice.

With the members of our Church in such a dislocated state, progression cannot be expected by simple attempts at conversion; even were the natives willing to embrace the true faith, they would have great difficulty in finding it amidst the crowd of adverse opinions. Without probing more deeply into these social wounds, I must take leave of the missionary labours in Ceylon, trusting that ere long the eyes of the government will be fixed upon the true light to guide the prosperity of the island, by framing an ordinance for the liberal education of the people.

CHAPTER XII.

The Pearl Fishery—Desolation of the Coast—Harbour of Trincomalie —Fatal Attack by a Shark—Ferocious Crocodiles—Salt Monopoly —Salt Lakes—Method of Collection—Neglect of Ceylon Hides—Fish and Fishing—Primitive Tackle—Oyster and Penknives—A Night Bivouac for a Novice—No Dinner, but a Good Fire—Wild Yams and Consequences—The Elephants' Duel—A Hunting Hermitage—'Bluebeard's' last Hunt—The Leopard—'Bluebeard's' Death —Leopard Shot.

WHILE fresh from the subject of government mismanagement, let us turn our eyes in the direction of one of those natural resources of wealth for which Ceylon has ever been renowned, the 'Pearl Fishery.' This was the goose which laid the golden egg, and Sir W. Horton, when governor of Ceylon, was the man who killed the goose.

Here was another fatal instance of the effects of a five years' term of governorship.

It was the last year of his term, and he wished to prove to the Colonial Office that 'his talent' had not been laid up in a napkin, but that he had left the colony with an excess of income over expenditure. To obtain this income, he fished up all the oysters, and ruined the fishery in consequence; from that day to the present time it has been unproductive.

This is a serious loss of income to the colony, and great doubts are entertained as to the probability of the oyster banks ever recovering their fertility.

Nothing can exceed the desolation of the coast in the neighbourhood of the pearl-banks. For many miles the shore is a barren waste of low sandy ground, covered for the most part with scrubby thorny jungle, diversified by glades of stunted herbage. Not a hill is to be seen as far as the eye can reach. The tracks of all kind of game abound on the sandy path, with occasionally those of a naked foot; but seldom does a shoe imprint its civilised mark upon these lonely shores.

The whole of this district is one of the best in Ceylon for deer-shooting, which is a proof of its want of inhabitants. This has always been the case, even in the prosperous days of the pearl fishery. So utterly worthless is the soil, that it remains in a state of nature, and its distance from Colombo (150 miles) keeps it in entire seclusion.

It is difficult to conceive that any source of wealth should exist in such a locality. When standing on the parched sand with the burning sun shining in pitiless might upon all around, the meagre grass burnt to a mere straw, the tangled bushes denuded of all verdure save a few shrivelled leaves, the very insects seeking shelter from the rays; there is not a tree to throw a shadow, but a dancing haze of molten air hovers upon the ground, and the sea like a mirror reflects a glare, which makes the heat intolerable. And yet beneath the wave on this wild and desolate spot, glitter those baubles that minister to man's vanity; and, as though in mockery of such pursuits, I have seen the bleached skulls of bygone pearl-seekers lying upon the sand, where they have rotted in view of the coveted treasures.

There is an appearance of ruin connected with everything in the neighbourhood. Even in the good old times, this coast was simply visited during the period of fishing. Temporary huts were erected for thousands of natives, who thronged to Ceylon from all parts of the east for the fascinating speculations of the pearl fishery. No sooner was the season over, than every individual disappeared; the wind swept away the huts of sticks and leaves; and the only vestiges remaining of the recent population, were the government stores and house at Arripo, like the bones of the carcass after the vultures had feasted and departed. All relapsed at once into its usual state of desolation.

The government house was at one time a building of some little pretension, and from its style it bore the name of the 'Doric.' It is now, like everything else, in a state of lamentable decay. The honeycombed eighteen-pounder, which was the signal gun of former years, is choked with drifting sand, and the air of misery about the place is indescribable.

Now that the diving helmet has rendered subaqueous discoveries so easy, I am surprised that a government survey has not been made of the whole north-west coast of Ceylon. It seems reasonable to suppose that the pearl oyster should inhabit depths which excluded the simple diver of former days, and that our modern improvements might discover treasures in the neighbourhood of the old pearl beds of which we are now in ignorance. The best divers, without doubt, could never much exceed a minute in submersion. I believe the accounts of their performances generally to have been much exaggerated. At all events, those of the present day do not profess to remain under water much more than a minute.

The accounts of Ceylon pearl fisheries are so common in every child's book that I do not attempt to describe the system in detail. Like all lotteries, there are few prizes to the proportion of blanks.

The whole of this coast is rich in the *biche de mer*, more commonly called the sea-slug. This is a disgusting species of mollusca, which grows to a large size, being commonly about a foot in length and three or four inches in diameter. The capture and preparation of these creatures is confined exclusively to the Chinese, who dry them in the sun until they shrink to the size of a large sausage, and harden to the consistence of horn; they are then exported to China for making soups. No doubt they are more strengthening than agreeable; but I imagine that our common garden slug would be an excellent substitute to any one desirous of an experiment, as it exactly resembles its nautical representative in colour and appearance. Trincomalie is the great depôt for this trade, which is carried on to a large extent, together with that of sharks' fins, the latter being used by the Chinese for the same purpose as the *biche de mer*. Trincomalie affords many facilities fcr this trade, as the slugs are found in large quantities on the spot; and the finest harbour of the east is alive with sharks. Few things surpass the tropical beauty of this harbour; lying completely land-locked, it forms a glassy lake surrounded by hills covered with the waving foliage of cocoa-nut trees and palms of great variety. The white bungalows, with their red-tiled roofs, are dotted about along the shore, and two or three men-of-war are usually resting at their ease in this calm retreat. So deep is the water, that the harbour forms a perfect dock; the largest vessel can lie so close to the shore that her yards overhang it; this enables stores and cargo to be shipped with great facility.

The fort stands upon a projecting point of land, which rises to about seventy feet above the level of the *galle face* (the race-course), which faces it. Thus it commands the land approach across the flat plain on one side, and the sea on the other. This same fort is one of the hottest corners of Ceylon, and forms a desirable residence for those who delight in a temperature of from 90° to 104° in the shade. Bathing is the great enjoyment; but the pleasure in such a country is destroyed by the knowledge that sharks are looking out for you in the sea, and crocodiles in the rivers and tanks; thus a man is nothing more than an exciting live-bait when he once quits terra firma. Accidents necessarily must happen; but they are not so frequent as persons would suppose from the great number of carnivorous monsters that exist. Still I am convinced that a white man would run greater risk than a black; he is a more enticing bait, being bright and easily distinguished in the water. Thus in places where the natives are in the habit of bathing with impunity, it would be most dangerous for a white man to enter.

There was a lamentable instance of this some few years ago at Trincomalie. In a sheltered nook among the rocks below the fort, where the natives were always in the habit of bathing, a party of soldiers of the regiment then in garrison went down one sultry afternoon for a swim. It was a lovely spot for bathing, the water was blue, clear, and calm, as the reef that stretched far out to sea served as a breakwater to the heavy surf, and preserved the inner water as smooth as a lake. Here were a fine lot of English soldiers stripped to bathe; and although the ruddy hue of British health had long since departed in the languid climate of the East, nevertheless their spirits were as high as those of Englishmen usually are, no matter where or under what circumstances. However, one after the other took a run, and then a 'header' off the rocks into the deep blue water beneath. In the long line of bathers was a fine lad of fifteen, the son of one of the sergeants of the regiment; with the emulation of his age he ranked himself among the men, and on arriving at the edge he plunged head-foremost into the water and disappeared. A crowd of men were on the margin watching the bathing; the boy rose to the surface within a few feet of them, but as he shook the water from his hair, a cloudy shadow seemed to rise from the deep beneath him, and in another moment the distinct outline of a large shark was visible as his white belly flashed below. At the same instant there was a scream of despair; the water was crimsoned, and a bloody foam rose to the surface;—the boy was gone! Before the first shock of horror was well felt by those around, a gallant fellow of the same regiment shot head-first into the bloody spot, and presently re-appeared from his devoted plunge, bearing in his arms *one half* of the poor boy. The body was bitten off at the waist, and the lower portion was the prize of the ground shark.

For several days the soldiers were busily employed in fishing for this monster, while the distracted mother sat in the burning sun, watching in heart-broken eagerness, in the hope of recovering some trace of her lost son. This, however, was not to be; the shark was never seen again.

There is as much difference in the characters of sharks as among other animals or men. Some are timid and sluggish, moving as though too lazy to seek their food; and there is little doubt that such would seldom attack man. Others, on the contrary, dash through the water as a pike would seize its prey, and refuse or fear nothing. There is likewise a striking distinction in the habits of crocodiles; those which inhabit rivers are far more destructive and fearless than the inhabitants of the tanks. The natives hold the former in great terror, while with the latter they run risks which are sometimes fatal. I recollect a large river in the south-east of Ceylon, which so abounded with ferocious crocodiles that the natives would not enter the water in depths above the knees, and even this they objected to, unless necessity compelled them to cross the river. I was encamped on the banks for some little time, and the natives took the trouble to warn me especially not to enter; as a proof of the danger, they showed me a spot where three men had been devoured in the course of one year; all three of whom are supposed to have ministered to the appetite of the same crocodile.

Few reptiles are more disgusting in appearance than these brutes; but, nevertheless, their utility counterbalances their bad qualities, as they cleanse the water from all impurities. So numerous are they, that their heads may be seen in fives and tens together, floating at the top of the water like rough corks; and at about five P.M. they bask on the shore close to the margin of the water, ready to scuttle in on the shortest notice. They are then particularly on the alert, and it is a most difficult thing to stalk them, so as to get near enough to make a certain shot. This is not bad amusement, when no other sport can be had. Around the margin of a lake, in a large plain far in the distance, may be seen a distinct line upon the short grass like the fallen trunk of a tree. As there are no trees at hand, this must necessarily be a crocodile. Seldom can the best hand at stalking then get within eighty yards of him, before he lifts his scaly head, and, listening for a second, plunges off the bank.

I have been contradicted for stating that a ball will penetrate their scales. It is absurd, however, to hold the opinion that the scales will turn a ball, that is to say *stop* the ball (as we know that a common twig will of course *turn* it from its direction, if struck obliquely).

The scales of a crocodile are formed of bone exquisitely jointed together like the sections of a skull. These are covered externally with a horny skin, forming no doubt an excellent defensive armour, about an inch in thickness; but the idea of their being impenetrable to a ball, if struck fair, is a great fallacy. People may, perhaps, complain because a pea rifle with a mere pinch of powder may be inefficient; but a common No. 16 fowling-piece, with two drachms of powder, will penetrate any crocodile that was ever hatched.

Among the most harmless kinds are those which inhabit the salt lakes in the south of Ceylon. I have never heard of an accident in these places, although hundreds of persons are employed annually in collecting salt from the bottom.

These natural reservoirs are of great extent, some of them being many miles in circumference. The most productive are about four miles round, and yield a supply in August during the height of the dry season.

Salt in Ceylon is a government monopoly, and it has hitherto been the narrow policy of the government to keep up an immense price upon this necessary of life, when the resources of the country could produce any amount required for the island consumption.

These are now all but neglected, and the government simply gather the salt as the wild pig feeds upon the fruit which falls from the tree in its season.

The government price of salt is now about three shillings per bushel. This is very impure, being mixed with much dirt and sand. The revenue obtained by the salt monopoly is about 40,000*l.* per annum, two-thirds of which is an unfair burden upon the population, as the price, according to the supply obtainable, should never exceed one shilling per bushel.

Let us consider the capabilities of the locality from which it is collected.

The lakes are some five or six in number, situated within half a mile of the sea, separated only by a high bank of drift sand, covered for the most part with the low jungle which clothes the surrounding country. Flat plains of a sandy nature form the margins. The little town of Hambantotte, with a good harbour for small craft, is about twenty miles distant, to which there is a cart road.

The water of these lakes is perfect brine. In the dry season the evaporation of course increases the strength until the water can no longer retain the amount of salt in solution. It therefore precipitates and crystallizes at the bottom in various degrees of thickness according to the strength of the brine.

Thus, as the water recedes from the banks by evaporation and the lake decreases in size, it leaves a beach, not of shingles, but of pure salt in crystallized cubes to the depth of several inches; sometimes exceeding half a foot. The bottom of the lake is equally coated with this thick deposit.

These lakes are protected by watchers, who live upon the margin throughout the year. Were it not for this precaution, immense quantities of salt would be stolen. In the month of August the weather is generally most favourable for the collection, at which time, the assistant agent for the district usually gives a few days' superintendence.

The salt upon the shore being first collected, the natives wade into the lake and gather the deposit from the bottom, which they bring to the shore in baskets; it is then made up into vast piles, which are subsequently thatched over with cajans (the plaited leaf of the cocoa-nut). In this state it remains until an opportunity offers for carting it to the government salt-stores.

This must strike the reader as being a rude method of collecting what nature so liberally produces. The waste is necessarily enormous, as the natives cannot gather the salt at a greater depth than three feet; hence the greater proportion of the annual produce of the lake remains ungathered. The supply at present afforded might be tripled with very little trouble or expense.

If a stick is inserted in the mud so that one end

stands above water, the salt crystallizes upon it in a large lump of several pounds' weight. This is of a better quality than that which is gathered from the bottom, being free from sand or other impurities. Innumerable samples of this may be seen upon the stakes which the natives have stuck in the bottom to mark the line of their day's work.

Were the government anxious to increase the produce of these natural reservoirs, nothing could be more simple than to plant the whole lake with rows of stakes. The wood is on the spot, and the rate of labour sixpence a day per man; thus it might be accomplished for a comparatively small amount.

This would not only increase the produce to an immense degree, but it would also improve the purity of the collection, and would render facilities for gathering the crop by means of boats, and thus obviate the necessity of entering the water; at present the suffering caused by the latter process is a great drawback to the supply of labour. So powerful is the brine, that the legs and feet become excoriated after two or three days' employment, and the natives have a great aversion to the occupation.

Nothing could be easier than gathering the crop by the method proposed. Boats would paddle along between the rows of stakes, while each stick would be pulled up, and the salt disengaged by a single blow:

the stick would then be replaced in its position until the following season.

Nevertheless, although so many specimens exist of this accumulation, the method which was adopted by the savage is still followed by the *soi-disant* civilized man.

In former days, when millions occupied Ceylon, the demand for salt must doubtless have been in proportion, and the lakes which are now so neglected must have been taxed to their utmost resources. There can be little doubt that the barbarians of those times had some more civilized method of increasing the production than the enlightened race of the present day.

The productive salt lakes are confined entirely to the south of Ceylon. Lakes and estuaries of sea-water abound all round the island; but these are only commonly salt, and do not yield. The north and the east coast are therefore supplied by artificial salt-pans. These are simple enclosed levels on the beach, into which the sea-water is admitted, and then allowed to evaporate by the heat of the sun. The salt, of course, remains at the bottom. More water is then admitted, and again evaporated; and this process continues until the thickness of the salt at the bottom allows of its being collected.

This simple plan might be adopted with great success with the powerful brine of the salt lakes, which might be pumped from its present lower level into dry reservoirs for evaporation.

The policy of the government, however, does not tend to the increase of any production. It is preferred to keep up the high rate of salt by a limited supply which meets with immediate demand, rather than to increase the supply for the public benefit at a reduced rate. This is a mistaken mode of reasoning. At the present high price, the consumption of salt is extremely small, as its use is restricted to absolute necessaries. On the other hand, were the supply increased, at one half the present rate, the consumption would augment in a far greater proportion, as salt would then be used for a variety of purposes which at the present cost are impossible,—viz., for the purpose of cattle-feeding, manures, &c. &c. In addition to this, it would vastly affect the price of salt fish (the staple article of native consumption); and by the reduction in the cost of this commodity there would be a corresponding extension in the trade.

The hundreds of thousands of hides which are now thrown aside to rot uncared for, would then be preserved and exported, which at the present rate of salt is impossible. The skins of buffaloes, oxen, deer, swine, all valuable in other parts of the world, in Ceylon are valueless. The wild buffalo is not even skinned when shot; he is simply opened for his marrow-bones, his tail is cut off for soup, his brains taken out for côtelettes, and his tongue salted. The beast himself, hide and all, is left as food for the jackal. The wandering native picks up his horns, which find their way to the English market; but the 'hide,' the only really valuable portion, is neglected.

Within a short distance of the salt lakes, buffaloes, boar, and in fact all kind of animals abound; and I have no doubt that if it were once proved to the natives that the hides could be made remunerative, they would soon learn the method of preparation.

Some persons have an idea that a native will not take the trouble to do anything that would turn a penny; in this I do not agree. Certainly a native has not sufficient courage for a speculation which involves the risk of loss; but provided he is safe in that respect, he will take unbounded trouble for his own benefit, not valuing his time or labour in pursuit of his object.

I have noticed a great change in the native habits along the southern coast, which exemplifies this, since the steamers have touched regularly at Galle.

Some years ago, elephants, buffaloes, &c., when shot by sportsmen, remained untouched except by the wild beast; but now within 150 miles of Galle every buffalo-horn is collected, and even the elephants' grinders are extracted from the skulls and brought into market.

An elephant's grinder averages seven pounds in weight, and is not worth more than from a penny to three halfpence a pound; nevertheless, they are now brought to Galle in large quantities to be made into knife-handles and sundry ornaments, to tempt the passengers of the various steamers. If the native takes this trouble for so small a recompense, there is every reason to suppose that the hides now wasted, would be brought into market and form a valuable export, were salt at such a rate as would admit of their preparation.

The whole of the southern coast, especially in the neighbourhood of the salt lakes, abounds with fish. These are at present nearly undisturbed; but I have little doubt that a reduction in the price of salt would soon call forth the energies of the Moormen, who would establish fisheries in the immediate neighbourhood. This would be of great importance to the interior of the country, as a road has been made within the last few years direct from this locality to Badulla, distant about eighty miles, and situated in the very heart of the most populous district of Ceylon. This road, which forms a direct line of communication from the port of Hambantotte to Newera Ellia, is now much used for the transport of coffee from the Badulla estates, to which a cheap supply of salt and fish would be a great desideratum.

The native is a clever fellow at fishing. Every

little boy of ten years old along the coast is an adept in throwing the casting-net; and I have often watched with amusement the scientific manner in which some of these little fellows handle a fine fish on a single line; Isaac Walton would have been proud of such pupils.

There is nothing like necessity for sharpening a man's intellect, and the natives of the coast being a class of ichthyophagi, it may be imagined that they excel in all methods of capturing their favourite food.

The sea, rivers, and in fact every pool, teem with fish of excellent quality, from the smallest to the largest kind, not forgetting the most delicious prawns and crabs. Turtle likewise abound, and are to be caught in great numbers in their season.

Notwithstanding the immense amount of fish in the various rivers, there is no idea of fishing as a sport among the European population of Ceylon. This I cannot account for, unless from the fear of fever, which might be caught with more certainty than fish by standing up to the knees in water under a burning sun. Nevertheless, I have indulged in this every now and then, when out on a jungle trip, although I have never started from home with such an intention. Seeing some fine big fellows swimming about in a deep hole is a great temptation, especially when you know they are grey mullet, and the *chef de cuisine* is short of the wherewithal for dinner.

This is not unfrequently the case during a jungle trip; and the tent being pitched in the shade of a noble forest on the steep banks of a broad river, thoughts of fishing naturally intrude themselves.

The rivers in the dry season are so exhausted that a simple bed of broad dry sand remains, while a small stream winds along the bottom merely a few inches deep, now no more than a few feet in width, then rippling over a few opposing rocks; while the natural bed extends its dry sand for many yards on either side. At every bend in the river there is of course a deep hole close to the bank; these holes remain full of water, as the little stream continues to flow through them; and the water in its entrance and exit being too shallow for a large fish, all the finny monsters of the river are compelled to imprison themselves in the depths. Here the crocodiles have fine feeding, as they live in the same place.

With a good rod and tackle there would be capital sport in these places, as some of the fish run ten and twelve pounds weight; but I have never been well provided, and while staring at the coveted fish from the bank, I have had no means of catching them, except by the most primitive methods.

Then I have cut a stick for a rod, and made a line with some hairs from my horse's tail, with a pin for a hook, baited with a shrimp, and the fishing has commenced.

Fish and fruit are the most enjoyable articles of food in a tropical country, and in the former Ceylon is rich. The seir fish is little inferior to salmon ; and were the flesh a similar colour, it might sometimes form a substitute. Soles and whiting remind us of Old England; but a host of bright red, blue, green, yellow, and extraordinary looking creatures in the same net, dispel all ideas of English fishing.

There are oysters in Ceylon; but here, alas! is a sad falling off in the comparison with our well-remembered 'native.' Instead of the neat little shell of the English oyster, the Ceylon species is a shapeless, twisted, knotty, rocky-looking creature, such as a legitimate oyster would be in a fit of the cramp or convulsions. In fact, there is no vestige of the true breed about it, and the want of flavour equals its miserable exterior.

There are few positions more tantalizing to a hungry man than being surrounded by oysters, without a knife. An oyster is an obstinate and perverse wretch that will not accommodate itself to man's appetite, and it requires a forcible attack to vanquish it ; so that every one eaten is an individual murder in which the cold steel has been plunged into its vitals, and the animal finds itself swallowed before it has quite made up its mind that it has been opened. But take away the knife, and see how vain is the attempt to force the stronghold. How utterly useless is the oyster; you may turn it over and over, and look for a weak place, but there is no admittance; you may knock it with a stone, but the knock will be unanswered. How would you open such a creature without a knife?

This was one of the many things that had never occurred to me, until one day, when I found myself with some three or four friends and a few boatmen on a little island, or rather a rock, about a mile from the shore. This rock was rich in the spasmodic kind of oyster, large detached masses of which lay just beneath the water, in lumps of some hundredweight each, which had been formed by the oysters clustering and adhering together. It so happened that our party were unanimous in the love of these creatures, and we accordingly exerted ourselves to roll out of the water a large mass; which, having accomplished, we discovered, to our dismay, that nothing but one penknife was possessed among us. This we knew was a useless weapon against such armour; however, in our endeavours to perform impossibilities, we tickled the oyster and broke the knife. After gazing for some time in blank despair at our useless prize, a bright thought struck one of the party, and drawing his ramrod, he began to screw it into the weakest part of an oyster; this, however, was proof, and the ramrod broke.

Stupid enough it may appear, but it was full a quarter of an hour before any of us thought of a successful plan of attack. I noticed a lot of drift timber scattered upon the island, and then the right idea was hit. We gathered the wood which was bleached and dry, and we piled it a few feet to windward of the mass of oysters. Striking a light with a cap and some powder, we lit the pile. It blazed, and the wind blew the heat strong upon the oysters which accordingly began to squeak and hiss, until one by one they gave up the ghost, and, opening their shells, exposed their delightfully roasted bodies, which were eaten forthwith.

How very absurd and uninteresting this is! but nevertheless it is one of those trifling incidents which sharpen the imagination when you depend upon your own resources.

It is astonishing how perfectly helpless some people are, if taken from the artificial existence of every-day life and thrown entirely upon themselves. One man would be in superlative misery, while another would enjoy the responsibility, and delight in the fertility of his own invention in accommodating himself to circumstances. A person can scarcely credit the unfortunate number of articles necessary for his daily and nightly comfort, until he is deprived of them. To realize this, lose yourself, wander off a great distance from everywhere, and be benighted in a wild country, with nothing but your rifle and hunting-knife. You will then find yourself dinnerless, supperless, houseless, comfortless, sleepless, cold, and miserable, if you do not know how to manage for yourself. You will miss your dinner sadly, if you are not accustomed to fast for twenty-four hours. You will also miss your bed decidedly, and your tooth-brush in the morning ; but if, on the other hand, you are of the right stamp, it is astonishing how lightly these little troubles will sit on you, and how comfortable you will make yourself under the circumstances.

The first thing you will consider is the house. The architectural style will of course depend upon the locality. If the ground is rocky and hilly, be sure to make a steep pitch in the bank or the side of a rock form a wall, to leeward of which you will lie when your mansion is completed by a few sticks simply inclined from the rock and covered with grass. If the country is flat, you must cut four forked sticks, and erect a villa after this fashion in skeleton work, which you then cover with grass.

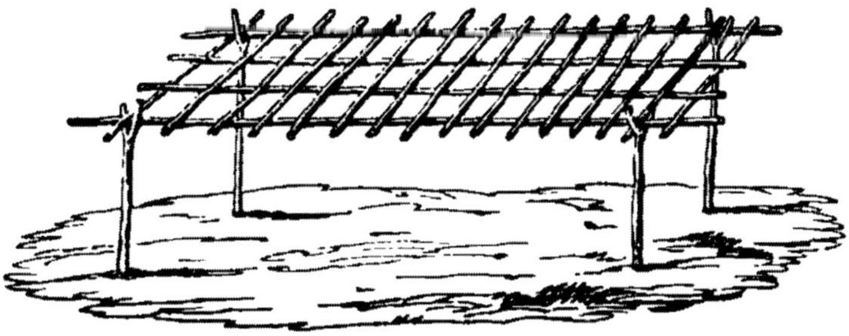

You will then strew the floor with grass or small boughs, in lieu of a feather bed, and tie up a bundle of the same material into a sheaf, which will form a capital pillow. If grass and sticks are at hand, this will be completed thus far in an hour.

Then comes the operation of fire-making, which is by no means easy; and as warmth comes next to food, and a blaze both scares wild animals and looks cheerful, I advise some attention to be paid to the fire. There must be a good collection of old fallen logs, if possible, together with some green wood to prevent too rapid a consumption of fuel. But the fire is not yet made.

First tear off a bit of your shirt and rub it with moistened gunpowder. Wind this in a thick roll round your ramrod just below the point of the screw, with the rough torn edge uppermost. Into these numerous folds sprinkle a pinch of gunpowder; then put a cap on the point of the screw, and a slight tap with your hunting knife explodes it and ignites the linen.

Now, fire in its birth requires nursing like a young baby, or it will leave you in the lurch. A single spark will perhaps burn your haystacks, but when you want a fire, it seldom will burn, out of sheer obstinacy; therefore take a wisp of dry grass, into which, push the burning linen, and give it a rapid circular motion through the air; this will generally set it in a blaze.

Then pile gently upon it the smallest and driest sticks, increasing their size as the fire grows, till it is all right ; and you will sit down proudly before your own fire, thoroughly confident that you are the first person that ever made one properly.

There is some comfort in that ; and having manufactured your own house and bed, you will lie down snugly and think of dinner, till you fall asleep, and the crowing of the jungle cocks will wake you in the morning.

The happiest hours of my life have been passed in this rural solitude. I have started from home with nothing but a couple of blankets and the hounds, and with one wrapped around me, I have slept beneath a capital tent formed of the other, with two forked sticks and a horizontal pole ;—the ends of the blanket being secured by heavy stones thus—

This is a more comfortable berth than it may appear at first sight, especially if one end is stopped up with boughs. The ridge pole being only two feet and a half high, renders it necessary to crawl in on all-fours; but this lowness of ceiling has its advantages in not catching the wind, and likewise in its warmth. A blanket roof, well secured and tightly strained, will resist rain for a much longer period than a common tent; but in thoroughly wet weather any woven roof is more or less uncomfortable.

I recollect a certain bivouac in the Augora patinas, for a few days' hunting, when I was suddenly seized with a botanical fit, in a culinary point of view, and I was determined to make the jungle subscribe something towards the dinner. To my delight I discovered some plants which, from the appearance of their leaves, I knew were a species of wild yam; they grew in a ravine on the swampy soil of a sluggish spring, and the ground being loose, I soon grubbed them up and found a most satisfactory quantity of yams about the size of large potatoes;—not bad things for dinner. Accordingly they were soon transferred to the pot. Elk steaks, and an Irish stew, the latter to be made of elk chops, onions, and the prized yams; this was the bill of fare expected. But, *misericordia!* what a change came over the yams when boiled; they turned a horrible slate colour, and looked like imitations of their former selves in lead.

Their appearance was uncommonly bad, certainly. There were three of us to feed upon them, viz. Palliser, my huntsman Benton, and myself. No one wishing to be first, it was then, I confess, that the thought just crossed my mind that Benton should make the experiment, but, repenting at the same moment, I punished myself by eating a very little one on the spot. Benton, who was blessed with a huge appetite, picked out a big one. Greedy fellow to choose the largest! but, *n'importe*, it brought its punishment.

Palliser and I having eaten carefully, were just beginning to feel uncomfortable, when up jumped Benton, holding his throat with both hands, crying 'My throat's full of pins. I'm choked.'

'We are poisoned, no doubt of it,' said Palliser, in his turn. 'I am choking likewise.' 'So am I.' There we were all three, with our throats in an extraordinary state of sudden constriction and inflammation, with a burning and pricking sensation, in addition to a feeling of swelling and stoppage of the windpipe. Having nothing but brandy at hand, we dosed largely instanter, and in the course of ten minutes we found relief; but Benton, having eaten his large yam, was the last to recover.

There must have been highly poisonous qualities in this root, as the quantity eaten was nothing in proportion to the effects produced. It is well known that many roots are poisonous when raw (especially the manioc), which become harmless when cooked, as the noxious properties consist of a very volatile oil which is thrown off during the process of boiling. These wild yams must necessarily be still worse in their raw state; and it struck me, after their effects became known, that I had never seen them grubbed up by the wild hogs; this neglect being a sure proof of their unfitness for food.

In these Augora patinas a curious duel was lately fought by a pair of wild bull elephants, both of whom were the *raræ aves* of Ceylon, 'tuskers.' These two bulls had consorted with a herd, and had no doubt quarrelled about the possession of the females. They accordingly fought it out to the death, as a large tusker was found recently killed, with his body bored in many directions by his adversary's tusks; the ground in the vicinity being trodden down with elephant tracks proved the obstinacy of the fight.

The last time that I was in this locality poor old Bluebeard was alive, and had been performing feats in elk-hunting which no dog could surpass. A few weeks later and he ran his last elk, and left a sad blank in the pack.

Good and bad luck generally come in turn; but when the latter does pay a visit, it falls rather heavily, especially among the hounds. In the same year I lost nearly the whole pack. Seven died in one week from an attack upon the brain, appearing in a form fortunately unknown in England. I lost no less than four of the best hounds by leopards, in addition to a fearful amount of casualties from other causes.

Shortly after the appearance of the epidemic alluded to, I took the hounds to the Totapella Plains for a fortnight, for change of air, while their kennel was purified and re-whitewashed.

In these Totapella Plains I had a fixed encampment, which, being within nine miles of my house, I could visit at any time with the hounds, without the slightest preparation. There were an immense number of elk in this part of the country; in fact this was a great drawback to the hunting, as two or more were constantly on foot at the same time, which divided the hounds and scattered them in all directions. This made hard work of the sport, as this locality is nothing but a series of ups and downs. The plains, as they are termed, are composed of some hundred grassy hills, of about a hundred feet elevation above the river; these rise like half oranges in every direction, while a high chain of precipitous mountains walls in one side of the view. Forest-covered hills abound in the centre and around the skirts of the plains, while a deep river winds in a circuitous route between the grassy hills.

My encampment was well chosen in this romantic spot. It was a place where you might live all your life without seeing a soul, except a wandering bee-hunter, or a native sportsman who had ventured up from the low country to shoot an elk.

Surrounded on all sides but one with steep hills, my hunting settlement lay snugly protected from the wind in a little valley. A small jungle about a hundred yards square grew at the base of one of these grassy hills, in which, having cleared the underwood for about forty yards I left the larger trees standing, and erected my huts under their shelter at the exact base of the knoll. This steep rise broke off into an abrupt cliff about sixty yards from my tent, against which the river had waged constant war, and, turning in an endless vortex, had worn a deep hole, before it shot off in a rapid torrent from the angle, dashing angrily over the rocky masses which had fallen from the overhanging cliff, and coming to a sudden rest in a broad deep pool within twenty yards of the tent door.

This was a delicious spot. Being snugly hidden in the jungle, there was no sign of my encampment from the plain, except the curling blue smoke which rose from the little hollow. A plot of grass of some two acres formed the bottom of the valley before my habitation, at the extremity of which the river flowed, backed on the opposite side by an abrupt hill covered with forest and jungle.

This being a chilly part of Ceylon, I had thatched the walls of my tent, and made a good gridiron bedstead, to keep me from the damp ground, by means of forked upright sticks, two horizontal bars, and numerous cross pieces. This was covered with six inches thickness of grass, strapped down with the bark of a fibrous shrub. My table and bench were formed in the same manner, being of course fixtures, but most substantial. The kitchen, huts for attendants, and kennel, were close adjoining. I could have lived there all my life in fine weather. I wish I was there now with all my heart. However, I had sufficient bad luck on my last visit to have disgusted most people. Poor Matchless, who was as good as her name implied, died of inflammation of the lungs ; and I started one morning in very low spirits at her loss, hoping to cheer myself up by a good hunt.

It was not long before old Bluebeard's opening note was heard high upon the hill-tops ; but at the same time a portion of the pack had found another elk, which, taking an opposite direction, of course divided them. Being determined to stick to Bluebeard to the last, I made straight through the jungle towards the point at which I had heard a portion of the pack join him, intending to get upon the track and follow up. This I soon did ; and after running for some time through the jungle, which, being young 'nillho,' was unmistakably crushed by the elk and hounds, I came to a capital though newly made path, as a single elephant, having been disturbed by the cry of the hounds, had started off at full speed; and the elk and hounds, naturally choosing the easiest route through the jungle, had kept upon his track. This I was certain of, as the elk's print sunk deep in that of the elephant, whose dung lying upon the spot was perfectly hot.

I fully expected that the hounds would bring the elephant to bay, which is never pleasant when you are without a gun; however they did not, but, sticking to their true game, they went straight away towards the chain of mountains at the end of the plain. The river in making its exit is checked by abrupt precipices, and accordingly makes an angle, and then descends through a ravine towards the low country.

I felt sure, from the nature of the ground and the direction of the run, that the elk would come to bay in this ravine; and after half an hour's run I was delighted, on arriving on the hill above, to hear the bay of the hounds in the river far below.

The jungle was thick and tangled, but it did not take long to force my way down the steep mountain side, and I neared the spot and heard the splashing in the river, as the elk, followed by the hounds, dashed across just before I came in view. He had broken his bay; and presently I again heard the chorus of voices, as he once more came to a stand a few hundred paces down the river.

The bamboo was so thick that I could hardly break my way through it; and I was crashing along towards the spot, when suddenly the bay ceased, and shortly after some of the hounds came hurrying up to me regularly scared. Lena, who seldom showed a symptom of fear, dashed up to me in a state of great excitement, with the deep scores of a leopard's claws on her hind-quarters. Only two couple of the hounds followed on the elk's track; the rest were nowhere.

The elk had doubled back and I saw old Bluebeard leading upon the scent up the bank of the river, followed by three other hounds.

The surest, although the hardest work, was to get on the track and follow up through the jungle. This I accordingly did for about a mile, at which distance I arrived at a small swampy plain in the centre of the jungle. Here, to my surprise, I saw old Bluebeard sitting up and looking faint, covered with blood, with no other dog within view. The truth was soon known, upon examination. No less than five holes were cut in his throat by a leopard's claws; and by the violent manner in which the poor dog strained and choked, I felt sure that the windpipe was injured. There was no doubt that he had received the stroke at the same time that Lena was wounded beneath the rocky mountain, when the elk was at bay; and nevertheless the staunch old dog had persevered in the chase till the difficulty of breathing brought him to a standstill.

I bathed the wounds, but I knew it was his last day, poor old fellow!

I sounded the bugle for a few minutes, and, having collected some of the scattered pack, I returned to the tent, leading the wounded dog, whose breathing rapidly became more difficult. I lost no time in fomenting and poulticing the part, but the swelling had commenced to such an extent that there was little hope of recovery.

This was a dark day for the pack. Benton returned in the afternoon from a search for the missing hounds, and, as he descended the steep hillside on approaching the tent, I saw that he and a native were carrying something slung upon a pole. At first I thought it was an elk's head, which the missing hounds might have run to bay; but on his arrival the worst was soon known.

It was Leopold, one of my best dogs. He was all but dead, with hopeless wounds in his throat and belly. He had been struck by a leopard within a few yards of Benton's side, and, with his usual pluck, the dog turned upon the leopard, in spite of his wounds; when the cowardly brute, seeing the man, turned and fled.

That night Leopold died. The next morning Bluebeard was so bad, that I returned home with him slung in a litter between two men. Poor fellow, he never lived to reach his comfortable kennel, but died in the litter within a mile of home. I had him buried by the side of old Smut; there are no truer dogs on earth.

A very few weeks after Bluebeard's death, I got a taste of revenge out of one of the race.

Palliser and I were out shooting, and we found a single bull elephant asleep in the dry bed of a stream; we were stealing quietly up to him, when his guardian spirit whispered something in his ear, and up he jumped. However, we polished him off, and having re-loaded, we passed on.

The country consisted of low thorny jungle and small sandy plains of short turf, and we were just entering one of these open spots within a quarter of a mile of the dead elephant, when we observed a splendid leopard crouching at the far end of the glade. He was about ninety paces from us, lying broadside on, with his head turned to the opposite direction, evidently looking out for game. His crest was bristled up with excitement, and he formed a perfect picture of beauty both in colour and attitude.

Halting our gun-bearers, we stalked him to within sixty yards: he looked quickly round, and his large hazel eyes shone full upon us, as the two rifles made one report, and his white belly lay stretched upon the ground.

They were both clean shots: Palliser had aimed at his head, and had cut off one ear and laid the skin open at the back of the neck. My ball had smashed both shoulders, but he was not fairly extinct. We therefore strangled him with my neck tie, as I did not wish to spoil his hide by any further wound. This was a pleasing sacrifice to the 'manes' of old Bluebeard.

E. Palliser had at one time the luck to have a fair turn up with a leopard with the dogs and hunting-knife. At that time he kept a pack at Dimboola, about nine miles from my house. Old Bluebeard belonged to him, and he had a fine dog named 'Pirate,' who was the heaviest and best of his seizers.

He was out hunting with two or three friends, when suddenly a leopard sprang from the jungle at one of the smaller hounds as they were passing quietly along a forest path. Halloaing the pack on upon the instant, every dog gave chase, and a short run brought him to bay in the usual place of refuge, the boughs of a tree.

However, it so happened that there was a good supply of large sharp stones upon the soil, and with these the whole party kept up a spirited bombardment, until at length one lucky shot hit him on the head, and at the same moment he fell or jumped into the middle of the pack. Here Pirate came to the front in grand style and collared him, while the whole pack backed him up without an exception.

There was a glorious struggle of course, which

was terminated by the long arm of our friend Palliser, who slipped the hunting-knife into him and became a winner. This is the only instance that I know of a leopard being run into and killed with hounds and a knife.

CHAPTER XIII.

Wild Denizens of Forest and Lake—Destroyers of Reptiles—The Tree Duck—The Mysteries of Night in the Forest—The Devil Bird —The Iguanodon in Miniature—Outrigger Canoes—The last Glimpse of Ceylon—A Glance at Old Times.

ONE of the most interesting objects to a tourist in Ceylon is a secluded lake or tank in those jungle districts which are seldom disturbed by the white man. There is something peculiarly striking in the wonderful amount of living creatures which exist upon the productions of the water. Birds of infinite variety and countless numbers,—fish in myriads,—reptiles and crocodiles,—animals that feed upon the luxuriant vegetation of the shores,—insects which sparkle in the sunshine in every gaudy hue;—all these congregate in the neighbourhood of these remote solitudes, and people the lakes with an incalculable host of living beings.

In such a scene there is scope for much delightful study of the habits and natures of wild animals, where they can be seen enjoying their freedom unrestrained by the fear of man.

Often have I passed a quiet hour on a calm evening when the sun has sunk low on the horizon, and the cool breeze has stolen across the water refreshing all animal life. Here, concealed beneath the shade of some large tree, I have watched the masses of living things quite unconscious of such scrutiny. In one spot, the tiny squirrel nibbling the buds on a giant limb of the tree above me, while on the opposite shore a majestic bull elephant has commenced his evening bath, showering the water above his head and trumpeting his loud call to the distant herd. Far away in the dense jungles the ringing sound is heard, as the answering females return the salute, and slowly approach the place of rendezvous. One by one their dark forms emerge from the thorny coverts and loom large upon the green but distant shores; they increase their pace when they view the coveted water, and belly deep enjoy their evening draught.

The graceful axis in dense herds quit the screening jungle, and also seek the plain. The short shrill barks of answering bucks sound clearly across the surface of the lake, and indistinct specks begin to appear on the edge of the more distant forests. Now black patches are dotted about the plain; now larger objects, some single and some in herds, make towards the water. The telescope distinguishes the vast herds of hogs, busy in upturning the soil in search of roots, and the ungainly buffaloes, some in herds, and others single bulls, all gathering at the hour of sunset at the drinking place. Peacocks spread their gaudy plumage to the cool evening air as they strut over the green plain; the giant crane stands statue-like among the shallows; the pelican floats like a ball of snow upon the dark water; and ducks and waterfowl of all kinds splash, dive and scream in a confused noise, the volume of which explains their countless numbers.

Foremost among the waterfowl for beauty is the water-pheasant. He is generally seen standing upon the broad leaf of a lotus pecking at the ripe seeds, and continually uttering his plaintive cry, like the very distant note of a hound. This bird is most beautifully formed, and the peculiarity of colour is well adapted to his shape. He is something like a cock pheasant in build and mode of carriage, but does not exceed the size of a pigeon. His colour is white, with a fine brown tinsel glittering head and long tail; the wings of the cock bird are likewise ornamented with similar brown tinsel feathers. These birds are delicious eating, but I seldom fire at them, as they are generally among the lotus plants in such deep water that I dare not venture to recover them on account of crocodiles. The lotus seeds, which they devour greedily, are a very good substitute for filberts, and are slightly narcotic.

The endless variety of the crane is very interesting upon these lonely shores. From the giant crane, who stands nearly six feet high, down to the smallest species of paddy bird, there is a numerous gradation. Among these the gaunt adjutant stands conspicuous as he stalks with measured steps through the high rushes, now plunging his immense bill into the tangled sedges, then triumphantly throwing back his head with a large snake writhing helplessly in his horny beak. Open fly the shear-like hinges of his bill—one or two sharp jerks, and down goes one half of an incredibly large snake! another jerk, and a convulsive struggle of the snake, one more jerk!—snap, snap goes the bill, and the snake has disappeared. The adjutant again stalks quietly on, as though nothing had happened. Down goes his bill presently with a sudden start, and again his head is thrown back; but this time it is the work of a moment, as it is only an iguana, which not being above eighteen inches long, is easy swallowing.

A great number of the crane species are destroyers of snakes, which in a country so infested with vermin as Ceylon, renders them especially valuable. Peacocks likewise wage perpetual war with all kinds of reptiles, and nature has wisely arranged that where these nuisances most abound, there is a corresponding provision for their destruction.

Snipes of course are numerous in their season

around the margin of the lakes; but the most delicious birds for the table are the teal and ducks, of which there are four varieties. The largest duck is nearly the size of a wild goose, and has a red fatty protuberance about the beak very similar to a muscovy. The teal are the fattest and most delicious birds that I have ever tasted. Cooked in Soyer's magic stove, with a little butter, cayenne pepper, a squeeze of lime juice, a pinch of salt, and a spoonful of Lea and Perrins' Worcester sauce, (which by the by, is the best in the world for a hot climate), and there is no bird like a Ceylon teal. They are very numerous, and I have seen them in flocks of some thousands on the salt-water lakes on the eastern coast, where they are seldom or never disturbed. Nevertheless they are tolerably wary, which of course increases the sport of shooting them. I have often thought what a paradise these lakes would have made for the veteran Colonel Hawker, with his punt gun. He might have paddled about and blazed away to his heart's content.

There is one kind of duck that would undoubtedly have astonished him, and which would have slightly bothered the punt gun for an elevation: this is the tree duck, which flies about and perches in the branches of the lofty trees like any nightingale. This has an absurd effect, as a duck looks entirely out of place in such a situation. I have seen a whole cluster of them sitting on one branch; when I first observed them I killed three at one shot to make it a matter of certainty.

It is a handsome light brown bird about the size of an English widgeon, but there is no peculiar formation in the feet to enable them to cling to a bough; they are *bonâ fide* ducks with the common flat web foot.

A very beautiful species of bald-pated coot, called by the natives keetoollée, is also an inhabitant of the lakes. This bird is of a bright blue colour, with a brilliant pink horny head. He is a slow flier, being as bulky as a common fowl, and short in his proportion of wing.

It is impossible to convey a correct idea of the number and variety of birds in these localities, and I will not trouble the reader by a description that would be very laborious to all parties; but to those who delight in ornithological studies, there is a wide field, which would doubtless supply many new specimens.

I know nothing more interesting than the acquaintance with all the wild denizens of mountain and plain, lake and river. There is always something fresh to learn, something new to admire, in the boundless works of creation. There is a charm in every sound in nature where the voice of man is seldom heard to disturb her works. Every note gladdens the ear in the stillness of solitude, when night has overshadowed the earth, and all sleep, but the wild animals of the forest. Then I have often risen from my bed, when the tortures of mosquitos have banished all ideas of rest, and have silently wandered from the tent to listen in the solemn quiet of night.

I have seen the tired coolies stretched round the smouldering fires sound asleep after their day's march, wrapped in their white cloths, like so many corpses laid upon the ground. The flickering logs on the great pile of embers crackling and sinking as they consume; now falling suddenly and throwing up a shower of sparks, then resting again in a dull red heat, casting a silvery moonlike glare upon the foliage of the spreading trees above. A little further on, and the horses standing sleepily at their tethers, their heads drooping in a doze. Beyond them, and all is darkness and wilderness. No human dwelling or being beyond the little encampment I have quitted;—the dark lake reflecting the stars like a mirror, and the thin crescent moon giving a pale and indistinct glare which just makes night visible.

It is a lovely hour then to wander forth and wait for wild sounds. All is still except the tiny hum of the mosquitos. Then the low chuckling note of the night hawk sounds soft and melancholy in the dis-

NIGHT SCENE

tance; and again all is still, save the heavy and impatient stamp of a horse as the mosquitos irritate him by their bites. Quiet again for a few seconds; when presently the loud alarm of the plover rings over the plain—'did he do it'—the bird's harsh cry speaks these words as plainly as a human being. This alarm is a certain warning that some beast is stalking abroad which has disturbed it from its roost, but presently it is again hushed.

The loud hoarse bark of an elk now unexpectedly startles the ear;—presently it is replied to by another, and once more the plover shrieks 'did he do it,' and a peacock waking on his roost gives one loud scream, and sleeps again.

The heavy and regular splashing of water now marks the measured tread of a single elephant as he roams out into the cooled lake, and you can hear the more gentle falling of water as he spouts a shower over his body. Hark! at the deep guttural sigh of pleasure that travels over the lake like a moan of the wind—what giant lungs to heave such a breath; but hark again!—There was a fine trumpet!—as clear as any bugle note blown by a hundred breaths it rang through the still air. How beautiful!—There, the note is answered; not by so fine a tone, but by discordant screams and roars from the opposite side, and the louder splashing tells that the herd is closing up to the old bull. Like distant thunder a deep roar growls across the lake, as the old monarch mutters to himself in angry impatience.

Then the long tremulous hoot of the owl disturbs the night, mingled with the harsh cries of flights of water-fowl, which, doubtless, the elephants have disturbed while bathing.

Once more all sounds sink to rest for a few minutes, until the low grating roar of a leopard nearer home warns the horses of their danger and wakes up the sleeping horsekeeper; he piles fresh wood upon the fires, and the bright blaze shoots up among the trees, and throws a dull ruddy glow across the surface of the water. Morning comes at length, ushered in, before night has yet departed, by the strong shrill cry of the great fish eagle as he sits on the topmost bough of some forest tree, and at measured periods repeats his quivering and unearthly yell, like an evil spirit calling. But hark, at that dull low note of indescribable pain and suffering!—long and heavy it swells and dies away. It is the devil-bird; and whoever sees that bird must surely die soon after, according to Cingalese superstition.

A more cheering sound charms the ear as the grey tint of morning makes the stars grow pale: clear rich notes, now prolonged and full, now plaintive and low, set the example to other singing birds, as the Bulbul, first to wake, proclaims the morning. Wild jungle-like songs the birds indulge in; not like our steady thrushes of Old England, but charming in their quaintness. The jungle partridge now wakes up, and with his loud cry subdues all other sounds, until the numerous peacocks, perched on the high trees around the lake, commence their discordant yells.

The name for the devil-bird is 'Gualama,' and so impressed are the natives with the belief that a sight of it is equivalent to a call to the nether world, that they sometimes die from sheer fright and nervousness. A case of this happened to a servant of a friend of mine. He chanced to see the creature sitting on a bough, and he was from that moment so satisfied of his inevitable fate, that he refused all food, and fretted, and died; as of course any one else must do, if starved, whether he saw the devil-bird or not.

Although I have heard the curious mournful cry of this creature nearly every night, I have never seen one; —this is easily accounted for, as being a night bird it remains concealed in the jungle during the day. In so densely wooded a country as Ceylon it is not to be wondered at that owls and all other birds of similar habits are rarely met with. I have never seen more than two woodcocks during my residence in the island.

From the same cause many interesting animals pass unobserved, although they are very numerous. The porcupine, although as common as the hedgehog in England, is very seldom seen. Likewise the manis or great scaled ant-eater, who retires to his hole before break of day, is never met with by daylight. Indeed I have had some trouble in persuading many persons in Ceylon that such an animal exists in the country.

In the same manner the larger kind of serpents conceal themselves by day, and wander forth at night, like all other reptiles except the smaller species of lizard, of which we have in Ceylon an immense variety.

Of this tribe the 'cabra goya' and the 'iguana' grow to a large size: the former I have killed as long as eight or nine feet, but the latter seldom exceeds four. I have often intended to eat one, as the natives consider them a great delicacy, but I have never been quite hungry enough to make the trial whenever one was at hand. The 'cabra goya' is a horrid reptile, and is not considered eatable even by the Cingalese.

One curious species of lizard exists in Ceylon: it is a little brown species with a peculiarly rough skin and a serrated spine. A long horn projects from the snout, and it is a fac-simile in miniature of the antediluvian monster the 'iguanodon,' who was about a hundred feet long and twelve feet thick.

Crocodiles attain an immense size, and it has frequently surprised me that they do not upset the small canoes in which the natives paddle about the lakes and rivers. These are formed in the simplest manner of very rude materials by hollowing out a log of wood, and attaching an outrigger. Some of these are so small that the gunwale is close to the water's edge when containing only one person.

Even the large sea-canoes are constructed on a similar principle; but they are very wonderful boats for both speed and safety.

A simple log of about thirty feet in length is hollowed out. This is tapered off at either end so as to form a kind of prow. The cylindrical shape of the log is preserved as much as possible in the process of hollowing, so that no more than a section of one fourth of the circle is pared away upon the upper side.

Upon the edges of this aperture, the top-sides of the canoe are formed by simple planks, which are merely *sewn* upon the main body of the log parallel to each other, slightly inclining outwards, so as to admit the legs of persons when sitting.

A vessel of this kind would of course capsize immediately, as the top weight of the upper works would overturn the flute-like body upon which they rested. This is prevented by an outrigger, formed of elastic rods of tough wood firmly bound together, which projects at right angles from the upper works. At the extremity of two rods, there is a tapering log of light wood, which very much resembles the bottom log of the canoe in miniature. This, floating on the water, balances the canoe in an upright position;—it cannot be upset until some force is exerted upon the mast which is either sufficient to lift the outrigger out of the water, or on the other hand to sink it altogether, either accident being prevented by the great leverage required. Thus when a heavy breeze sends the little vessel flying like a swallow over the waves, and the outrigger to windward shows symptoms of lifting, a man runs out upon the connecting rod, and squatting upon the outrigger adds his weight to the leverage. Two long bamboos, spreading like a letter V from the bottom of the canoe, form the masts, and support a single square sail, which is immensely large in proportion to the size and weight of the vessel.

The motion of these canoes under a stiff breeze is most delightful; there is a total absence of rolling, which is prevented by the outrigger, and the steadiness of their course under a press of sail is very remarkable. I have been in these boats in a considerable surf, through which they fly like a fish; and if the beach is sandy, and the inclination favourable, their own impetus will carry them high and dry.

Sewing the portions of a boat together, appears ill adapted to purposes of strength; but all the Cingalese vessels are constructed upon this principle: the two edges of the planks being brought together, a strip of the areca palm stem is laid over the joints, and holes being drilled upon each plank, the sewing is drawn tightly over the lath of palm; this being thickly smeared with a kind of pitch, keeps the seams perfectly water-tight. The native dhonies, which are vessels of a hundred and fifty tons, are all fastened in this simple and apparently fragile manner; nevertheless they are excellent sea boats, and ride in safety through many a gale of wind.

The first moving object which met my view on arrival within sight of Ceylon was an outrigger canoe, which shot past our vessel as if we had been at anchor.

The last object that my eyes rested on, as the tall cocoa-nut trees of Ceylon faded from sight, was again the native canoe, which took the farewell lines to those who were left behind. Upon this I gazed till it became a grey speck upon the horizon, and the green shores of the eastern paradise faded from my eyes for ever.

* * * * *

How little did I imagine when these pages were commenced in Ceylon, that their conclusion would be written in England!

An unfortunate shooting trip to one of the most unhealthy parts of the country, killed my old horse 'Jack,' one coolie, and very nearly extinguished me, rendering it imperative that I should seek a change of climate in England. And what a dream-like change it is!—past events appear unreal, and the last few years seem to have escaped from the connecting chain of former life. Scarcely can I believe in the bygone days of glorious freedom, when I wandered through that beautiful country, unfettered by the laws or customs of conventional life.

The white cliffs of Old England rose hazily on the horizon, and greeted many anxious eyes as the vessel rushed proudly on, with her decks thronged with a living freight, all happy as children in the thoughts of home. The sun shone brightly, and gave a warm welcome on our arrival; and as the steamer moored alongside the quay, an hour sufficed to scatter the host of passengers who had so closely dwelt together, as completely as the audience of a theatre when the curtain falls. That act of life is past, '*exeunt omnes*,' and a new scene commences. We are in England!

A sudden change necessarily induces a comparison, and I imagine there are few who have dwelt much among the tropics who do not acquire a distaste for the English climate, and look back with lingering hopes to the verdant shores they have left so far behind. The recollection of vanished years, which seem to have been the summer of life, makes the chill of the present feel doubly cold, and our thoughts still cling to the past, while we strive against the belief that we never can recall those days again.

How, as my thoughts wander back to former scenes, every mountain and valley reappears in the magic glass of memory! Every rock and dell, every old twisted stem, every dark ravine and wooded cliff, the distant outlines of the well-known hills, the jungle paths known to my eye alone, and the far, still spots where I have often sat in solitude, and pondered over the events of life, and conjured up the faces of those so far away; doubtful if we should ever meet again. Thus even now I picture to myself the past; and so vivid is the scene that I can almost hear the fancied roar of the old waterfalls, and see the shadowy tints which the evening sun throws upon the tree tops. My old home rises before me like a dissolving view, and I can see the very spot where it was my delight to live, where a warm welcome awaited every friend. And, lastly, the faces of those friends seem clear before me, and bring back the associations of old times. Those who have shared in common many of these scenes, I trust to meet again, and look back upon the events of former days as landscapes on the road of life that we have viewed together.[1]

For me Ceylon has always had a charm, and I shall ever retain a vivid interest in the colony.

I trust that a new and more prosperous era has commenced, and that Ceylon having shaken off the incubus of mismanagement, may, under the rule of a vigorous and enterprising governor, arrive at that prosperity to which she is entitled by her capabilities.

The governor recently appointed (Sir H. Ward) has a task before him which his well-known energy will doubtless enable him to perform.

[1] It is a deep satisfaction that the early friendships formed in Ceylon have endured through life.